THE MAKING OF EUROSCEPTIC BRITAIN

The Making of Eurosceptic Britain

CHRIS GIFFORD
University of Huddersfield, UK

LONDON AND NEW YORK

First published 2014 by Ashgate Publishing

Published 2016 by Routledge
2 Park Square, Milton Park, Abingdon, Oxon OX14 4RN
711 Third Avenue, New York, NY 10017, USA

Routledge is an imprint of the Taylor & Francis Group, an informa business

Copyright © 2014 Chris Gifford

Chris Gifford has asserted his right under the Copyright, Designs and Patents Act, 1988, to be identified as the author of this work.

All rights reserved. No part of this book may be reprinted or reproduced or utilised in any form or by any electronic, mechanical, or other means, now known or hereafter invented, including photocopying and recording, or in any information storage or retrieval system, without permission in writing from the publishers.

Notice:
Product or corporate names may be trademarks or registered trademarks, and are used only for identification and explanation without intent to infringe.

British Library Cataloguing in Publication Data
A catalogue record for this book is available from the British Library

The Library of Congress has cataloged the printed edition as follows:
Gifford, Chris, 1966–
　　The making of Eurosceptic Britain / by Chris Gifford. – Second Edition.
　　　pages cm
　　Includes bibliographical references and index.
　　ISBN 978-1-4094-5758-9 (hardback)
　　1. European Economic Community–Great Britain. 2. European Union–Great Britain. 3. Great Britain–Politics and government–1945– 4. Great Britain–Foreign economic relations. I. Title.
　　HC240.25.G7G54 2014
　　337.1'420941–dc23
　　　　　　　　　　　　　　　　　　　　　　　　　　　　　　　　　　　2014011769

ISBN 9781409457589 (hbk)

Contents

Preface and Acknowledgements   *vii*

1	Introduction	1
2	The Post-Imperial Crisis	15
3	Britain and the Beginnings of European Integration	31
4	British Membership and its Opponents	53
5	Eurosceptic Thatcherism	79
6	A European Crisis of the British State	103
7	Labour in Power: The Rise and Fall of Anglo-Europe	131
8	The Eurosceptic Challenge to the Coalition Government	155
	Conclusion	171

Bibliography   *175*
Index   *197*

Preface and Acknowledgements

This second edition has been completely revised. It includes a new introduction that reflects the growing literature and debates in the study of Euroscepticism. I have also drawn more fully on the two official histories of Britain and the European Community for the earlier chapters (Milward 2002; Wall, 2013). Writing in 2012–2013, I was able to provide a more complete account and assessment of the Labour governments' approach to Europe than was possible in the first edition. A new chapter explores the extensive mobilisation of Eurosceptic forces in opposition to the Coalition government and the Conservative leadership's European policy. The full implications of recent developments, including the prospect of a referendum on British membership, remains to be seen; however, they seem to confirm my central argument that Euroscepticism is a persistent and institutionalised feature of British politics. While demonstrating there is a structural logic to the historical unfolding of Eurosceptic Britain, I have attempted to do justice to the conflicts and struggles through which this is expressed. The central paradox is that Eurosceptic Britain continues despite Europeanisation; the latter, I would argue, has yet to find significant normative expression within UK citizenship and until it does, Britain's European journey remains open to challenge and reversal.

Some of the material for this book represents a reworking of material published in journals (see Gifford 2006, 2007, 2010, 2014). I am particularly grateful to the reviewers of these articles, as I am to those who reviewed the first edition and my proposal for a second edition. Their constructive criticism, and generosity towards flaws and weaknesses, provided the motivation to revisit my earlier work. I would like to thank Robert Cook in helping with preparing the text for publication and this edition is dedicated to him.

Chris Gifford

Chapter 1

Introduction

Britain's[1] relationship with the European Union[2] has been a matter of intense political debate since the Macmillan government first proposed British membership in 1961. In the emergent post-imperial context, the issue went to the heart of British political identity and organisation. It encapsulated the extent to which the British political and social order was in transition, and the tensions that arose as a consequence of these changes. Britain's European trajectory seemed to have been secured when Edward Heath signed the Treaty of Rome in 1972 and there was a resounding vote in support of membership in the 1975 referendum. Nevertheless, it has been accompanied by the persistent rise of a domestic Euroscepticism centred on the fundamental belief that the true sentiments and interests of 'the British people'[3] are antithetical to European integration. Its impact was demonstrated in 2013, the fortieth anniversary of British accession, when David Cameron committed the Conservative party to holding a second referendum on membership. The decision underlined the extent to which Britain's position in the EU remained highly uncertain and intensely critical.

This book argues that a point has been reached where opposition to European integration can no longer be viewed as a contained or temporary facet of British politics but is both essential and systemic to what Britain has become. Thus it explores the historical unfolding of the institutionalisation of Euroscepticism as part of its post-imperial trajectory. This opening chapter sets out the key debates and the general direction of the book. In so doing it makes the case for shifting our perspective from British Euroscepticism to the making of Eurosceptic Britain.

The Concept of Euroscepticism

The origins of the term Euroscepticism can be traced back to articles in *The Times* in 1985 and 1986 (Spiering, 2004, p. 127). It was a term used to refer to the emergence

---

1 While I use 'Britain' throughout this book, I acknowledge that it is a problematic construction that excludes Northern Ireland and can fail to grasp the multi-national dimensions of the United Kingdom and Northern Ireland. Nevertheless, the book is a contribution to debates on 'Britain and Europe' and the terms used thus reflect that wider discourse.

2 I will refer to either the European Community (EC), or to the European Union (EU) when discussing general or recent developments. I will also refer to 'Europe' as shorthand for European institutions and the integration project.

3 When referring to 'the British people' or 'the people' I have used quotation marks to indicate that this is a populist construction rather than an empirical reality.

of a section of the British right within the Conservative party that was increasingly opposed to the second wave of integration initiated by the Delors Commission.[4] Over the following decades, the term has morphed from journalese to becoming a distinctive area of academic political research. A pre-existing socially constituted meaning has become subject to investigation in order to deepen, systematise and, ultimately, explain a facet of contemporary political reality.

The maturation of the academic study of Euroscepticism was demonstrated by Mudde's (2012) characterisation of the field as consisting of two distinct Schools: Sussex and North Carolina. The Sussex School stems from the work of Paul Taggart and Aleks Szczerbiak (2008a, 2008b) while the North Carolina School is associated with Lisbet Hooghe, Gary Marks and Leonard Ray (Ray, 1999; Hooghe and Marks, 2005, 2007, 2009). If the Sussex School has focused on detailed national case studies and definitional refinements, the North Carolina School has stressed broad ideological positions and their connection to parties and public opinion across Europe. In their mapping of the configuration of Eurosceptic politics, Szczerbiak and Taggart made their well-known distinction between hard and soft Euroscepticism (2008a, pp. 7–8; 2008b, pp. 247–8). They conceived of hard Euroscepticism as principled opposition to the integrationist project, whether opposed to its institutional and constitutional foundations or to its overarching policy agenda. Soft Euroscepticism, meanwhile, was concerned with a more qualified opposition that rejected and criticised specific policies, or gave prominence to national concerns and interests in opposition to integration (2008a, pp. 7–8). While soft Euroscepticism may include contestation of the EU as an ongoing project of integration, hard Euroscepticism would also include those who may nominally support it but wish to see a fundamental redrawing of the terms of their country's membership (p. 8). In contrast, the North Carolina School has focused on ideology and the relationship between party ideology and public opinion. In so doing they highlighted a left/right socio-economic divide on European integration, but this was soon eclipsed by a focus on political identities and their GAL (green/alternative/libertarian) versus TAN (traditionalism/authority/nationalism) classification (Hooghe and Marks, 2009, p. 16). The two Schools have therefore predominantly focused on mapping Euroscepticism, drawing on teams of national experts to develop in-depth case studies in the case of Sussex, or quantitative surveys and large scale data sets in North Carolina.

The importance of this body of work became apparent when, post-Maastricht, it was clearly evident that Euroscepticism was a significant and persistent feature of the dynamics of European integration. However, this also highlighted weaknesses with the dominant approaches. As Euroscepticism became more ubiquitous, complex and diverse, it was clear that broad comparative maps of the political

---

4 The Delors Commission refers to the three terms (1985–1994) that Jacques Delors presided over the European Commission. The second wave of European integration is associated with this period that included the Single European Act (1986) and the Treaty on European Union (1992).

parties and public attitudes could not do justice to specific contexts and the array of actors involved. In this regard, Usherwood and Startin's (2013) call for more holistic, nuanced and interdisciplinary approaches was an astute and significant contribution. In the British case, an extensive literature had documented the problems Britain's politicians experienced with European integration both before and after membership (see Kaiser, 2002), but these were not explicitly viewed through the lens of Euroscepticism.

At the start of the twenty-first century this began to change when Stephen George (2000) argued that Britain was no longer simply an 'awkward partner' but should be considered as a 'Eurosceptic state', because of the complex and persistent expressions of Euroscepticism within and across a range of domestic actors and institutions. Forster (2002) was more explicit in his criticism of existing approaches, which, he argued, failed to provide a systematic explanation of the role and influence of sceptical groupings on government policy. In a compendious work of contemporary political history, Forster documented the key factors that explained how Eurosceptics were able at certain times to act as a significant force of opposition and influence the direction of European policy. Forster was therefore primarily concerned with the expression of Euroscepticism as a fragmented movement of opposition within mainstream party politics.

A central concern is the extent to which Euroscepticism can be explained by the institutions of British representative democracy. The main proposition of the party-based comparative literature is that Euroscepticism can be broadly explained in terms of the organisation of competitive political systems that are characteristic of liberal democratic states. In line with this, Szczerbiak and Taggart summarised two main findings from the research on party-based Euroscepticism:

> The first is that opposition to the EU brings together 'strange bedfellows' of some very different ideologies. Opposition extends from new politics, old far left politics through regionalism to new populism and neo-fascism in the far right. The second point is that opposition to the EU seems to be related to the positions of parties in their party systems. It differentiates between parties at the core and those at the periphery in the sense that wholly Eurosceptical parties are at the peripheries of their party systems while parties at the core are generally not Eurosceptical. (2000, p. 5)

In the British case, studies have focused on the factional nature of Euroscepticism within political parties and this has been accounted for in terms of the distinctiveness of British political institutions in structuring opposition (Aspinwall, 2000; Usherwood, 2002). In those countries characterised by power sharing governments, a range of institutional mechanisms enables the 'Eurosceptic social voice' to be 'filtered out' (Aspinwall, 2000, p. 433). In comparison, British governments operating in a system of one party rule have to give greater consideration to backbench Eurosceptic opinion than proportional representation systems that tend to produce broad centrist governments. Governments in this situation have been shown to adopt negative positions towards European integration as a consequence of strong opposition within party ranks, particularly when faced with small majorities (pp. 434–6). A further feature of these institutional dynamics has been the externalisation of Eurosceptic opposition (Usherwood, 2002). The fudging of European policy, the failure to manage powerful Eurosceptic factions and a lack of salience across public opinion results in a radical extra-parliamentary Eurosceptic mobilisation that has major implications for party cohesion. From this perspective, the significance of Euroscepticism is to be found in a specific set of British institutional dynamics that has allowed Eurosceptic factionalism within the main parties to take on a particular significance. In summary, the peculiarities of the British political system creates comparatively more opportunities for Eurosceptics to influence mainstream party positions and government policy, and is that much harder to 'filter out'.

Both Aspinwall and Usherwood downplay explanations of British Euroscepticism in terms of ideological factors; however, their analyses suggest a crisis of political leadership and party cohesion that clearly has a significant ideological dimension. If we address issues of ideology, and of political culture more widely, then the focus on Euroscepticism as the politics of factionalism and opposition becomes problematic. Baker, Gamble and Seawright (2002), for instance, drew attention to the ideological dimensions of Euroscepticism across British Conservatism. On this view, recent Euroscepticism in the Conservative party has been fundamentally driven by a powerful hyperglobalist ideology at the very centre of the party. The key elements of this ideology include national economic and political independence within a global free market that implies a fundamental opposition to European integration. Gamble (2003) expanded on these tensions more broadly in his study of *Between Europe and America: the Future of British Politics*. In advocating a 'traditional open seas policy of seeking the most rapidly growing markets and the cheapest sources of supply', Eurosceptics combined nationalism with globalism, reviving powerful 'world island' narratives (Gamble, 2003, p. 130).

The prevalence of a distinctive ideological Euroscepticism within British political parties makes it essential to connect developments in the party system to the wider historical and cultural context. It is the very 'otherness' of a European identity *en masse* that Spiering argued was so particular to the British case; 'in other European countries such a differentiation makes no sense' (2004, p. 145). What is more the emotiveness of 'Europe' constituted as a national threat meant it easily became a resource for politicians and the press to exploit (p. 145). Spiering pointed to deep cultural antecedents of contemporary British Euroscepticism, which shaped more contingent political forces (p. 146). In a similar vein, from a constructivist approach, Daddow noted that 'Europe has, historically, been heterotypified as a hostile Other in popular discourse of an "exceptional" British identity' (2011, p. 133). His central argument, however, concerned the inability of the premierships of Blair and Brown to significantly challenge this discursive domain defined by European 'otherness'. Indeed, in adhering to traditional, establishment conceptions of British foreign policy and the national interest, they found themselves complicit in its reproduction. The failure of New Labour's Europeanism was indicative of its failure to reinvent a common British identity in the context of an increasingly plural and diverse society and in the face of the forces of separatist nationalism that had come to the fore with devolution. This pointed to the deeper set of cultural dynamics associated with the post-imperial demise of Britishness that Wellings argued was driving Euroscepticism (2012). On this account, Euroscepticism emerged from the 1960s onwards as the expression of an English nationalism embedded in the timeless endurance of Anglo sovereignty, ingrained in the deep bonds with the old Commonwealth and, importantly, un-yielding in the face of Nazism. With entry into the EC the old allegiances of the Anglo-sphere were expected to be sacrificed and sovereignty surrendered to an unknown *finalité* of European unity. It was the final proof that England may have won the war but it had 'lost the peace' (Wellings, 2010). Thus, imagined as a fundamental threat to the nation, Europe provided the 'other' against which a popular and populist Englishness could be mobilised. For Wellings Euroscepticism enables us to explain English nationalism but it also emerges as a lens through which political cultural change can be viewed.

The literature therefore points to British Euroscepticism as a persistent phenomenon within contemporary British politics; however, its treatment as a cumulative and independent political force, institutionalised over time, remains underdeveloped. While it manifests in a variety of forms across parties, the media, public opinion and civil society, it is not reducible to any particular one or any combination of these, and should therefore be approached systemically. As such, it is the contention of this book that Euroscepticism emerges in the interplay between agency and structure, played out within specific contexts, where its presence becomes embedded over time. From this viewpoint, Eurosceptic *outcomes* are identified by a historically grounded analysis of political interaction and contextualised struggle. These outcomes in turn determine what is feasible and legitimate action over Europe that ultimately comprises a complex duality of structure and agency (Hay and Wincott, 1998, p. 956). The analysis presented of Britain and Europe identifies both the idealist and materialist tensions that underpin this relationship, and their reproduction and re-articulation by political actors within changing historical circumstances.

Definitions and Explanations

Any workable definition of Euroscepticism has to combine inclusivity with sensitivity to context. While the hard/soft distinction has proved particularly productive, the problem emerges that soft Euroscepticism has, in today's Europe, become so ubiquitous that it becomes too inclusive to shed light on specific contexts (Mudde, 2012, p. 201). One option proposed by de Wilde and Trenz (2012, p. 540), and utilised here, is to define Euroscepticism as polity contestation and not as policy contestation. On this view it is a public discourse, not reducible to political parties, that concerns the legitimacy of European integration. Eurosceptics take issue with the competencies and constitutional architecture of the EU and its underlying integrationist *raison d'etre*. This definition aligns with Taggart and Szczerbiak's hard Euroscepticism but is located within a broader conception of the de-legitimation of the EU. While this form of Euroscepticism may be comparatively new in many European countries, the point about the British case is that it is well-established and quite nuanced. Political actors, from governing elites to populist outsiders, have consistently contested the legitimacy of an integrating Europe, even when they have recognised the necessity of British membership. Hence, a broad definition of hard Euroscepticism informs the arguments presented in this book. Taking this view more extreme forms of British Euroscepticism may represent a radicalisation of mainstream political ideas and positions, and align with varying degrees to wider attitudes and beliefs. In Mudde's (2010) terms they are not an exception to the normal politics of a contemporary democratic state but part of a 'pathological normalcy'. This is not to exclude the reality and possibility of British Europeanism but, for the most part, political actors occupy an institutionalised Eurosceptic environment that shapes their political positions on the EU. This environment is characterised by three overarching features summarised below, which, when taken together, explain the making of Eurosceptic Britain.

A Eurosceptic Populism

A central proposition of this book is that developments in British politics have embedded a *structural susceptibility* to populist politics that has taken on a significant Eurosceptic dimension. In a context of imperial decline, political actors have looked to regenerate the 'nation' by identifying 'others' against which a 'new' Britain can be redefined. Recent analyses of populism have shifted the focus on to the autonomous capacity of discursive practices to independently constitute political subjects (Laclau, 2005; Mouffe, 2005). It involves the re-aggregation of differences within a political subject and the construction of an internal frontier with an enemy clearly identified on the other side of that frontier (Laclau, 2005 pp. 37–9). The point here is that populist strategies and movements do not represent any stable or coherent collective actors beyond which they discursively and antagonistically constitute. Once the theoretical core is specified, other characteristics can be identified as potentially part of the general logic of populism (Canovan, 1999, pp. 3–7; Meny and Surel, 2002, pp. 12–13). It has a characteristic mood that sets it apart from everyday, routine politics and adopts a specific style of politics that involves simple and direct language, analyses and solutions to problems. In so doing complex political debates are presented in dichotomous terms: the central opposition of 'the people' and 'the other' give rise to simplistic moral discourses of 'right' and 'wrong' and 'good' and 'bad'. Finally, populist movements structure the political debate, forcing 'more habitual participants into a defensive posture and into changing the way discussion takes place, issues are framed, and constituencies mobilised' (Taggart, 2002, p. 78); hence, they re-imagine political identities in ways that can have a wide significance across political cultures.

A populist and exclusive British Euroscepticism should be situated within a post-imperial context and conceived as a broad-based, albeit fragmented, populist movement mobilising and configuring national and political identities. As such it transcends the mainstream party system to include populist protest and anti-establishment parties; policy, pressure and interest groups; civil society organisations independent of political parties and, importantly, a large segment of the national press. Membership of the EC could not be debated without invoking the nation and 'the people'. Europe was re-imagined by Eurosceptic forces as the 'other' of British political identity and interests. It was symbolically constituted as a threat to Britain's exceptional social and political development. By turning Europe into a fundamental political issue, what we find is that it was no longer contained by the party system and the capacity to establish the kind of political consensus on the issue that was evident in other member-states proved impossible. While Eurosceptic mobilisations and episodes evidently manifest within the established British party system, they are not reducible to it. Instead, Euroscepticism intermeshes with mainstream politics, furthering the crisis of the British party system and the capacity of governing elites to achieve an effective and stable European policy.

The book then discusses three key populist moments in the British politics of Europe. The first period of Eurosceptic mobilisation took place from the 1971 'Great Debate' on membership, to accession and the 1975 referendum. The 1970s signalled the rise of populist Euroscepticism as a political phenomenon that could profoundly determine the structure and direction of mainstream British politics; politicians on both the left and right were prepared to sacrifice party unity for an issue they considered to be fundamental to 'the British people'. The subsequent two Eurosceptic mobilisations discussed in this book focus on the Conservative party but are not limited to the party system. First: the rebellions over the Maastricht Treaty that divided the party and went on to dominate the Major government's period in office. Second: the Eurosceptic opposition to the Coalition government's European policy and the campaign for an IN/OUT referendum. Populist Eurosceptic mobilisations are a defining feature of Eurosceptic Britain, each wave contributing to its further institutionalisation.

A Eurosceptic Governing Code

Populist Euroscepticism has looked to de-legitimise Britain's relationship with Europe by direct appeals to 'the people' against governing elites. In so doing, it has challenged the attempt to accommodate to Europe within the existing traditions of depoliticised rule structurally embedded within British governing institutions. Buller (2000a, 2000b) has identified depoliticisation with underlying assumptions concerning the problems and methods for governing the UK that are distinguishable from, albeit interconnected with, party ideologies and government policies. The defining feature of this *governing code* has been the pursuit of autonomy, which simply meant maintaining freedom from societal forces in order to have the authority to carry out effective and competent government. Implicit within this basic definition is the historical complexity of British modern government characterised by multi-territorial political and economic interests and pressures. In this context, being able to autonomously exercise executive power is considered to be the essence of British political authority. There are two areas which stand out and demonstrate how this code operates as an institutionalised norm. First, the ideology of parliamentary sovereignty has acted to de-legitimise alternative expressions of interests while fusing executive and legislative power through the doctrine of the Crown-in-Parliament. Second, a strict separation between the political and the economic developed during the nineteenth and twentieth centuries, whereby politicians agreed not to intervene or constrain the freedom of business and finance to pursue their private economic interests (Buller and Flinders, 2005, p. 532). Central to this has been the maintenance of an open economy by the institutions of high finance. Hence the governing code has sought to construe the national interest in terms of the external disciplines of the market, thus limiting domestic expectations and insulating governments from societal pressures.

While membership of the EC was often seen to represent a radical departure for Britain, it was in fact consistent with a conservative approach to government. In this regard, the perceived economic benefits have been particularly associated with its role in exposing the domestic economy to external disciplines. While this has at times led British governments to Europeanise monetary policy, it is more evident in the consistent belief that a highly integrated, competitive European market acts as a force for socio-economic good. In the run up to membership, the official documents emphasised the advantages of the dynamic effects on the economy that would offset any negative consequences (Haack, 1972, p. 143). The economic case for membership was increasingly expressed in terms of a competitiveness discourse which claimed that exposure to the pressures of new markets would help modernise the British economy. At the point at which attempts to impose domestic reforms on the British economy had proved impossible, Europe entered as an external alternative to programmes of national modernisation that had proved chronically unsuccessful. Thereafter the single market was integral to a national neo-liberal approach to transnational economic governance; in other words, an important external constraint on governments forcing them to engage in policy competition to create environments favourable to mobile capital. Notwithstanding the significant tensions over the Europeanisation of monetary policy, Europe's political economy had become an established element of the British governing code.

The incorporation of Europe into economic governance was compatible with shifting ideas of governing autonomy. In a post-imperial context, in which British influence and role in the world was in chronic decline, established conceptions of governing autonomy had to be reformed to accommodate the reality of interdependence (Buller 2006, pp. 398–9). Pro-European elites were at the forefront of a post-imperial reformulation of traditional conceptions of sovereignty, as a constitutional property articulating national power and independence, and proposed that sovereignty should be viewed pragmatically as a state's capacity to exert its influence (Howe, 1990). It therefore follows that British influence is most effectively realised in cooperation with other states within a European institutional framework. Nevertheless, this was also aligned with the governing code: the national interest remains at its core and the British constitution provides elites with the flexibility to exercise autonomy and exert power in foreign affairs. This emphasis on governing autonomy also implies that British governments exercise influence against other states and European institutions in order to realise the British interest. An established governing position therefore lends itself to Euroscepticism: a predominantly state-centric Europe must be maintained so that distinctive British objectives can be perceived to be autonomously expressed and achieved. In this respect, support for integration normally implies a cooperative or qualified Euroscepticism rather than Europeanism. These positions have come to be presented as pragmatic and realistic approaches to Europe; however, they mask more fundamental ideological differences, marked by polity contestation.

Eurosceptic Globalisation

Britain's governing code reflects a history of multi-national political rule, often resistant to territorial containment. A central argument of this book is that globalisation is essential for understanding British modern development and its relationship with European integration. While recent reassertions of state variation are an important corrective to more exaggerated arguments concerning globalisation, a return to a methodological nationalism makes little sense when we examine the British case (Gifford, 2007). It was British political rule that enabled the global integration of markets and peoples that reached unprecedented levels by the end of the nineteenth century and remains its historical legacy. The dramatic extension of capitalist social relations was not the product of blind market forces as depicted by Marx and Engels, but was made possible by the political leadership of Britain, the world's most powerful state (Arrighi, 1999, p. 219). According to Arrighi's world-systems approach, there were three features of this: first, the British capacity to secure a European balance of power; second, British led liberalisation of Western trade and third, British empire building, both formal and informal, in the non-Western world. These three dimensions were mutually reinforcing. Britain provided huge export opportunities for other Western states, which could be paid by the extraction of resources from its empire, particularly India. In the latter part of the nineteenth century, British supremacy was challenged by the spread of Western industrialisation. However, even as its own industrial power waned, its hegemony was reinforced by its position as the world centre for commercial and financial transactions and the continuation of sterling as the global currency. It was the cost of the First World War that eventually exhausted British capacities to sustain financial supremacy, and its growing reliance on US loans signalled a transfer of global leadership.

This political economic experience meant that British modern development was intrinsically interconnected with globalisation as a generalising force, which has had a significant impact upon its post-hegemonic trajectory. Martell neatly captures this when he describes Britain as 'a very globalised and globalising country, both an importer and exporter of globalising structures and processes' (2008, p. 452). A critical proposition of this book is that the analysis of British politics has to work with the distinctive interconnectedness of the categories of the 'global' and the 'national'. Expressions of national interests are not easily distinguishable from transnational interests, particularly economic. Concerns about British geopolitical status and influence are often profoundly implicated in national decision-making. Britain should, first and foremost, be viewed as a global-national state and its relationship with Europe can only be understood in relation to this primary materialisation (Gifford, 2007). If European integration has mediated the relationship of European states to globalisation, then in the British case the argument here is that globalisation mediates its relationship to the EU. It has had a more direct relation to processes of global restructuring and the 'European' is constituted *within* a global-national framework.

Chapter Outline

These overarching themes are explored in the coming chapters by a chronological discussion of the emergence and embedding of Euroscepticism within the British state and politics. Chapter 2 discusses the post-war context and counterposes European integration as a project of political economic modernisation with a British imperial state in decline. As Alan Milward (1992) has shown, there was an interdependent relationship between national modernisation and European integration that resulted in a post-war European rescue of the nation-state. European integration linked national projects of modernisation with the political and economic organisation of Western Europe. This was missing in the British case. Britain's distinctive global interconnectedness and imperial governing code is therefore shown to be central to its post-war development. However, its decline as a global power and the post-imperial crisis that ensues shapes its relationship with European integration. Specifically, Eurosceptic Britain is configured in the context of a crisis of political economy and of national identity and the political struggles that emerge out of this.

In Chapter 3 the problem of British modernisation is shown to be critical in explaining the failure of British governments to constructively engage with the process of European integration in the 1950s. The British problem with European integration is explained in terms of the continuation of institutions and policies associated with imperialism that were becoming exhausted by global structural change towards the end of 1950s. The problem of British decline was fundamental to the decision by the Conservative government under Harold Macmillan to apply for EC membership in the early 1960s. However, it was conceived as a conservative strategy designed to secure core elements of the British state.

Chapter 4 argues that the decision of the Labour government of Harold Wilson to apply for membership establishes Europe as fundamental to a post-imperial governing strategy. However, it was highly contested within the Labour party, and from the end of 1960s onwards a populist opposition emerges on the left against Europe. In particular, the *exclusion of Europe* becomes entrenched within the national political discourse and European integration is constructed as the 'other' of British identity. The Conservative government under Heath then takes Britain into the Community at a point when both main parties are divided on the issue. The decision to hold a referendum is the direct result of splits in the Labour party and, despite the comprehensive victory for the *Yes* campaign, British political leaders look to depoliticise an issue that had become politically toxic. Moreover, by the end of the 1970s, a Eurosceptic governing strategy looks increasingly consistent with a revived Anglo-American project of economic globalisation.

In Chapter 5 the central claim is that, at its core, the Thatcherite settlement was anti-European, because it was primarily concerned with the national legitimation of a global neo-liberal economic strategy. On a host of issues including the single market, the European budget and monetary union, Thatcher governments re-asserted Eurosceptic Britain contra European integration. This meant it was structurally incapable of adjusting to the second wave of European integration initiated by Delors. The attempt, however, to recast Thatcherism as a populist Eurosceptic re-assertion of British exceptionalism proved highly divisive within the governing elite. The eventual consequence of this was a crisis in the relationship between Britain and the EC that came to a head during the Major premiership.

A European crisis of the British state is revealed in Chapter 6 by the failure of the Major government's European economic policy and the Eurosceptic rebellion over the ratification of the Maastricht Treaty. It is argued that during the period 1990–1993 the attempt to revise the Thatcherite settlement through a renewed Europeanism was fundamentally flawed and crisis-prone. Neither the economic nor the political basis for a constructive British engagement with the second wave of integration was in place and the attempts of the Major government to accommodate these developments backfired. This created the opportunity for an extraordinary attack on the governing elite by a right wing populist Eurosceptic movement. The consequence of this was the further entrenchment of Euroscepticism within the British political order.

Chapter 7 explores the extent to which the New Labour project was pro-European and how the Labour governments managed the European issue. In contrast to the Conservatives, New Labour represented a fresh start on Europe and the Blair government placed itself in the mainstream of European policy-making.

This reflected its Third Way political project and commitment to the modernisation of British state and society. In the European context, this meant convincing its European partners that reform along British lines, involving accommodating to financially-driven globalisation, should be the basis for the future of the EU. The capacity of Labour to influence European policy agendas was hampered by its absence from the Euro and its key role in supporting the US-led invasion of Iraq. Labour's position on Europe became increasingly defensive, attempting to depoliticise European policy agendas in the face of Eurosceptic opposition. While the Brown government found some success in its response to the financial crisis, the overall impact of the crisis was to discredit Labour's economic model. The overall argument is that Labour's European strategy was framed within a distinctly British global-national policy agenda. A positive and proactive European policy was only achievable when it was successfully aligned with this, a task which proved increasingly difficult to achieve.

The coming to power of a Coalition government brought together a Eurosceptic Conservative party with the pro-European Liberal Democrats. However, a working political compromise on Europe seemed achievable. Both parties were committed to referenda on further integration, the Conservatives were prepared to put on hold their calls for repatriation and the Liberal Democrats ruled out Euro membership for the duration of the parliament. Nevertheless, the significant number of Conservatives for whom Euroscepticism was a defining political cause had been swelled by the 2010 election and they proved quick to mobilise in opposition to the Coalition's European policy. In parallel with earlier mobilisations, it was not confined to parliament but was a broad based movement on the right of British politics. Of particular note was the rise of UKIP under the leadership of Nigel Farage. The defining feature of this mobilisation was once again populism. The identities and interests of 'the British people' were antithetical and threatened by integration, which had now been fully discredited by the Eurozone crisis. The focus for this Eurosceptic mobilisation was a referendum on Britain's continued membership. When Cameron conceded this, it signalled a hardening of Euroscepticism on the part of the political class with the Labour party accommodating to the Conservative position. Chapter 8 argues that the period 2010–2013 witnessed an unravelling of the British governing approach to Europe.

Conclusion

The book shows that it is possible to trace a multi-dimensional British Eurosceptic trajectory from the 1950s up until the Coalition government in 2013. British decline was evident throughout the first half of the twentieth century but it was most acute from the late 1950s as it entered a post-imperial phase. This situation created the momentum for the 'turn to Europe'. However, this was concomitant with the reproduction of Britain as a Eurosceptic state, in which traditional conceptions of British interests and identity were to be defended within this context of change. This took a populist turn as Eurosceptics embraced anti-elite appeals to 'the people'. In summary, Euroscepticism becomes central to the reproduction of a distinct and exceptional British state, and its institutionalised politics, in a context of globally-induced structural change and domestic political crisis.

Chapter 2
The Post-Imperial Crisis

Introduction

The starting point of this chapter is Alan Milward's (1992) seminal account of European integration. From Milward's perspective, British approaches towards European integration diverge markedly from the post-war European reconstruction that takes place in the core countries of Western Europe. The chapter goes on to argue that Britain in the 1950s was principally an imperial power entering a period of post-imperial crisis, and it is this context that determines its relation to integration. Its post-war institutions were not those of a nationally organised capitalist welfare state, but of a global power wrestling with relative economic, and absolute political, decline. The consequence of these developments was a crisis both of political economy and of political identity, which projects of national renewal failed to resolve. Thus, British membership of the EC emerges as a conservative strategy, but one that lacked consensus and provided a new opportunity to contest the nation. This chapter sets out this context in broad terms, before documenting its implications for the policy and politics of Britain and Europe in Chapters 3 and 4.

The Missing European Rescue of the British State

It is the emergence of a common state model across Western Europe after the Second World War that is, according to Milward, the basis for the formation of the European Communities. He argues that European integration was a core dimension of the post-war establishment of a new state form, the Keynesian welfare state. This model of the nation-state was predicated on the securing of legitimacy by responding to a greater set of demands from citizens than ever before (p. 26). It was organised in terms of a wider social consensus than had been seen in the past, including 'labour, agricultural producers, and a diffuse alliance of lower and middle income beneficiaries of the welfare state' (p. 27). There was a virtual guarantee of full employment via Keynesian demand management, and political parties competed with one another for electoral support on the basis of their commitment to welfare programmes (p. 31). The success of this post-war welfare state has been identified in its twin settlements (Offe, 1984, p. 147). Firstly, the productivist or redistributive settlement, which formally incorporated organised labour into collective bargaining and recognised its role in public policy formation. With varying degrees of success, this reconfiguration of the power relationship between labour and capital was the mechanism by which the capitalist welfare state attempted to overcome the disruptive struggles and contradictions of liberal capitalism, and enable Fordist economic modernisation to take place. Secondly, the state secured legitimation by a redistributive settlement institutionalised in the extension of welfare provision and the establishment of the 'social wage' (Rhodes, 2000). The implication of Milward's analysis is, however, that for a number of Western European states the construction of the welfare state involved a third settlement, one that redefined the relations between these states and secured future growth and stability. The welfare state was dependent on economic growth and the EC was a key mechanism that secured and stimulated the burgeoning European market (Milward, 1992, p. 223). National protectionism had been seen as one of the main causes of economic instability in the pre-war period, thus it was in the interests of these European states to avoid it. There was a need for a system which allowed governments to subsidise, protect and modernise industries without using tariffs and quotas which closed national borders to trade. This was achieved by the limited surrenders of national sovereignty within the framework of a European Community (Milward, 1992; Milward and Sorenson, 1993). For Milward, the key political goal behind the integrationist project was to secure the allegiance of citizens to the nation-state, which had been weakened by the catastrophe of the Second World War. This went hand in hand with the need to incorporate West Germany into a European commercial and political framework.

In placing Milward's classic account of integration within a broader framework,[1] it is therefore useful to identify the EEC with the post-1945 Fordist solution to the problem of maintaining capitalist growth and stabilising state boundaries. Integration put in place an organised European economic space that allowed capitalism to expand in the interests of the nation-state. In this sense, it was part of a mode of regulation that involved:

> highly diversified attempts within different nation-states to arrive at political, institutional and social arrangements that could accommodate the chronic

---

1   European integration can be viewed as part of a global Fordist mode of regulation. Fordism has been characterised as a form of social organisation typical of the twentieth century. It involves the economic dominance of mass production and semi-skilled labour, the centralised organisation of both large-scale capital and labour, and a more economically and socially interventionist state (Aglietta, 1979; Lipietz, 1985; Hall and Jacques, 1989; Harvey, 1989; Rustin, 1989; Overbeek, 1990). After the Second World War in Western Europe, Fordism was also more likely to be characterised by formal democratic structures, and included features such as constitutionalism. The project of European integration was an expression of the intensification of international relations between Fordist European states. This occurred to the extent that integration is usefully conceptualised independently of nation-state power as an emergent system of regional governance. This is important to the present study because it is this profound transformation and modernisation of European state relations that has been persistently problematic for the British state.

incapacities of capitalism to regulate the essential conditions of its own reproduction. (Harvey, 1989, p. 129)

From the perspective of this model of post-war political economy, European integration provided a regional solution to regulation; a solution that was between the nation-state and the broader set of international institutional arrangements that came into place after the war under American hegemony. The elitist and technocratic features of the integrationist project were part of the international spread of Fordist political economic structures. These structures established national societies of citizens whose lifestyles were geared to consumption and who had expectations of rising standards of living. It was in this respect that Milward can legitimately argue that integration was primarily 'a response of national governments to popular demand' (1996, p. 65).

Nevertheless, Milward understates the role of post-national political developments in the process of European integration and, in particular, federalist forces (Anderson, 1997, p. 59). The post-war problem of allegiance led to the extension of the formally rational structures, of political authority of which the European Communities were a part. In the nation-state, these structures organised and neutralised political conflict by the extension of bureaucratic institutions that processed the claims of citizens (these included corporative arrangements, welfare organisations, mass political parties, interest groups and parliaments) (Habermas, 1976, p. 37; Offe, 1984, p. 163, 1996, p. 14). Underpinning these developments were modern principles of political legitimacy, legal constitutionalism and popular sovereignty (Anderson, 1992, p. 340). In Germany and Italy, new forms of regional and federal government were imposed in the wake of fascism. While France remained a unitary state, the solution to its post-war imperial crisis involved the rewriting of the constitution and the establishment of the Fifth Republic. The formal implementation of European integration, the Treaties of Paris (1951) and Rome (1957), were an extension of processes of political modernisation and were part of broader processes of constitution-making that underpinned post-war reconstruction. The Treaties linked together elites (national ministers, officials and interest group representatives) within a formal framework of institutionalised rules and rule making, which enabled the pursuit of defined economic and political objectives (W. Wallace, 1990, p. 79). Within this elite context, the principles of federalism and the possibilities of European unity had real political meaning and challenged the reestablishment of post-war Europe purely on the basis of national sovereignty (Lipgens, 1982).

In summary, European integration saw the emergence of a distinctively European post-national corporatist regime that was consistent with global politico-economic restructurings occurring under the patronage of American hegemony. It was against this background of state reorganisation and post-national modernisation that British opposition to European integration must be understood.

At first sight the social and economic consensus that brought the EC into being was also evident in Britain (Milward, 1992, p. 436). The 'ambitions and functions' of the British state were extended in a variety of ways, including: a commitment to full employment; agricultural protection; demand management and state control over industry, and the extension of welfare (p. 345). A key difference, however, was that on the continent these goals were underpinned by an industrial and commercial policy explicitly designed to support the modernisation of industry and to encourage an export-led recovery of national industry, primarily within a European trading bloc. Milward argues a British commercial policy centred on money rather than trade was in marked contrast to a regional solution to the economic problems of the post-war era (p. 433). British post-war economic policies were based on the Bretton Woods agreements and related Anglo-American agreements for a 'one-world' economic system (p. 347), in which the reconstruction of the national economy was firmly linked with the international financial system and Britain's leading role within it. As such, a central feature of the relevant agreements was the re-establishment of sterling as an international currency in exchange for a substantial dollar loan. The resultant problem, however, was that it put into place a system of fixed exchange rates that could only secure sterling as an international currency against a strong dollar. This proved unrealistic and the 1947 experiment with conversion led to a sterling crisis and had to be abandoned in a matter of weeks. Both 1949 and 1951 witnessed further runs on the reserves as a consequence of balance of payments crises that confirmed sterling's weakness. Nevertheless, governments remained committed to sterling's global role and with it the restoration of Britain's decision-making authority over the global economy (p. 354). From early on this brought British governments into conflict with specific European economic arrangements, such as the European Payments Union: a soft-currency zone that supported European trade and allowed European countries to obtain credit on easy terms (p. 350). For British elites, it diverted trade away from hard currency markets and between 1950 and 1957 they attempted to have it dissolved and lead Europe into a 'one world system' (p. 352, p. 387).

Milward therefore argues that the failure of British governments to take seriously European integration reflected the continued historical dominance of finance over industry (p. 395). The pursuit of currency convertibility and the 'one world system' reflected the interests of the City of London, and the desire to restore its international business. The City was in no position to facilitate the introduction of policies of economic modernisation, as it was a 'closed social circle protected by its own restrictionist politics' (p. 395). Its dominance over economic policy continued because of the weakness of industry; the British state lacked the deep association between commercial and industrial policies that had been developed elsewhere. Industry had a far more limited role in government compared to the Bank of England and the Treasury, which favoured finance. Industry itself did not challenge government policy, but rather pursued economic strategies that were defensive, retreating into what were perceived to be 'safe' world markets and failing to take advantage of European opportunities (pp. 403–24). Hence the new political consensus that was typical of the reconstructed European state was absent in Britain. Indeed, the developments underway in Europe were to a large extent an anathema to the British governing elites, 'a hermetically sealed system with so little outward vision that no understanding of European developments could be possible', reflecting, in part, the continued dominance of key institutions by a socially prejudiced and amateurish upper class (p. 431).

When Milward came to write the official history of the United Kingdom and the European Community, he came to a rather different verdict on the actions and approaches of British politicians and civil servants:

> There were elements of sentimental grandiosity, but not such as to constitute a fundamental critique of British policy towards Western Europe. Where pragmatism made mistakes it was more through ignorance, or through the pressure of party politics, than through conceit ... (2002, p. x)

While the earlier work emphasised the comparative weakness of the British post-war consensus as explaining the failure to fully engage with European developments, the 'official history' is suggestive of a form of British consensus, but one that was structurally different to that which had emerged on the continent. From the official record, it is possible to identify the contours of a *national strategy*: a clear sense of where the country was heading that gave rise to fixed and coherent goals and guided the first phase of Britain's relations with European integration (p. 7). Many of the key objectives of this strategy were global in nature, reflecting not grandiosity but a realistic assessment of Britain's place in the world, and the advantages that could be traded in by maintaining and extending these connections. In addition, they were underpinned by a concern with the national community (living standards, employment, welfare and security) rather than with world power status: 'these were the goals of a medium-sized materialist democracy' (p. 4).

Milward's work on Britain and the early years of European integration points in two directions: a failure of modernisation, associated with the inability to break culturally and institutionally with Empire, and a rational and coherent national strategy that was, in the end, unsustainable. Yet to conceptualise a strategy that was largely driven by external concerns as national is problematic; moreover, to conceive it as imperial does not necessarily mean it is regressive and delusional. This book problematises the concept of a national strategy and proposes that we view Britain's relationship with Europe in terms of imperial and post-imperial strategies.

A Very British Consensus

The extent to which we can apply the idea of a post-war consensus to Britain requires clarification. Hay points out that 'consensus is perhaps the most disputed term in the academic vernacular of post-war British political history' (1999, p. 20). The concept is used to describe a degree of bipartisan convergence that existed in the post-war period (Beer, 1982; Miliband, 1973; Gamble, 1974; Barnett, 1986; Lowe, 1990; Addison, 1994). The clearest demonstration of this convergence was when the 1951 Conservative government took office and retained the commitment to full employment and the welfare state (Jessop, 1980, p. 29). However, the extent to which a consensus existed amongst British elites, let alone across society as a whole, remains highly debatable (Pimlott, 1988; Addison, 1994, pp 279–92; Hay, 1996, pp 44–8). Consensus can be used to refer to agreements on policy objectives across the main parties. However, it becomes more analytically significant when it is used to illustrate a broader political settlement, characterised by the structured acceptance and reproduction of the broad parameters of the state.

One of the fruits of victory in 1945 was the survival of Britain's cultural and institutional heritage, to the point where the post-war settlement was markedly continuous with what had been in existence before (Cain and Hopkins, 1993b, p. 266; Hay, 1994, p. 45). This inheritance consisted of the dominant institutions of the British imperial order that had been gradually adapted to the development of mass democracy in the late nineteenth and early twentieth centuries. The threat posed by working and middle class radicalism in the eighteenth and nineteenth centuries led to the formation of a cadre of intellectuals and administrators, imbued with the elite ethos by the institutions of the public schools, Oxford and Cambridge, who were able to actively constitute a hegemonic order (Gowan, 1987). An imperial status order was established, organised around hierarchies of social and political identities in which 'property was no longer the basis of the suffrage, but "race", gender, labour and level of civilisation now determined who was included in and excluded from the political nation' (Hall, 1994, p. 27).

These developments were indicative of piecemeal and conservative forms of state rationalisation that took place in the nineteenth century in reaction to domestic pressures, and included the extension of the franchise and the establishment of elementary state education. However, it was in the context of a combination of internal and external threats at the beginning of the twentieth century that the British state went through a more intense period of rationalisation. This was a response to a crisis of the British state that stemmed from German and US threats to its global hegemony and the rejection of the authority of the state by Irish nationalists, suffragettes and a growing minority of anarcho-syndicalists in the labour movement (Leys, 1983, p. 39). Significantly, these threats gave rise to a strategy of social imperialism that was centrally dependent on a programme of social reform and attempted to institutionalise conflicts over class, gender and nation (Nairn, 1979, p. 54; Leys, 1983, p. 50). This strategy saw the Labour party fully incorporated into the state and accepting the 'soundness of Constitution and Parliament' (Nairn, 1979, p. 54). It was a particular form of British state rationalisation established as a necessary condition of state survival. British elites committed to the construction of a national political order and established the hegemony of a more revisionist liberal ideology. During the 1920s, this included a system of imperial preferences that allowed newly emerging Fordist industries, such as the car industry, to flourish (Overbeek, 1990, p. 76). Such developments co-existed with the continuation of a liberal economic orthodoxy, and a commitment to the central principles of *laissez faire*.

The British post-war consensus was, therefore, largely a modification of this social imperial consensus, which had been intellectually fashioned towards the end of the nineteenth century and established at the beginning of the twentieth century. The popular 'radicalism' that emerged during the war in support for social reform was consistent with the imperial order. The tremendous support for the Beveridge proposals represented a Gramscian passive revolution controlled from above, encapsulating the principles of a revisionary imperialist liberalism (Hay, 1996, p. 30). Moreover, a Keynesian economic strategy that promised full employment and material prosperity did not challenge City and Treasury dominance and the role of sterling in the global economy.

The post-war Labour government was entrenched within an existing imperialist political order, within which the national political community was to be made compatible. Nairn points out that the Second World War provided the Labour party with a 'real opportunity' to move forward but was 'circumscribed', as the war also validated the existing ethos and class structure (Nairn, 1979, p. 60). Labour's incorporation was evident on taking office: the new government ended its hostility to imperialism and 'hoisted the burdens of Empire with all the enthusiasm of the converted' (Cain and Hopkins, 1993b, p. 277; see also Fieldhouse, 1984). Initially, Britain was to be the third force in global politics between America and the USSR, although this ambition was quickly modified to being the junior partner of the US. Crucial to securing this world power status was the extension and reinforcement of the concept of Empire (Cain and Hopkins, 1993b, pp. 276–7). The Colonial Office was reinvigorated and set about coordinating a post-war renewal of the imperial project (Lee, 1977). This strategy could not be dismissed as either inept or based on nostalgia for the past, but rather 'the renewed commitment to Empire was as much a matter of calculation as it was of sentiment. Quite simply the imperial option appeared to be far more promising than the alternatives, especially in war torn Europe' (Cain and Hopkins, 1993b, p. 276).

The immediate post-war British state remained primarily a world state because of its immense colonial possessions, the position of its institutions in the global economy and the role of British elites in global governance. It was believed that economic recovery would follow from an eventual revival of the 'one world' system. The economic strategy to enable this to take place initially involved a form of imperial preferential trading and the establishment of the sterling bloc, and later by a return to multilateralism and convertibility. The belief in the symbiotic relationship between the international interests of financial capitalism and the national interest was instinctively accepted by British governing elites, and was evident in the post war Labour administration's attitude to the City and the role of sterling. The so-called City-Bank of England-Treasury nexus re-emerged as a distinct source of power, ensuring that the value of sterling continued to be the marker of British economic competency (Ingham, 1984; Cain, 1997). The Attlee government 'was active in Commonwealth conferences in promoting the solidarity of the sterling area and the use of sterling as a reserve currency. It also took the first tentative steps towards reopening the doors of the London market-place' (Strange, 1967, p. 232). However, this was now fundamentally dependent on the US:

> the role of the City in the world economy changed and its place was now clearly defined by the contours of the Atlantic economy and Pax Americana, and by the dominance of those fractions of capital associated with that of American hegemony – the internationalizing 'Fordist' industries such as automobiles, chemicals, and consumer electronics. (Overbeek, 1990, p. 107)

The continuation of sterling's role as a reserve currency was underpinned by US financial support, which had been agreed during the Anglo-American Loan negotiations of 1945. It meant that the 'special relationship' developed on the basis of an institutionalised conjunction of financial interests.

The British post-war political order remained imbued with a cosmopolitan-imperial model of political development that set it apart from Western Europe and its post-war national corporatist trajectory. In Chapter 3 this context is shown to be decisive in British governments' response to European integration. However, it is a position that begins to change towards the end of 1950s, and this culminates in the decision of the Macmillan government to apply for membership of the EC in 1961. The shift in Britain's position is explained by a changing context that is characterised by a post-imperial crisis of political economy and political identity.

A Crisis of Political Economy

The failure of national accumulation strategies during the 1960s and 1970s has been explored in considerable depth (Bacon and Eltis, 1978; Glyn and Harrison, 1980; Pollard, 1980; Fine and Harris, 1985; Coates and Hillard, 1986; Overbeek, 1990; Gamble, 1994). Jessop (1991) has usefully termed the crisis of the British economy that had become chronic by the 1970s as a crisis of flawed Fordism. He notes:

> It involved a limited expansion of mass production, relatively poor productivity growth, union strength producing wage increases from 1960s onwards not justified by productivity growth, a precocious commitment to social welfare and jobs for all, growing import penetration from the 1960s to satisfy the mass consumer market, and from the mid-1970s, to meet demand for capital goods. (p. 138)

Jessop argues that liberal, corporatist and *dirigiste* strategies all failed to work in Britain and resulted in a chronically flawed Fordist economy and state (pp. 140–41). Liberal strategies were constrained by the lack of modernisation and poor management within British industry. Corporatist strategies failed because both capital and labour were fragmented and disorganised. *Dirigiste* solutions were limited because of the state's incapacity to influence the economy at a micro level. A major cause of these failures was the range of powerful and particularised producer groups and organisations in Britain (Marquand, 1981, p. 27). These groups acted in terms of their own interests and lacked a conception of the wider general interest. They behaved conservatively and inhibited change. Ultimately the state relied on the blunt instruments of legal restraints (e.g. prices and incomes) and money (e.g. subsidies) to coerce organisations to behave in the way they wanted (Jessop, 1980). In particular, a powerful and voluntarist labour movement, conditioned by a history of operating inside an imperial regime, compounded the problem of constructing a class compromise organised around a stable corporatist settlement. The implication of this was that 'conflict around the issue of the social wage remained central to problems of economic management and renewal' (Rhodes, 2000, p. 168). Governments failed to appreciate the importance of securing the social wage, and they were faced with a comparatively dysfunctional, and often militant, labour movement that asserted its independence in relation to the state.

From the perspective developed here, this flawed Fordism can also be seen as an expression of the extent to which the British political economic order continued to be post-imperial, rather than national, with a considerable but problematic international orientation. This meant a commitment to shrinking markets, investment going overseas and the pursuit of a high and stable exchange rate that disadvantaged domestic industry. Consequently attempts to maintain full employment, stimulate domestic demand and maintain capital investment were from the outset fundamentally compromised (Hay, 1994, p. 45; Anderson, 1992, p. 166). Most strikingly, it meant,

> policy lurched between contracting the economy when a failure to achieve balances, above all in foreign payments, threatened sterling, and expanding it when unemployment started to rise. The excessive use of monetary and fiscal instruments to engineer deflation was highly damaging to investment – both public and private. (Rhodes, 2000, p. 166)

In effect successful Keynesian policies depended on a strong national economy and expansion of productive investment in order to avoid balance of trade deficits. This proved impossible to achieve in Britain because the state was incapable of reorganising industry or curtailing British commitments abroad. Therefore expansion of the economy fuelled wage demands, sucked in imports and created balance of payments crises. The consequence of this was a loss of confidence in sterling, the threat of currency devaluation and the acceleration of the trend to invest large amounts of British capital abroad. Governments therefore resorted to policies of retrenchment in order to restore the confidence of the financial markets, which they believed depended on the status of sterling as a reserve currency. They continued to shore up the value of sterling through austerity measures and international loans in order to secure confidence in the City as a world financial centre and avoid a flight of capital. This was deeply problematic considering the inexorable decline of sterling and the globalised role of the City, whose interests had increasingly become divorced from those of sterling. The sustained speculation on the pound culminated in the devaluation crisis of 1967, which exhausted the official defences and, in effect, led to the acceptance that sterling was never going to rival the dollar. The adoption of floating exchange rates during the 1970s did not, however, prevent the intensification of speculation against the pound from financial markets that had little faith in the British economy. The politics of sterling had disastrous effects on programmes of reform designed to construct a national political order. They led to high interest rates, investment crises and inflationary pressures that proved disastrous for the domestic economy and persistent attacks on the welfare state that undermined wider social relations.

The relative weakness of the British economy led large-scale transnational capital interests to look for ways to disengage themselves from domestic politics. Gradually, the City began to accept this as the most fruitful strategy for the renewal of financial interests. The clearest example of this was the Eurocurrency market that grew rapidly from the late 1950s onwards.[2] This provided the City with a new role as a 'global offshore centre' servicing the large quantities of dollars that were now looking for a European home. These found their base in London because there were few controls on the foreign currency holdings of non-residents, in contrast to the restrictions on the outflow of sterling, which was in order to avoid speculative attacks and maintain the balance of payments. Burn (1999) has demonstrated how the establishment of the Eurodollar market reflected the historically depoliticised facets of British economic governance. The City was effectively 'quarantined' from the domestic economy by the system of exchange controls introduced after 1931, and was 'accorded *de facto* offshore status', allowing it to deal in the currencies and deposits of non-domiciles as unrestrictedly as it had in the nineteenth century (p. 236). This did not occur, according to Burn, as a consequence of some kind of coordinated action on the part of the Bank-City-Treasury nexus, but emerged outside of political scrutiny precisely because this nexus operated in such a way that the Bank of England acted to shield the City from political control. His key insight here is that that this nexus permitted the national interest to be construed in such a way that it included unregulated, transnational capitalist interests. In this context, the Treasury devolved political power to the Bank that in turn devolved it to the City. The nationalisation of the Bank of England in 1946 had incorporated the Bank within the state whilst, paradoxically, allowing it to adopt a policy position at variance with an elected government and in line with particular private interests, yet configured as the national interest (p. 246). The benefits of the Eurodollar market were now obvious. It meant less dependence on sterling, which meant less dependence on the state and the politics of the domestic economy. It was not then the case that

---

2 By at least $150m between 1963 and 1974 and by considerably more following the recycling of OPEC oil profits in the second half of the 1970s (Hobsbawm, 1995, p. 278).

the British state actively nurtured the Eurodollar market, but that its institutional architecture allowed this to emerge free from any democratic political oversight. Whilst this market may have prefigured the globalisation of finance, and the loss of government control over the money supply and exchange rates that was evident by the early 1990s, in the case of the UK it was in part domestically driven by a political and institutional opportunity structure.

The Eurodollar was then symptomatic of a political economy that was undergoing a post-imperial reorientation, which was also continuous with its liberal imperial past. The failure to achieve successful domestic economic modernisation meant that the UK economy was, in certain respects, open and transnational without the strength to effectively compete overseas. What was characteristic of Fordist multinationals, based on the US model, was their hierarchical organisation, integrating activities and coordinating across different functions to provide more extensive control over production, and building upon an already strong presence in the domestic market. In contrast, many of the British 'multinationals' that had emerged in the nineteenth century lacked any such domestic base and many operated exclusively abroad. They were promoted and often managed by City investment houses as a way of accessing and maximising overseas investment opportunities, particularly mining and utilities, in the context of formal and informal imperialism (Cox, 1997, p. 11). In the immediate post-war period, the incentives for change were weak because of the security of trade with Commonwealth and former imperial markets. However, as these went into decline, UK business found itself out-competed abroad and faced with the incursion of foreign multinationals at home, particularly from the US. Between 1950 and 1962, of the 376 new subsidiaries established in the UK, 81 per cent of these were US multinationals (p. 26). Relative economic decline particularly highlighted the lack of successful 'national champions' in the UK that could extend their reach overseas, accumulating profits that could then be repatriated.

How far governments would have been able to reverse these trends remains debatable. However, they appeared naïve in their attitudes to the impact of financial markets on Britain, and this was evident in their failure to actively advance a European solution. Any reform of the economy would therefore have required the state to ensure that the interests of financial and transnational capital were subordinated to the national interest; instead, governments persisted in the belief that the international priorities of the City-Bank-Treasury nexus were those of the nation. The financial markets were, therefore, effectively able to exercise a veto over key aspects of economic policy. This was exacerbated by the breakdown of the Bretton Woods agreements on regulated exchange rates and the increase in speculative attacks on currencies. In this context, the Labour government in 1976 opted for an international solution to Britain's economic crisis in order to regain market confidence in the form of austerity policies imposed in agreement with the International Monetary Fund. From this point onwards, national economic policy was firmly subordinated to a new wave of global financial market integration.

A Crisis of National Identity

A predominantly political economy approach to understanding the British post-imperial crisis and problems of political modernisation does not, however, detail the extent to which this crisis is also a crisis of national political identities. From this perspective, the end of Empire did not mean the emergence and consolidation of a British nation-state but, instead, a highly contested post-imperial political order. As we shall see, this has specific implications for understanding the relationship between the British state and the project of European integration.

Three features of this stand out. Firstly, there have been persistent struggles over ethnicity, citizenship and the position within British society of minorities from former colonies and other non-Western countries (Halsey, 1986, pp. 67–76; Gilroy, 1987; Anthias and Yuval Davies, 1992, pp. 40–60). Britishness had been established as a global form of identification and the right to settle in Britain had been established as a justifiable right in respect of obligations fulfilled to the British Empire, notably military service. In 1948 automatic citizenship, including the franchise, was granted for newly arrived Empire and Commonwealth migrants. At the same time, the British government promoted immigration to address the shortage of young male workers that had occurred as a consequence of wartime losses. A net inflow of migration started in the 1950s as a result of a large increase in immigration from Commonwealth countries, particularly those of South Asian origin. The legacy of Empire was therefore an openness to migrants, and an *ad hoc* multiculturalism, as the formal inclusionary and exclusionary statuses and mechanisms, associated with a territorially based citizenship, were absent. Yet, in a context of rising ethnic and racial tensions and economic crises, governments put in place increasingly restrictive immigration controls that particularly focused on limiting the entry of non-white people, culminating in the British Nationality Act of 1981. Nevertheless British citizenship policy remained ambiguous and complex (Hansen, 2000). The post-imperial period was marked by a continued struggle to reconfigure British imperial subjects as national citizens, indicative of the extent to which Britain remained somewhat at a variance from other modes of state building, and their particular but established routes to citizenship and nationality (Brubaker, 1989, 1992).

Secondly, there have been conflicts over the internal boundaries of the United Kingdom and, in particular, over the status of the 'subordinate nations' of Scotland, Wales and Northern Ireland within the Union. Clearly, the most violent of these struggles occurred in Northern Ireland where, by the 1960s, the historical subordination and political exclusion of the sizeable Catholic minority led to a wave of civil rights protests and the establishment of a paramilitary republican movement. The emergence of a correspondingly hard-line British Loyalism, including paramilitary forces, alongside an increasingly coercive state response to the conflict, meant a political solution proved elusive until the breakthrough that led to the 1998 Good Friday Agreement. While far more limited, Welsh nationalism was from the 1950s characterised by movements that employed violent means.

However, its mainstream expression was the defence of a distinctive cultural and linguistic heritage that eschewed demands for full political independence. The case of Scotland was different again: the Scottish Nationalist Party emerged as a significant force by the 1970s and, in campaigning for separation from the rest of the United Kingdom, it could point to a long history of independent statehood.

The final dimension of this post-imperial crisis of national identity was the fracturing and fragmentation of British institutional politics. This included the persistent decline in the share of the national vote that the main political parties were able to obtain. This was concomitant with electoral volatility including a weakening of party loyalties, particularly associated with processes of class de-alignment, alongside a generalised political disengagement evidenced by declining electoral turnouts. While the political system still favoured Conservative and Labour party dominance, a multi-party politics emerged that included the distinctive politics of devolved governments. The idea that the interests and preferences of British citizens could be translated into identification with mass political parties and stable forms of public participation in British democratic life proved increasingly problematic.

European integration therefore enters the political landscape at a point of British political disintegration. This is the context for understanding the relationship between Britain and Europe and the emergence of Eurosceptic Britain.

The Post-Imperial Making of Eurosceptic Britain

The British post-imperial crisis most clearly expressed itself in the struggles of successive governments to carry out national modernisation and manifesting in chronic problems of territorial rule. It was a crisis of transition that was fuelled by the absence of a coherent and successful national accumulation strategy, together with a lack of any reconfiguration of national political identities.

In relation to the national political economy, the pursuit of membership of the EC was viewed as critical. It was a liberal strategy of economic modernisation, aimed at improving the competitiveness of the British economy by exposing it to the market forces of a European common market. This was to provide the necessary stimulus to Britain's international Fordist companies that could be the basis to reinvigorate the British economy (Overbeek, 1990, pp. 100–101). However, it was a strategy that potentially replaced, rather than complemented, the modernisation of the British economy. Crucially, it was a significant change that the state could bring with some autonomy from domestic constraints, because it was within the realms of foreign policy decision-making. Yet, without economic modernisation, it was a blunt economic strategy that proposed the revival of the British economy by exposing it to European competition and giving the economy a 'short, sharp shock'. In this sense it was a traditional free trade approach to British economic problems. By the mid 1960s, the concern was that this strategy would have a negative impact on the British balance of payments, because the inadequacies of British industry would be exposed by the intensification of foreign competition (Crossman, 1979, pp. 259–60; Young, 1998, pp. 195–6). By the early 1970s, the European strategy became, at best, a short-term instrument of crisis management, aimed at shoring up dominant fractions of British capital in the context of the crisis in US hegemony and a global economic downturn. From a longer-term perspective, an economic relationship between Britain and the EC was being established, in which a key rationale for membership was to secure Britain as a gateway to Europe for transnational capital.

At the heart of the failure to construct a consensus around a programme of substantive social and economic change, was the institutionalisation of the political class within a structure that worked against change. Governments and parties then continued to support the semi-rational structures of imperial rule. However, as these structures declined in legitimacy and new forms of representation, such as corporatism, failed to replace them, the state resorted to forms of coercion and populism (Jessop, 1980, pp. 54–65). The continued conservative belief in the established institutions of the British state underpinned and held together both the Labour and Conservative parties, despite the intensification of divisions during the 1960s and 1970s (Nairn, 1977; Marquand, 1988; Anderson, 1992). Thus, despite the unique historical conjuncture that the post-imperial crisis represented, the response by the British political class was mostly regressive. They liberated international economic interests and asserted the power of the state in order to secure a renewal of accumulation. The personalised visions of a European British trajectory that were articulated by pro-European politicians were often compromised and confused, and did not form the basis for a coherent reconstruction of either the economy or national-political identities. The deep institutionalised visions of the relationship between politics and the economy, that were identifiable in other European member states and drove integration forward, were absent in the British case.

This struggle to reconfigure political identities was especially evident in relation to British membership of the EC, which was consistently presented by governing elites as a continuation, rather than a transformation, of the political order. The conservative European strategy put together by the Macmillan government saw Europe as a way of stabilising and strengthening pre-existing conceptions of British interests and identities in the wake of imperial decline. However, the unintended consequence of governing elites' European strategy during the 1960s and 1970s was the intensification of Euroscepticism, as Europe became something to mobilise against in order to construct and assert conceptions of British national identity and alternative projects for national renewal. For sections of the political class, the debate on EC membership offered a false resolution of the post-imperial crisis by resurrecting and recreating British imagined communities (Anderson, 1991) in the face of the project of European integration. Here it is evident that, while the opportunity to reconstruct the British state as a European nation-state through membership of the EC arose, the realisation of this was fundamentally constrained by existing traditions and identities reasserted within the post-imperial crisis. Indeed, 'new' or modified forms of legitimation were emerging in this post-imperial situation, that foresaw only a limited role for European initiatives, and centred on populist conceptions of British exceptionalism (Hall, 1979; Gamble, 1988). Evidently, the British nation was being imagined, and the contestation over the relationship with European integration was a fundamental part of that process.

Conclusion

This Chapter has counterposed European integration as an example of post-war organised capitalism, with a British imperial state and its post-imperial crisis. Milward's discussion of the interdependent relationship between national and European modernisation was shown to be missing in the British case. It was argued that Britain's highly globalised modern development, its post-war decline as a global power and the post-imperial crisis is the context through which we must understand its relation to European integration. Specifically, Eurosceptic Britain was being configured in the context of a crisis of political economy and of national identity, and the political struggles that emerged out of this. It is from this perspective of structural continuity and discontinuity that the next two chapters explore the early history of Britain's relationship with European integration.

Chapter 3
Britain and the Beginnings of European Integration

Introduction

This chapter explores the British response to the first wave of European integration. The lukewarm reception from British governing elites to integration is shown to reflect the post-war social imperial consensus of the time. It implied a commitment to the reconstruction of British state power within a context of global, rather than European, interdependencies that would re-establish British power. In this respect, the key objective of policy was to secure a wider Atlantic community consisting of the United States, the British Empire and Commonwealth, and Western Europe. On the one hand, British policy contributed towards the wider geopolitical framework which enabled European integration to take place (Deighton, 1993). On the other, British European priorities were framed within a set of global and national parameters that excluded participation in the European Coal and Steel Community (ECSC) and the European Economic Community (EEC). This is shown to change once the realities of British decline are fully manifest. The chapter explores how Europe became a solution to the emerging post-imperial crisis for the Macmillan government that culminates in the first failed application for EC membership. Yet it is argued that both in the crafting of this strategy, and the political response to it, we can begin to identify the contours of Eurosceptic Britain.

The Labour Government and the Schuman Plan 1950

The formal beginnings of European integration can be traced to the Schuman Declaration of May 1950, when the French Foreign Minister put forward the idea of a supranational European authority to govern coal and steel industries:

> the French government proposes to take action immediately on one limited but decisive point ... to place Franco-German production of coal and steel under a common High Authority, within the framework of an organisation open to the participation of the other countries in Europe. (cited in Pinder, 1991, p. 1)

The ECSC was the brainchild of Jean Monnet, the head of the French Commissariat du Plan that formed the basis of post-war French reconstruction. Monnet persuaded Robert Schuman of the idea, because it was seen at the time as a solution to containing a reconstructed Germany. By placing the German steel industry under a supranational authority, the backbone of the German economy was secured within a European framework. European control over the German steel industry eventually meant any future German rearmament could be monitored and contained. It also resolved the problem of the Ruhr Authority, which had been set up in 1948 to watch over Germany's main steel making region.

The question that arises is: why did the solution to the control of the Ruhr encompass the wider ambition of European federalism? Anderson raises this issue in his discussion of Milward's intergovernmentalist analysis of the origins of the European Community, and argues that Milward understates the role of federalist forces (1997, p. 58). In particular, Anderson points out that it was the role of Monnet that led to the proposal of a supranational solution to post-war European cooperation. Monnet was an exceptional historical figure who was capable of turning a supranational vision into a practical reality. European security and prosperity was to be guaranteed by placing Germany on an equal footing with other states, within an overarching supranational legal framework. It was a solution that was fully supported by the smaller nations of Europe, which had come to the conclusion that their futures depended upon a federal Europe, but also because of the influence of Monnet in the United States and the support he received for the goal of a United Europe (Grosser, 1980, p. 104).

When the Schuman Declaration was published, it made explicit reference to the goal of political union. This position was restated by the German Chancellor, Konrad Adenauer, who made it clear that the project 'was above all political not economic' (cited in Nugent, 1994, p. 39). While the immediate concerns were economic growth and the position of Germany within Europe, the technocratic solution envisaged by Monnet had the wider ambition of binding the relations between European states within a legal constitutional order. The ECSC was to be composed of a regulatory body, the High Authority, independent of national governments, a court of law to enforce the Treaty, and a parliamentary assembly. As such, it clearly reflected the ambitions of Monnet and his supporters for a federal Europe that had been born out of resistance to fascism and then to Stalinism. In the ECSC, they believed they had found a practical method for achieving their goals; over time there would be a gradual transfer of national sovereignty to a supranational community, as national governments came to recognise its effectiveness in achieving specific policy goals. In this sense, its legitimacy stemmed not from direct support amongst electorates for the European ideal, but from an acceptance of the social and economic benefits that accrued from integration. The task of the ECSC was to provide 'economic expansion, growth of employment and a rising standard of living in the Member States' (European Communities – Commission, 1987, p. 23). On this view, a federal Europe would be founded on a form of civic supranationalism that mirrored the civic nationalism that formed the basis for post-war reconstruction. It reflected the federalist principle that the peoples and states of the six members were, at least notionally, equal. Citizenship was partially delinked from traditional ideas of national assertion and re-linked to economic growth and welfare.

The reaction of the British Labour government to the ECSC indicated the extent to which there was a fundamentally different consensus at work in Britain. The initial plans for a supranational Europe surprised the British. Ernest Bevin, Foreign Minister at the time, was shocked and angered by the French proposals and, in particular, at the lack of prior consultation. Both the Germans and the Americans were aware of the impending declaration, while the British were taken unawares because they were not consulted on the proposal (Lord, 1996, p. 6). British annoyance with the French proposal was unsurprising, as it represented a significant shift in French foreign policy. The British were keen to promote European cooperation through the framework of the Council of Europe and the Organisation for European Economic Cooperation (OEEC), an approach the French appeared to support. The British policy was to support gradual moves towards European unity based on intergovernmental cooperation, an approach that was designed to secure a particular form of British leadership of Western Europe. In fact, Bevin had gone so far as to propose the idea of a European 'Third Force', based on Anglo-French cooperation and, in particular, using French and British colonial possessions in Africa as a basis for European recovery (Greenwood, 1992, p. 66). Yet it appears that Bevin was unable to change the fundamental direction of an Atlanticist policy that was being pursued by the Treasury:

> On every occasion when Bevin actively tried to get the customs union rolling, the economic departments kicked it into touch, the Americans who opposed regional economic arrangements would be offended, that trade with the Commonwealth might be injured and that, anyway, economic integration with the dislocated French economy held no advantage. (p. 65)

This reflected the post-war consensus on foreign policy that Churchill encapsulated in his 'three circles' speech in 1950. The three circles were the British Commonwealth, the United States and Europe. Churchill had stated that there was an order of priority to these circles: 'The first circle for us is naturally the British Commonwealth and Empire ... then there is the English speaking world ... and finally there is Europe' (cited in Lord, 1996, p. 62). Evidently, considering British immediate post-war financial and military weakness alongside the emerging Soviet threat, only the security of the 'special relationship' could provide the basis for post-war re-establishment of Britain as a global power (Deighton, 1993, p. 13). On this view, British elites associated traditional notions of governing autonomy, associated with global rule and influence, with what was in reality increased dependence on the US.

Consequently, the British position was to participate in increased European cooperation, but this was to occur alongside the construction of a wider Atlantic community. It was believed that this would allow Britain to support European co-operation and maintain its independence and sovereignty as a global power. The French were sceptical, however, of the British commitment to Europe, and the supranationalism of the Schuman Declaration therefore represented a new direction in French European policy that broke with the strategy being pursued by the British. This change of direction by the French was given added impetus by American support for greater Western Europe unity (Grosser, 1980, p. 119).

The Labour government's official rejection of a closer economic union was laid down in a paper presented by Bevin and the Chancellor, Stafford Cripps (Moon, 1985, p. 71).[1] It reflected the traditional economic priority of the British state which was to secure sterling as an international currency, the economic importance of the Commonwealth, and a multilateral 'open world' system. Moon points out that these 'effectively distanced the Cabinet from European aspirations of economic unification ... and became its official policy' (p. 71). The British government did not, however, reject the Schuman Declaration out of hand (which was impossible anyway, considering it now had US backing), and recognised its contribution to Franco-German reconciliation. A Foreign Office report argued that the plan would be a pragmatic solution to the German problem, and that Britain should join it, or at least be positive about it, while acknowledging that supranationalism remained a major problem. However, the Cabinet position was that they were not prepared to enter into talks unless the supranational principle was negotiable. What is clear from these events is that the British government was not prepared to accept a proposal that would limit governing autonomy and the global role by committing Britain to European unity. The formal decision not to participate in the ECSC was taken on 2 June 1950, and identified the prior commitment to submit resources to the jurisdiction of the High Authority as the fundamental reason for non-participation:

> M. Schuman's original memorandum said in terms that his plan would be a step towards the federation of Europe. It has been our settled policy hitherto that in view of our world position and interests, we should not commit ourselves irrevocably to Europe either in the political or the economic sphere unless we could measure the extent and effects of the commitment. (PRO, CAB 129/40, C.P. (50) 120, 2 June 1950 cited in Gowland and Turner, 2000b, p. 25)

The Labour party's response to the issue was the publication of a pamphlet by the National Executive Committee entitled *European Unity* (1950 cited in Gowland and Turner, 2000b, pp. 70–71). This rejected the Schuman Plan because it appeared to threaten the Labour party's economic policies; in particular, the coal and steel industries were regarded as part of the commanding heights of the economy and needed to be nationalised in order to maintain full employment. The reluctance of other European governments to nationalise their industries meant that the British nationalised coal and steel industries would be combined with private industries in an 'unstable market'. The High Authority was seen as too weak to regulate these

---

[1] However, opposition to European integration did not represent the opinion of the Labour party as a whole. The party remained split on the issue with a substantial minority of the Labour movement in favour of a federal Europe. A motion proposed by a backbench MP at the 1948 conference for a United States of Europe was accepted by the Conference and opposed by the NEC (Moon, 1985, p. 74).

industries in comparison to national governments. There was also the fear that the Authority would be dominated by a non-socialist majority. *European Unity* argued that it was better to go with the 'winner takes all' British political system. The threat to the Labour government's national governing strategy had been summed up by Herbert Morrison's famous remark that 'it's no good. We can't do it. The Durham miners will never wear it' (cited in Young, 1998, p. 64), reflecting the militant opposition of the National Union Mineworkers to any change to the industry's newly established nationalised status. *European Unity* went on to refer to how closer involvement in Europe could jeopardise relations with the Commonwealth. It stated that Britain 'is the nerve centre of a world-wide Commonwealth which extends into every continent'; the Commonwealth, it argued, was the 'nucleus of a potential world society based on free cooperation' (1950 cited in Gowland and Turner, 2000b, p. 71). The document went on to express fears over the implications of the plan for domestic control of defence matters, the Sterling Area and on relations with the United States. *European Unity* encapsulated the Labour party's position and alternative views 'achieved no prominence at all within the anatomy of the issue derived from the Parliamentary debate' (Moon, 1985, p. 81).

For the Labour government, involvement in the Schuman plan would have meant challenging some of the core elements of the British state. The priority of the government was to maintain strong single party rule. Indeed, membership of the ECSC was perceived as a weakening of a strategy designed to secure the representation of an organised working class within the British state. This can be seen as paradoxical, since the opposition was part of a national class project that was already chronically weakened by its support for the structures of the imperial state. Nowhere was this more evident than in the failure of Labour's nationalisation policy to restructure the 'commanding heights' of the economy and to secure the representations of labour that were found in industry on the continent (Cronin, 1991; Hay, 1996).

These economic, political and geopolitical constraints on British participation within the Schuman Plan reflected the underlying social imperial consensus within the British political order. The ECSC implied a territorial and capitalist reorganisation of the British state that was profoundly unacceptable at the time. This opposition was most succinctly summarised in a Foreign Office memorandum of 12 December 1951, which outlined a commitment to Atlanticism and Empire/Commonwealth that was to remain unchallenged until the late 1950s:

> The United Kingdom cannot seriously contemplate joining in European integration. Apart from geographical and strategic considerations, Commonwealth ties and the special position of the United Kingdom as the centre of the Sterling Area, we cannot consider submitting our political and economic system to supranational institutions. Moreover, if these institutions did not prove workable, which their dissolution would not be serious for the individual countries which would go their separate ways again; it would be another matter for the United Kingdom which would have had to break its Commonwealth and Sterling Area connexions to join them. Nor is there, in fact, any evidence

that there is real support in this country for any institutional connection with the continent. Moreover, although the fact may not be universally recognised, it is not in the true interests of the continent that we should sacrifice our present unattached position which enables us, together with the United States, to give a lead to the free world. (DBPO [1986], Series II, Vol. I, No. 414 cited in Gowland and Turner, 2000b, pp. 29–30)

The dismay and anger at the Schuman Plan indicated the extent to which the British conception of the European order was being challenged. However, its rejection by British elites also indicated a continued confidence in the principles of British liberal imperialism. The latter was not based on formal legal constitutional arrangements and Fordist economic organisation but on a more informal political domination from London (which in the aftermath of the Second World War meant in partnership with Washington). The British position was to support looser, more intergovernmentalist arrangements, such as the OEEC, that limited its obligations to Europe and enabled it to concentrate on orchestrating the global political arena. It was informal global political domination that mattered and in this respect Britain seemed to view Europe, the third of Churchill's three circles, in the same way as the colonies of white settlement. The trappings of formal political independence were often necessary to secure informal political domination:

> As they [former colonies] increased their formal political independence, so they became reliant on flows of British capital to an extent that limited their freedom of action in crucial respects and tied export interests and their political representatives to policy norms, the rules of the game, set by London. (Cain and Hopkins, 1993a, p. 469)

The point here is that real power remained in London; in the case of Europe, the attitude was similar. Ultimately, power within Europe was not considered to lie in its sovereign nation-states or in the pooled sovereignty of a unified Europe and its supranational institutions, but in the partnership between Washington and London and the establishment of the 'one world' system. While it caused some disturbance for the Labour government, the importance of the ECSC should not be overemphasised. There was a general belief that it was unlikely to succeed. To the extent that it was perceived as a challenge to existing forms of global governance, it was not considered to be a particularly strong one. Its importance as a fundamental reorganisation of global power relations was therefore underestimated.

The Failure of the European Defence Community 1951–1954: A British Victory

We may characterise the emerging British position as one of tolerating the moves towards formal integration so as not to jeopardise the ideal of an Atlantic community. European integration was therefore to be viewed as a peripheral element of a form of association that had been enshrined in NATO and the Bretton Woods agreements. This policy hid a deeper British opposition towards European integration that emerged in response to the setting up of the ECSC. This opposition continued with attempts to form a European Defence Community (EDC).

The background to the EDC was the intensification of the Cold War that occurred as a consequence of the attack by North Korea on the South, and a growing concern that the same fate awaited a divided Germany. The overwhelming superiority of Soviet forces compared to NATO compounded these fears. As a solution to this the Americans promised extra troops for Europe but in return wanted to see German rearmament, a proposition that deeply concerned European governments. The response of the French was the Pleven Plan, named after the French Defence Minister and close Monnet associate, which advocated a European army, an independent European Defence Minister and eventually a European foreign policy, under the control of federal institutions that were to be devised by the Assembly of the ECSC and outlined in a new treaty for a European Political Community. The Labour government's reaction to these developments was critical. In the House of Commons Bevin stated: 'Europe is not enough; it is not big enough, it is not strong enough, and it is not able to stand by itself. It is this great conception of an Atlantic Community that we want to build up' (cited in Evans, 1975, p. 15).

Nevertheless, the Pleven Plan had strong American support and the British government recognised that some solution to the rearmament of Germany had to be found. Herbert Morrison, who had replaced Bevin at the Foreign Office, stated that Britain wanted to see 'the closest possible association with the European continental community' (cited in Gowland and Turner, 2000a, p. 58). In September 1951 a joint declaration was signed by France, the US and Britain supporting the EDC but without any commitment to British participation.

The election of a Conservative government in October 1951 under Churchill did not change the official policy. On 28 November Eden, as Foreign Secretary, informed a NATO meeting that British troops would not be part of a European defence force. This was seen by many as a reversal in Conservative thinking, as Churchill had been a strong supporter of European unity during the war and while in opposition; indeed, in August 1950, he had spoken out in favour of a European army. Eden himself had criticised Labour's isolationism and their refusal to join the Schuman negotiations. However, once in power, the Conservative party's support for European unity appeared to be more a matter of the politics of opposition.[2] Churchill's rhetorical support for European unity was carefully worded in such a way that Britain was not included, as a Cabinet note of 1951 made clear:

> Our first object is the unity and the consolidation of the British Commonwealth and what is left of the former British Empire. Our second 'fraternal association'

---

2 Young refers to a speech by Eden made at Columbia University in 1952, in which he stated that European federation was something 'we know in our bones we cannot do' (1998, p. 74).

of the English speaking world; and third, United Europe, to which we are a separate closely and specially-related ally and friend. (PRO, CAB 129/48 C. 51, 29 November 1951 cited in Gowland and Turner, 2000b, p. 29)

While the British government remained outwardly supportive of the EDC proposals, at no stage did they seriously countenance anything more than associate status. Nevertheless, the Conservative government moved to accommodate developments in ways that would not have been countenanced in 1950; without doubt US pressure was a significant factor in this change of course. The government became increasingly supportive of the EDC, to the point where by April 1952 Eden proposed a treaty with the EDC that would guarantee mutual defence (Milward, 2002, p. 104). Meanwhile, the political difficulties posed by the supranational structures of the ECSC and EDC were to be addressed by the 'Eden Plan', which proposed linking the European Communities with the Council of Europe. Milward argues that by 1954 Britain was 'constitutionally closer to the European Communities than it was again to be before 1973', although 'this was of course not through any sympathy with federalist aspirations' (p. 124). Key members of the Conservative government, notably Harold Macmillan, wanted to see more pro-active British leadership in Europe, in opposition to the forces of supra-nationalism and federalism that were at this point in the ascendant (2002, pp. 97–8). With the coming to power of a new French government under Mendes-France, commitment to both the EDC and EPC waned, and when the treaty finally reached the National Assembly, he and his ministers abstained and it was rejected. Notwithstanding the British government's accommodation of the EDC and EPC, in the end its refusal to join remained a significant factor in their failure and, it is argued, directly contributed to the refusal of the French Assembly to ratify the Treaty (Northedge, 1974, p. 166).

The failure of the EDC opened the space for a British initiative for extending the Treaty of Brussels to include Italy and Germany. This new organisation, the Western European Union (WEU), was a loose consultative organisation, which put in place procedures for checking German remilitarisation. Its primary objective was therefore to incorporate Italy and Germany back into the Western defence system. For the British government, NATO remained the most important international defence organisation and the WEU was viewed as the best way of maintaining Anglo-American leadership of the West European bloc. However, the damage had been done; Maxwell Fyfe, Home Secretary at the time, stated that the refusal to commit British troops to the EDC 'destroyed Britain's name on the continent' (cited in Turner 2000, p. 50).

The Conservatives under Churchill appeared more supportive than the Labour government of the idea of European unity. However, the general attitude in the Conservative party reflected a confidence in the 'solidity and superiority of British institutions and this made the European vision of transcending existing political structures unacceptable' (Morris, 1996, p. 125). On the issue of supranationalism, there was no similarity between the European Christian democratic parties and the

British Conservatives. Yet some sort of leadership role within Western Europe was a fundamental feature of British foreign policy at the time, and the failure of the EDC and the formation of the WEU was viewed as a success by the Conservative government. However, this did not prevent the widening of the gap between Britain and her West European allies.[3]

For both the Labour and Conservative governments during the period in question, the relationship of Britain with Western Europe was framed within the broader parameters of the state's global strategic objectives. Central to this was the idea of Anglo-American hegemony, and the belief that this could only be realised if Britain had sufficient independence as a global power. Within this paradigm, governing elites were prepared to be supportive of proposals for greater European unity, but were reticent when it came to British involvement in organisations that set up supranational authorities with federal intentions. Attempts to establish some form of institutional bridge with the EDC and ECSC proved exceptionally difficult to negotiate and in the end amounted to very little. While elites looked for compromises, one has to conclude that competing visions of Europe and its post-war organisation were at work at the time, and the federalist drive for European unity was antithetical to British ambitions.

Britain and the Treaty of Rome

The failure of the EDC did not end the drive for further integration of Western Europe. Proposals for an economic union were put forward in a memorandum from the Benelux countries presented to the ECSC in 1955. It contained measures for the establishment of a common market as well as for joint action in the areas of transport and energy and, in particular, for atomic energy. The Benelux proposals, plus Monnet's plans for an atomic energy community, were examined at the Messina Conference in 1955 and the outcome of this was the Messina Resolution. This committed the member-states of the ECSC to continue the creation of a united Europe through an expansion of common institutions, the gradual integration of national economies, the creation of a common market, and increased coordination of social policies (Nugent, 1994, p. 44).

The result of the Messina Conference was the setting up of the Spaak Committee (named after the Belgian Foreign Minister) to put together specific proposals in line with the resolution. The British were invited to participate, and agreed to do so on the understanding that they had 'special difficulties' with any proposal for a European common market (Camps, 1964, p. 30). This was in line with the official position of appearing to be a benevolent supporter of moves towards integration,

---

3 The Six were also frustrated by the depoliticisation of the OEEC that was being orchestrated by the British and was evident in the opposition to using the OEEC as a framework to discuss tariffs. Instead, the British insisted that this could only take place inside GATT (Kaiser, 1996, pp. 25–6).

yet the government hoped to steer the talks 'along the most sensible lines' (PRO, CAB 134/1026 MAC (55) 20th, 16 June 1955, cited in Young, 1993, p. 95), which meant back towards the intergovernmentalism of the OEEC and the completion of trade liberalisation and convertibility.

The British representative at the negotiations was not a Minister but rather a civil servant, Russell Bretherton, an Under Secretary in the Board of Trade. This appeared to demonstrate the low priority awarded to participation, but was appropriate considering his role as a representative on the OEEC Steering Committee on Trade. Bretherton was not in a position to contribute constructively to negotiations unless non-supranational moves to integration were to be adopted. The Treasury had made it clear that any benefits that might accrue from membership of a common market would be offset by its negative implications for Commonwealth arrangements, effectively terminating these arrangements, and the 'one world' strategy (Milward, 2002, pp. 201–2). Nevertheless, it was clear that governments were prepared to negotiate on British conditions for entry and wanted to see the country's participation in a common market. Indeed, in August 1955, Bretherton informed his superiors that they were in a position to shape the negotiations to suit British interests (Young, 1998, p. 91). The possibility of negotiating free trade arrangements, rather than a fully fledged common market with a common external tariff, appeared to become a possibility. In the end this option was not supported by Spaak, and once the French government came out in support of a common market, the British ability to influence the direction of negotiations in line with their objectives was effectively over. By November 1955, the British had withdrawn from the Spaak Committee.

There was growing concern in government circles about the potential success of the Spaak Committee (Kaiser, 1996, p. 48). Recognition within both the Board of Trade and the Treasury over the economic consequences of British exclusion from European developments had been acknowledged (Young, 1995, p. 94; Kaiser, 1996, pp. 34–6). On 7 November 1955 Sir Frank Lee, Permanent Secretary of the Board of Trade, stated that in his view economic advantage lay in joining a European common market (Milward, 2002, p. 214). Nevertheless, the political implications of the proposals were beginning to be viewed as a direct challenge to British post-war policy, as Peter Thorneycroft's (President of the Board of Trade) letter to Macmillan in January 1956 made clear:

> I am convinced that the Americans are living in a fools' paradise about Messina, and I strongly recommend that you and the Foreign Secretary should seek to bring home to President Eisenhower the gravity of the dangerous situation which is rapidly developing against the interests of both our countries and all our joint work since the war to build up a 'one-world' trading system. (cited in Milward, 1992, p. 428)

Thorneycroft went on to charge the integrationist project with 'undermining our security and economy' and stated that it would inevitably lead to German domination of Europe (p. 429). The need for a British counter proposal to the common market had become a matter of urgency by the beginning of 1956. The response was Plan G, a proposal for a European industrial free trade area (FTA) that would preserve British Commonwealth trade and protect British agriculture, while opening up the markets of the Six to British industry. For Thorneycroft and the Board of Trade the proposals represented a radical reorientation of British commercial policy, which involved removing Britain's protectionist trade legacy, although it was certainly conceived to be entirely consistent with the 'one-world' approach.

The non-involvement in the process of European integration for both Labour and Conservative governments during the 1950s can be explained by the continued attempts by elites to secure the British state as a cosmopolitan-imperial power. To a large extent, decisions were being made on the basis of an assessment of the short term disadvantages of membership to Britain's global status, rather than any critical assessment of the chronic nature of British decline. While the free trade area negotiations with the six countries of the EC were occurring, it was clear that the world order was no longer conducive to the continuation of British power. Britain's economic decline, demonstrated by the weakness of its balance of payments, meant that it was not in a position to lead the world towards trade liberalisation and currency convertibility. This is in line with many commentators on British decline, who consider the late 1950s to be central to understanding the sequence of British decline (Gallagher, 1982; Tomlinson, 1982; Holland, 1984; Cain and Hopkins, 1993b); the key event in this respect was the 1956 Suez crisis (Louis and Owen, 1989; Cain and Hopkins, 1993b). It was in this context that the first British application for membership of the Community was conceived (Young, 1998, p. 99; Turner, 2000, p. 51).

The Suez Crisis and the Turn to Europe

The decision by the British Conservative government under Anthony Eden to invade Egypt, in coalition with France and Israel, was in reaction to Colonel Nasser's nationalisation of the Suez canal. The grounds for this action were that Nasser wanted to block oil reaching Europe and was intent on invading Israel. The invasion of Egypt by the combined forces of the three powers was met with universal condemnation and, most importantly, was not supported by the US. The failure of the attack led to an immediate sterling crisis in Britain, and American support for economic stabilisation was only agreed if Britain removed her troops. The impact of Suez on the Conservative party was dramatic and led to the resignation of Eden. The tensions in the party at the time were between the progressive One Nation Tories, who were increasingly anti-Empire and pro-Europe; and Empire Tories, such as the backbench Suez group, who pressurised Eden to take action over Suez to restore 'Britain's imperial mission and destiny' (Amery cited in Turner, 2000, p. 50). Harold Macmillan was successful in succeeding Eden as Prime Minister because he was seen to be a compromise candidate able to unite the Conservative party. Yet it was Macmillan who recognised that the Empire was largely over and that Britain's post-imperial future would, in some shape or form, involve the EC. Macmillan came to link EC membership with modernisation, which was consistent with his position as one of the leading corporate liberals within the Conservative party, who supported state intervention into the economy and emphasised science and technology as a national priority.

The consequence of Suez was also to seriously tarnish Britain's reputation amongst members of the Commonwealth (Sanders, 1990, p. 148). Many members began to support the movement amongst prominent third world leaders towards a position of non-alignment with either East or West. This reflected the growing anti-imperialism of both colonies and former colonies, and the growing importance of nationalism. As the Empire came to an end, Britain's status as a global power declined. In the relationship between the superpowers, British diplomacy was proving limited. Britain had not established a tripolar world and, if any power was to emerge as a third force, it was more likely to be the EC. It was becoming clear that the US was taking the Community very seriously and by the early 1960s viewed a United Europe as a potential junior partner (Grosser, 1980, pp. 200–201).

The economic benefits of Commonwealth and Empire were also becoming far less certain. With the decline in the prices of raw materials after the Korean War and their reduced import purchasing power, the export potential of these countries grew more slowly (Cain and Hopkins, 1993b, p. 286). Commonwealth markets were also being penetrated by Japan, the US and the EC (Jessop, 1980, p. 70). Furthermore, problems in the British economy were being made worse by money going out of the country into the Empire, and this was combined with the high cost of defence to maintain a global role (Cain and Hopkins, 1993b, pp. 282–3). The new economic opportunities that began to open up were in Europe and Japan and, as a result, British trading and investment patterns began to shift towards the former (Cain and Hopkins, 1993b, p. 287; Jessop, 1980, p. 70; Sanders, 1990, p. 151). Yet, rather ironically, the British economy was actually performing better than at any time since before the 1880s. The problem, however, was the extent to which it was being out performed by its rivals (Gamble, 1994, p. 20). As Cain and Hopkins point out, Britain's decline as an imperial power became effective only when these relativities changed (1993b, p. 312). The real problem was that the economy was not growing sufficiently enough to sustain extensive external and domestic commitments. The consequence of this was recurring current account deficits that provoked currency speculation. This was exacerbated by colonies and other countries holding sterling assets that exceeded the value of foreign reserves and resulted in the so-called 'sterling balances problem' (Schenk, 2002, p. 347).

The British crisis was therefore a crisis of a world state that was being forced back into its national and regional base by external forces. The immediate problem for the political classes was how to adapt to this new reality. Britain seemed unable to take advantage of these structural changes in the global situation in the way that countries such as Germany and Japan were successfully doing. By the end of the 1950s the reality of decline was clearly apparent (Jessop, 1980; Gamble,

1994). The growing concern with 'what is wrong with Britain?' focused on the lack of modernisation of the major institutions of the British political order, from the economy to the civil service and universities (Jessop, 1980, p. 79; Gamble, 1994, p. 24). The structural boundaries and parameters of the British state appeared uncertain, and the contestation over British nation-statehood became the organising principle of political strategies from the 1960s onwards.

These structural developments and shifts in the politico-economic order resulted in a range of policy developments and institutional reforms. In the aftermath of Suez defence cuts were introduced and decolonisation was speeded up. There was also a strong recognition that British policy had to be more firmly linked to that of the US; as Macmillan noted when reflecting on Suez, 'it was the action of the United States which really defeated us in attaining our object ... This situation with the United States must at all costs be prevented from arising again' (PRO, AIR 8/1940, COS 220, 11 October 1957, cited in Hennessy, 2000, p. 258).

There was no immediate change of policy regarding joining the EC in the aftermath of Suez, yet it undoubtedly resulted in a radical shift in thinking amongst the party elite; Macmillan became increasingly alarmed by developments on the continent and their implication for the country. Edward Heath, Chief Whip at the time, concludes in his account of the Suez crisis,

> perhaps the greatest legacy of Suez was that it forced many of the British establishment to accept that the sun was setting on the British Empire and that America was the new superpower. This in turn forced many who had hitherto been sceptical about European unity to realise that our future lay in our own continent and not in distant lands which our forebears had coloured pink on the map. Even Eden, who had crucially kept our seat empty at Messina in 1955, acknowledged this fact in one of the last memos he circulated as Prime Minister. On 28 December 1956, he wrote that 'the consequences of this examination may be to determine us to work more closely with Europe'. (Heath, 1998, pp. 177–8)

Three weeks after the Suez cease-fire in November 1956, a debate on the FTA proposals took place in the House of Commons. When it was clear that Labour were not prepared to oppose the FTA, the government was ready to enter into talks within the institutional framework of the OEEC. In fact it was not until the Treaty of Rome had been signed that negotiations actually begun, by which point, with de Gaulle's return to power, the French government had already decided against any agreement. In less than a month negotiations had come to an end with French rejection of the British plan, which it was soon apparent lacked the systems of bargains and sacrifices that characterised the EC and guaranteed mutual benefits to its members. Indeed, the scheme would allow Britain to import relatively cheaply from outside of Europe because of its system of Commonwealth preferences, and still take advantage of a free trade area for exporting within Europe. In short it implied 'commercial advantage with fewer obligations' (Camps, 1964, p. 167; Gowland and Turner, 2000a, p. 108); notably it lacked the commitment to wider

European unity that such obligations implied. Negotiations quickly became polarised between the British and the French; the former being concerned with international free trade, the latter with European unity. Although it was de Gaulle who actually vetoed the free trade proposals, in the end the 'free trade area was defeated by loyalty to the Treaty of Rome' (Camps, 1964, p. 172).

It was quickly apparent that the integrationist project was not going to be the failure predicted by many British elites; tariff reductions were occurring earlier than had been envisaged, and the Community was thriving with growth rates double those of Britain (Milward, 2002, p. 179). Politically the EC had put paid to British leadership of Europe; Britain had assumed this would be its role after ending the war victorious. What had emerged amongst the British governing elite was an 'increasingly desperate antagonism to the Six' (Young, 1998, p. 116). When FTA negotiations finally failed, Macmillan told a small meeting of colleagues that 'there were three elements who wanted supranationalism and who were playing no small part on the Commission ... the Jews, the Planners and the old cosmopolitan elite' (cited in Young, 1998, p. 118). The EC was viewed as an inward-looking protectionist bloc that was antithetical to the 'one world system' envisaged by British governing elites. Nevertheless, by the late 1950s the main vehicle the British relied upon to achieve its goals, the OEEC, was effectively redundant, eventually replaced by the Organisation for Economic Development and Cooperation (OECD), which was not restricted to Europe. In 1960, out of the remnants of the British free trade area proposals, a European Free Trade Association was established consisting of Britain, Denmark, Norway, Sweden, Austria, Switzerland and Portugal. However, it was less significant economically for Britain than the EC and lacked the leverage to bring about some form of association between the two. In short it proved to be of 'marginal utility' (W. Wallace, 1990, p. 79); by 1960 a new strategy was required.

The First Application

The decision to apply for membership of the EC, as revealed by Foreign Office and Cabinet papers, can be viewed as a largely conservative and tactical shift in British policy (Ellison, 2000). The decision was designed to secure fundamental geopolitical objectives in the context of decline (Young, 1993). Indeed Lord argues that 'the 1961 application was in many ways grounded in traditionalist categories of foreign policy thought' (1996, p. 13). Largely without exception, the analytic focus has been on the actions of elites intended to maintain Britain's strategic position by the pursuit of EC membership. However, the argument presented here is that to view the first application as a matter of geopolitical decision-making is problematic, unless this is located in the context of the pressures for a profound restructuring of the British state regime. The move towards membership of the EC might be seen as part of a strategy of modernisation, by repositioning Britain within the most significant economic and political reorganisation of states in post-war

Europe. Yet it was also a compromised strategy and, as such, a distinctively post-imperial strategy designed to secure core elements of the British state.

By the early years of the 1960s there was a re-examination of relations with Europe and a questioning of the assumptions that had been governing European policy since the end of the war (Camps, 1964, p. 280; Gowland and Turner, 2000a, pp. 120–23). For the Macmillan government, membership of the EC was perceived to be a vital strategy of modernisation at a time of terminal decline. It implied the necessary modernisation of Britain's economy and external relations. Furthermore, the adoption of a modernising European discourse was viewed as essential for revitalising the Conservative party and creating a new image (Kaiser, 1996, p. 146). Evidently it was a way of uniting both party and national interests.

In many respects the Foreign Office and the Treasury were responsible for refining the European strategy (Young, 1993, p. 102). By the end of the 1950s the Foreign Office began to view Europe as a new arena for establishing British influence in the context of imperial decline and as a way of strengthening Anglo-American relations post-Suez (Beloff, 1963, pp. 89–90). The European conversion of the Treasury was also occurring with the appointment of Sir Frank Lee as Joint Permanent Under Secretary in January 1960. Lee believed that British economic success now depended on participation within the European Community. He chaired the influential Economic Steering Committee which recommended British entry. The combined impact of Lee and the Economic Steering Committee was illustrated by the reaction of one Treasury official, in which he stated that 'in 1959 the very idea caused him (as an advocate of EC membership) to be written off as a long haired eccentric, in 1960 it was getting to be all right, and by 1961, you were a stick in the mud if you thought otherwise' (cited in Moon, 1985, p. 171).

During 1960 Macmillan became increasingly convinced of the necessity of British membership and in July he made the significant appointment of two 'Europeans' to key positions in his government. Christopher Soames became Minister of Agriculture and Duncan Sandys was moved to the Ministry of Commonwealth Relations in order to deal with any potential opposition. Another key appointment was that of Edward Heath, who was made Foreign Office Minister with responsibility for European affairs. In the domestic arena, the press were increasingly supportive of membership and there was also a strong European movement in the country which encouraged the government that a shift in policy would be conducive to positive public opinion (Camps, 1964, p. 294). In the negotiations over membership the international orientations of British policymaking resurfaced in the concern to secure commitments to both the Commonwealth and to the EFTA. Initially, the government pushed ahead with the idea of a modified Customs Union that would link together the EC and the EFTA. Yet the Six were explicit that the only option open to Britain was full membership. It became clearer to the British government that the EC was more than an economic arrangement and that any political influence Britain was to have could only be secured by full membership. The climate inside the EC was seen to be becoming more favourable to Britain. On the 31 July 1961 Macmillan made the announcement to the House of Commons of British intention to seek membership of the European Community. In so doing, however, he emphasised the conservative elements of this strategy and played up its role in securing British world power status. Macmillan made it clear that the 'dominant considerations in his mind were political ones'; 'our right place is in the vanguard of the movement of greater unity of the free world, and that we can lead better from within than outside' (cited in Camps, 1964, p. 359). Inherent within this statement was also a degree of caution, emphasising the continued importance of the Commonwealth. Macmillan stated that 'if a close relationship between the United Kingdom and the countries of the EC was to disrupt the long-standing and historic ties between the United Kingdom and the other nations of the Commonwealth the loss would be greater than the gain' (cited in Evans, 1975, p. 28).

The strategic continuities in the British decision to apply for membership of the EC can be illustrated by the geopolitical objectives of the governing elite at the time. EC membership was viewed as necessary to maintain Britain's key strategic relationship with the United States; indeed, it was partly a consequence of pressure from the United States. The continuation of this key external relationship was viewed as fundamental to British security; in particular, the continuation of British power in the world became associated with maintaining an independent nuclear deterrent. However, by the late 1950s it was clear that Britain lacked both the resources and technological know-how to develop its own system. Any continuation of Britain as a nuclear power, and thereby its world role, depended on US support for an independent national deterrent (Kaiser, 1996, p. 129). In return, the Americans wanted to see British membership because it was believed the British would be more favourable to American interests and keep the Community from becoming an 'inward looking club' (George, 1990, p. 31; Kaiser, 1996, p. 130). Indeed, it was believed that Britain could help undermine de Gaulle's attempts to assume leadership of Western Europe and to make it more independent of American control (Grosser, 1980, pp. 183–90).

In 1961 Macmillan met President Kennedy in Washington and became convinced that the US was even more strongly in favour of British membership than it had been in the past, and that the continuation of the special relationship was dependent on membership. The architect of this policy was George Ball, who was appointed by Kennedy to Under Secretary for Economic Affairs. Ball was a European specialist, having been legal adviser to the West European unification movement. He was committed to the EC and convinced Kennedy that British membership of this organisation was vital for Western unity. In a meeting with Edward Heath, he argued that outside of Europe, Britain would be a 'force for division rather than cohesion since she is a giant lodestar drawing with unequal degrees of force on each member state' (cited in Evans, 1975, p. 144). The position of the US put British governing elites under pressure to join but it also seemed to reinforce an idea that Britain could regain its leadership role within Europe. In these terms Britain's role was clearly to be that of a constraining force, controlling and directing European integration in ways that were in line with American interests.

From such a point of view, membership of the EC was not seen as threatening to Anglo-American relations but in fact was a way of consolidating the 'special relationship' (Kaiser, 1996, p. 130).

The 'special relationship' was not a British illusion but continued to reflect shared political economic interests. From the end of the 1950s, the US joined the UK in persistent balance of payments deficits while the Six accrued surpluses (Schenk, 2002, p. 350). This was only possible because both countries had reserve currency status and their deficits were financed by trading partners holding their currencies as reserves (p. 351). It was a policy objected to by the Six because of its inflationary pressures. While the Six wanted to see a reduction in US and UK balance of payments, the Americans and the British sought ways to finance their deficits through changes in international monetary policy (p. 353). The consequence of this was a 'series of secret meetings at official and ministerial level between the United States and the United Kingdom designed to develop joint positions on international monetary issues' (p. 353). It was evidence of what Strange referred to as the instinctive conjunction of financial interests that underpinned the 'special relationship' and reinforced the differences between Britain and mainland Europe (1971, pp. 72–3).

In fact the Treasury believed that EC membership would reinvigorate sterling's international role and that the City of London would become Europe's financial centre (Schenk, 2002, p. 355). This was particularly noticeable in the continued commitment to sterling as a reserve currency, which it believed was essential for the continuation of the City as a financial centre. After a return to convertibility in 1958, the City was once again provided with a medium of exchange that enabled a rapid revival (Strange, 1971, p. 233). Government monetary policy until the late 1960s was then determined by the need to uphold the value of sterling through international loans and high interest rates. The underlying weaknesses of the British economy, and a comparatively de-regulated City, meant this was difficult to sustain and there was intense speculation against sterling. Nevertheless it was argued that once EC trade resolved Britain's balance of trade deficit, sterling would strengthen as it would be backed by the balance of payments of the EC as a whole (Milward, 2002, p. 349).

By 1960 Macmillan's European policy was combined with a programme of economic modernisation. The domestic response to the problems of economic decline was expansionist policies and a more interventionist approach that aspired to the model of French economic planning (Pollard, 1980, p. 398; Jessop, 1980, pp. 39–40; Overbeek, 1990, pp. 131–2). This included the revival of a corporatist strategy with the setting up of the National Economic Development Council in 1962 as a common forum involving management, government, labour and some independents in an attempt to consider ways of encouraging economic growth. It also implied a new settlement between capital and labour in the form of a National Incomes Commission (Hennessy, 2000, p. 260). Yet there were weaknesses with this approach; overall economic control remained with a Treasury that avoided direct state intervention into production. The outlook of an intensification of

European competition for the less advanced sections of the British economy were, however, likely to be negative. Nevertheless, the belief was that entry into the EC would reinvigorate the British economy by giving it 'a much needed dose of stiff competition' and end its excessive reliance on the Commonwealth and Sterling Area (Young, 1998, p. 120; Gowland and Turner, 2000a, p. 121). The modernising implications of this European policy therefore had much in common with traditional approaches to the domestic economy that enforced greater domestic competition through the external sanction of free trade (Gamble, 1994, p. 115).

While much of British industry remained weak and uncompetitive, the City and large multinationals were successfully adapting to a changing economic environment. Despite the declining economic importance of the Commonwealth, the historical internationalisation of the British economy meant it was well placed to become a gateway to European markets for outward-looking British multinationals, as well as the increasing number in foreign ownership; the penetration of US capital had been reinforced in 1958 by the relaxation of foreign exchange controls and the consequent growth of the Eurodollar market (p. 109). In July 1961, the Federation of British Industry (FBI), which was dominated by big international corporations, came out in favour of EC membership (Overbeek, 1990, p. 101).

The most significant aspect of the negotiations on British membership was the attempt to bridge the intricate network of Commonwealth and colonial trade, and commercial relationships, with the interests of what was in effect a protectionist regional trade bloc. Milward points out that the British application 'arrived still wrapped and garlanded in Britain's long international mercantile and imperial history, the history that had briefly made it a world power' (2002, p. 420). A complex array of Commonwealth and imperial preferences were in place that the government had committed itself to trying to protect; moreover, the hope was to win over the Commonwealth by gaining preferences for its members inside the EC. For Macmillan this was of particular importance for retaining Britain's power and influence, as well as for securing legitimacy for the government's strategy. Commonwealth leaders were not reassured and expressed their disapproval of the British application, viewing it as Britain turning away from its historical global responsibilities and giving in to US pressure. The response of the EC to the proposals for Commonwealth preferences was categorical:

> The Six decided that it conflicted with their objectives, was not acceptable in respect of third countries against which it created a permanent discrimination and reduced chances of reasonable worldwide agreements. In the transitional period special arrangements could be made on a product by product basis, but they must be degressive and could not continue beyond the transitional period. For the full common market regime the negotiating objective had to be worldwide commodity agreements, but as far as relations with third countries were concerned, these would have to be non-discriminatory. They could make not make a distinction between the Commonwealth and others. (pp. 382–3)

In the end the government was able to secure some preferences for Commonwealth food products for the transitional period, but when compared to the position they had set out in 1961 they had achieved relatively little. The extent to which the government was willing to relinquish its established global markets to secure entry to the EC meant the end of the post-war strategy of using the Commonwealth, and remaining colonies, to secure British power and influence in the world. However, as the political debate demonstrated, this was not just a matter of economics but also one of identity.

On the right of the Conservative party there was an outburst of 'Empire loyalism', fuelled by the Beaverbrook press, which accused Macmillan of putting 'Europe ahead of the Commonwealth' (Young, 1998, p. 141; George, 1990, p.34). The dissenters within the Conservative party were the imperialist right wing of the party who numbered between 30 and 40 MPs and, although they did not threaten a government with a majority of 100, they proved themselves to be particularly vocal. The Conservative MP Walker Smith, the first back-bencher to be called in a debate on pursuing membership, put into words the problem that, in due time, would tear the Conservative party apart (Young, 1998, pp. 154–5). Walker Smith's essential point concerned the distinctiveness of Britain compared to Europe; he noted that 'their evolution has been continental and collective, ours has been insular and imperial' (p. 155). The question of entry went beyond mere economics, he cautioned; it went to the heart of the British state's post-imperial future and the extent to which this implied a continuation with its past. As far as Walker Smith was concerned, membership implied an undesirable break with that past. This early Eurosceptic speech reflected the underlying unease within Conservative ranks about the decision to pursue membership, and this was not restricted to the back benches but was also evident in the Cabinet (Gowland and Turner, 2000a, p. 124).

The government also faced the growing opposition of the Labour party; its leader, Hugh Gaitskell, issued a statement in September 1962 against entry on the government's terms. The Labour party was divided over membership. A section was strongly in favour as a matter of principle, including many on the right such as the Deputy Leader George Thomas. The majority of Trade Unions were also firmly in support of membership by the early 1960s on pragmatic grounds (Kaiser, 1996, p. 173). Conversely opponents of membership, mostly on the left, viewed the EC as a 'capitalist club' and a threat to the independent economic policy of a future Labour government. Gaitskell, however, was part of a section of the party that could be said to be agnostic on the issue. When faced with a divided party, he proved to be extraordinarily erratic in attempting to oppose the Conservative government's position without fully objecting to British membership. By the time Gaitskell came to deliver his speech to the Labour party conference in October 1962, he had chosen the course of opposition:

> After all, if we could carry the Commonwealth with us, safeguarded, flourishing prosperous; if we could safeguard our agriculture, and our EFTA friends were all

in it, if we were secure in our employment policy, and if we were able to maintain our independent foreign policy and yet have this wider, looser association with Europe, it would be a great ideal. But if this should not prove to be possible; if the Six will not give it to us; if the British Government will not even ask for it, then we must stand firm by what we believe, for the sake of Britain, and the Commonwealth and the World; and we shall not flinch from our duty if that moment comes. (Gaitskell, 1962, p. 37)

To become a member of a federal Europe would, he argued, mean 'the end of Britain as an independent European State' and 'the end of a thousand years of history' (p. 23). The speech was well received. It reflected the continued significance of the Commonwealth for many on the left and the right of the party as the main alternative to the Empire, both as a source of renewed political identity and as a viable economic partner (Young, 1998, pp. 156–61). The Commonwealth, therefore, was a significant factor in the opposition to a European membership within both parties and, however vague, seemed to offer an alternative trajectory that was more continuous with Britain's past. It was the Commonwealth option that Dean Acheson, the former US Secretary for State, ridiculed for its lack of unity, political structure or strength when in 1962 he famously described Britain as having 'lost an Empire' without yet 'having found a role' (p. 171).

The opposition to membership gathered pace and began to influence the opinion polls; by 1962 they showed a decline in support for entry (Gowland and Turner, 2000a, p. 131). European integration was, therefore, becoming symbolically constituted across sections of the political class as a threat to British identity and interests, and was proving to have potential as a political discourse around which electorates could be mobilised. In general Macmillan and Cabinet ministers attempted to depoliticise the issue, denying the federal intentions of the Community and emphasising that membership would not undermine existing commitments and institutions (Young, 1998, p. 129; Turner, 2000, p. 56). Examining the political debates on the issue and the way it was presented by government spokesmen, Moon argues that a disproportionate amount of attention was given to dealing with subjects associated with criticism of entry rather than setting out a positive course (1985, p. 167). The tone of the debate was reflected in a Guardian editorial: 'the plunge is taken but, on yesterday's evidence, by a shivering Government' (cited in George, 1990, p. 33).

It is argued that Macmillan remained 'reticent about the full implications of membership of the Community' (Camps, 1964, p. 513). In April 1961, the Lord Chancellor, Viscount Kilmuir, made clear the significant losses of sovereignty that would result from signing the Treaty of Rome; however, the issues he raised were obfuscated and concealed from the public (Young, 1998, pp. 126–9; Milward, 2002, p. 448). In the debate in the House of Commons on 2 August 1961, Macmillan told MPs that moves towards a federal Europe would be resisted. It was believed that supranationalism had been undermined by de Gaulle and that Britain would be entering an organisation that was largely intergovernmental[4] (W. Wallace, 1997, p. 27). This opened the way for British leadership within an association of nation-states; by a sleight of hand, Empire was to be replaced by Europe (Turner, 2000, p. 52). The possibility of British membership was abruptly ended by de Gaulle's veto of the British application in January 1963, when he concluded that Britain had failed to prove its European credentials in the negotiations on membership. The strategic alliance with the United States and differences on agriculture and trade were cited as the main stumbling block (Kaiser, 1996; Wilkes, 1997).

Conclusion

By applying for membership of the EC, the Macmillan government recognised the need for modernisation. However, modernisation was typically associated with geopolitical adjustments within an already established set of parameters; specifically, the increased dependence of post-war Britain on the US. Nevertheless, the hope was that a declining imperial state could become a leading capitalist state within an association of nation-states and thereby renew its global authority and reinvigorate the domestic economy. Europe was to replace Commonwealth and Empire and provide the basis for Britain to lead an Anglo-American dominated Western bloc. This was a strategy of change based on deep continuities with the past and contrasted with the radical restructuring that European integration implied and that the original six member-states had committed themselves to. It involved the pursuit of distinctive British objectives that, as the negotiations on membership demonstrated, were unacceptable to other member-states. The inability to secure Commonwealth preferences not only demonstrated the incompatibility between established British interests and the Community, but were seized upon by the opponents of membership as issues fundamental to the future of the nation. The first application therefore saw the emergence of Eurosceptic politics – clear divisions within the main parties, a growing concern with public opinion, accusations of betrayal by governing elites and a belief that integration was antithetical not just to British interests but to British identity.

---

4 Three years after Macmillan made his statement that Britain intended to seek membership of the Community, the European Court of Justice declared in an historic ruling that European law took precedence over national law (Meehan, 1993, p. 57). This radical assertion of the Community as an independent legal order reinforced the constitutional nature of the Treaties, the formal supranationalism on which European integration was founded.

Chapter 4

British Membership and its Opponents

Introduction

In the previous chapter we have seen that the decision to apply for membership of the EC was a limited strategy of conservative modernisation primarily concerned with post-imperial survival. This chapter explores the Labour government's decision to come out in support of membership following the election of 1966. It charts the limitations and constraints on a strategy that failed to command authority as a vision for national renewal. When Edward Heath finally signed the Treaty of Rome in 1972, it was against a backdrop of significant splits in both main parties and the emergence of a distinctively populist Euroscepticism. Despite a significant vote in support of membership in the 1975 referendum, the argument here is that British elites distanced themselves from Europe in the face of the rise of Euroscepticism. By the end of the 1970s it is argued that a British European trajectory was subordinated to the broader imperatives of globalisation.

Labour's Volte Face

In Chapter 3 it was demonstrated that the position of the Labour party under Hugh Gaitskell to membership of the Community had been one of hostility. It was highly critical of the terms of entry negotiated by the Conservatives and only considered the possibility of membership on terms that were never likely to be accepted by the Six. The unifying impact of the position was illustrated by the general lack of opposition within the party to Gaitskell's speech to the 1962 conference. This speech, described by Nairn as 'tear jerking patriotism and invocation of the imperial relics' (1973, p. 46), was clearly concerned with using the prospect of British membership of the Community as a basis for party and public mobilisation. The death of Gaitskell in 1963 and the election of Wilson did not seem to imply any change in policy, especially as Wilson had defeated the longstanding pro-European George Brown in the leadership contest. Nevertheless, in the 1961 Commons debate on the decision to open negotiations, Wilson clearly set out a position on Europe that was consistent with an emerging governing approach. The abrogation of national sovereignty was, he argued, fully consistent with political progress. While roundly rejecting federalism, he raised concerns that the EC was a discriminating and autarchic trading bloc. Conversely Britain was outward looking and should oppose 'little' Europeanism, yet the economic implications of exclusion were formidable (Wall, 2013, pp. 47–9). Moreover, consistent with the Gaitskell line, it was quite clear that the politics of Europe meant invoking the nation. On the failure of the entry negotiations, Wilson spoke of a 'national humiliation', the surrendering of 'vital national and Commonwealth interests' and the need for British leadership in Europe to re-assert our 'national strength and national independence' (pp. 50–51). The 1964 election manifesto restated that Britain's first priority was the Commonwealth, although it was careful not to rule out membership (Frey, 1968; Young, 1998). On entering office, it was clear that alternatives to the EC were limited and the Foreign Office was advocating for membership. During 1965, those on the left were becoming increasingly concerned about a drift into the common market (Castle, 1980, p. 33). By December of that year, Michael Stewart, the Foreign Secretary, made it clear in a paper to Wilson that Britain should declare its readiness to negotiate entry (Wall, 2013, p. 108). Stewart's concerns were political and reflected fear of a French-dominated Europe following de Gaulle's hostility to the European Commission and the subsequent French boycott of the Community, although this checking of supranationalism was also viewed as working to Britain's advantage. Early in 1966, Wilson approved the formation of a top-level committee to examine the implications of membership (Young, 1998, p. 186).

In a significant speech during the 1966 election campaign, Wilson sought to make political capital out of the failure of the Conservative negotiations, and accused Heath of giving in to the French: 'One encouraging gesture from the French government and the Conservative leader rolls on his back like a spaniel' (cited in Gowland and Turner 2000a, p. 157). Yet during the same speech Wilson explicitly stated that the government was ready to join the EC if British and Commonwealth interests could be safeguarded (Wall, 2013, p. 116). With the election victory of 1966 securing a Labour majority of 97, the shift in policy became more pronounced with the appointment of George Brown as Foreign Secretary in August 1966 (Frey, 1968, pp. 199–200). In May 1966 Brown had made a speech to the Socialist International in Stockholm that was emphatically pro-European:

> We want an expanded EEC ... We want to be a member of it and we want to find the basis on which this would be possible. And the Labour government in Britain, deeply conscious of its responsibilities to Europe, and Europe's responsibilities to the world, is determined to play its full part in bringing about the European unity which is so fundamental to both. (cited in Wall, 2013, p. 120)

In October 1966 a meeting was held at Chequers on membership of the Community, by which point officials had produced a considerable range of documents examining the pros and cons of British entry. Crossman reflected in his diaries, after reading papers distributed by Brown and Michael Stewart (who took over at the Department of Economic Affairs from Brown) that it was clear that they 'now wanted full backing from the Cabinet for a new European initiative and it was also clear that ideally they would have liked a declaration of intent to sign the treaty (of Rome)' (Crossman 1979, p. 259). At this meeting Wilson announced that he and George Brown would tour the European capitals to clarify the issues and sound out opinion; this initiative became known as the 'probe'. The Cabinet was split and Crossman recounts a discussion in which he spoke up for a position that placed domestic considerations first:

> I regard little England as the precondition for any successful socialist planning whether inside or outside the Common Market. Whatever happens, we need to cut back our overseas commitments and withdraw our troops from the Far East and the Middle East. (p. 261)

Crossman went on to argue for devaluation, suggesting that his colleagues should not view going into Europe as a way of retaining world power status. He also regretted that a paper on a North Atlantic free trade area was not taken seriously (p. 262). These views reflected the position of the opponents of integration on the left[1] of the party who primarily wanted to see Britain as a strong socialist nation-state although maintaining its internationalist and Atlanticist outlook. At this time, however, the extent to which membership of the EC was a threat to this vision did vary across the left.[2] The same could be said for those on the centre and right of the party[3] (Bilski, 1977, p. 310). Nevertheless, undoubtedly, the core of the anti-Europeans was on the left, while pro-Europeans were on the right.[4]

---

1   Key figures here included Barbara Castle, Michael Foot and Peter Shore.

2   An interesting example of this was Tony Benn. Benn was opposed to British membership during the 1950s and early 1960s but came out in support of the Government's application in 1967 because of a growing sense of British isolation (Benn 1996, p. 121, p. 171, p. 177). In 1970 he was commenting that the EC was the right organisation necessary to control international companies (p. 222). However, he came out in opposition in 1971 because he did not want to align himself with pro-European Labour politicians on the right of the party. He increasingly regarded this group as a threat to socialism and, in working with the Conservative Europeans, he claimed they represented 'a new political party under the surface in Britain' (p. 240). He came to see the anti-market case as a way of maximising support for the left (p. 241). However, it was also Benn who put forward the case for a referendum in 1971 in an attempt to unite the party (pp. 238–9). In doing this, he was also attempting to subvert the emerging governing position on Europe that depoliticised the issue. In considering the implications of a referendum, he expressed concern over the public's reluctance to participate, which, he believed, 'had been told by its liberal elites that it shouldn't be interested in these things' (p. 251). Benn's approach to the issue reflected his general concern over the lack of democracy in British politics on both the left and the right and his position on EC membership did not demonstrate the crude opportunism and nationalism of many of his colleagues on the left. However, in this attempt to bring about some sort of symbiosis between the British state and democratic socialism, Benn ended up in the debate over the EC defending the traditional state structure.

3   Dennis Healey was an example of a politician who demonstrated both principled opposition and pragmatic accommodation (Young 1998, p. 268).

4   The main supporters were the European social democrats led by Roy Jenkins and included George Thomson, Harold Lever, David Owen, Roy Hattersley, Shirley Williams and Bill Rodgers.

It is essential that the change in policy that occurred in the autumn of 1966 is viewed in relation to the crisis of the Labour administration. The Wilson government of 1964 was elected on a platform of domestic modernisation. Warde describes the project as a form of technocratic collectivism that redefined socialism in terms of 'purposeful administration by a meritocratic elite' (1982, p. 97). The economic proposals included state directed industrial investment and state economic planning in order to address the incompetence of private sector management. The Wilson government put in place a set of reforms that included a Department of Economic Affairs, which was to produce a five-year plan and promote long term growth. It was inspired by the post-war French planning system and was intended to be a counterweight to the powers of the Treasury (Leys, 1983, p. 71). The dilemma was that in order for this economic policy to succeed it required an expansion of the economy, but this in turn threatened the value of the pound. Leading members of the government, including Wilson, seemed to underestimate the economic realities of the British economy and the implications of the proposals for economic expansion contained within the National Plan (Hennessy, 2000, pp. 303–4). Only months after taking office in July 1966, a run on the pound led to pressure to deflate the economy, and the extensive and expensive policy commitments that had been promised in the Labour manifesto had to be curtailed.[5] The overriding goal of the government then became the traditional one of restoring international confidence in the pound through deflationary policies. This occurred alongside inflationary wage rises negotiated by a fragmented labour movement. After 1966 there was a return to stop-go, compulsory wage restraint and legislation was proposed to restrict strikes (Warde, 1982, p. 108). The government had failed to use demand management to secure the cooperation of the trade unions on long term incomes policy commitments (Rhodes, 2000, p. 167).

This effectively meant the end of the government's National Plan and, as Crossman reflected, 'the destruction of the Wilson myth' (1979, p. 232). The rest of the Labour government's period in office was dominated by the sterling crisis. Despite a devaluation in 1967 by 1968 the pound was in the words of Roy Jenkins, the Chancellor at the time, 'staring over the precipice into the abyss' (cited in Hennessy, 2000, p. 316). The weakness of sterling and fragility of the Bretton Woods system of exchange controls meant that the pound came under intense speculation and was only shored up by a 4 billion dollar line of credit (Jenkins, 1989, p. 230). Neither was the government able to bring about wage restraint and wages exploded, alongside a dramatic increase in strike activity during 1969–1970. Clearly the Labour governments of the 1960s were struggling to challenge orthodox economic priorities and were overwhelmed by the problems of sterling and the balance of payments (Jessop, 1980, p. 40; Warde, 1982, p. 107).

---

5   This measure aimed to prevent the government from having to face the humiliation of devaluing the pound; however, this became inevitable after another sterling crisis in the autumn of 1967.

Membership of the EC came to fill the void in economic policy; however, it was clear in the paper presented by officials in September 1966 that, at least in the short term, the implications of membership would expose British industry to competition, further exacerbating the stop-go cycles in which the British economy had been caught since the end of the war: 'We should be forced to pursue deflationary policies to safeguard the balance of payments ... and this would lead to stagnation of output, low investment and slow growth of productivity' (cited in Wall, 2013, p. 133).

A shift in the orientation of foreign policy also became particularly urgent as political relations with the Commonwealth deteriorated. This was most clearly evident over the issue of Rhodesia. When the white Rhodesian government declared unilateral independence, Wilson announced economic sanctions that he predicted would bring down the regime, but they failed to do so. The failure to solve this problem affected the unity of the Commonwealth nations and British prestige amongst them. Further problems concerning Britain's world role emerged in its continued military commitments East of Suez, including patrolling the Indian Ocean and the Persian Gulf and maintaining a presence in Malaysia. The Labour government committed Britain to maintaining these costly symbols of world power status in order to secure US support for oil sanctions on Rhodesia (Crossman, 1979, p. 165; Gowland and Turner, 2000a, p. 155). These defence commitments, however, were to prove too expensive to sustain, and by the beginning of 1968 the decision had been made to withdraw all forces East of Suez, apart from those in the Persian Gulf and Hong Kong, by the end of 1971. Such developments intensified the need for alternative international arenas within which the British state could continue to be a significant global power.

What we begin to see at this time is a worsening of the post-imperial crisis. Even before the economic crisis of 1966, and pre-empting the second application for membership, Benn was commenting in his diaries that 'this country is so decrepit and hidebound that only activities in a wider sphere can help us to escape from the myths that surround our politics' (Benn, 1996, p. 121).

In more general terms there was 'a steady deterioration in the authority of the state and the dominant ideas of the political order' (Leys, 1983, p. 63). This was precipitated by the deteriorating economic position of Britain relative to the rest of the industrialised world.[6] A diverse range of challenges to the social order were emerging including, a rise in the number of strikes, ethnic and racial tensions, civil rights movements and urban guerrilla warfare in Northern Ireland. As Halsey points out, these 'domestic discontents fanned by economic stagnation, class and status inequalities were less and less easily contained by the traditional remedies of political liberalism, gentlemanly culture and civic incorporation' (1986, p. 151).

---

6   Between 1961 and 1978 Britain's share of world exports of manufacturing goods fell from 15.7 per cent to 9.5 per cent and the overall rate of profit declined from 14.2 per cent in 1960 to 4.7 per cent in 1978 (Leys 1983: 64).

The breakdown of the old imperial order had reached a critical point by the mid-1960s, a position that was exacerbated by the Labour government's failed programme of modernisation.

It is within this context that the second application for membership of the EC took place. For the Labour government, a primary feature of this policy was that it was the only way of retaining British power in the world; conversely, outside of the EC Britain would be bypassed by the US and would be a declining fourth force in a world dominated by the US, Europe, China and the Soviet Union (Wall, 2013, p. 138). At the October 1966 meeting, it was presented by Brown and Stewart as the 'only way to make sure that Britain kept her place at the top table' (Crossman, 1979, p. 259). Membership of the EC seemed to offer the possibility of a return to great power status combined with opportunities for economic renewal through a revised external policy. In this sense, it appeared to enable the Labour government to recapture its place as the party of post-imperial reconstruction, without having to engage with the chronic problems of the domestic politico-economic structure.

Europe emerged as the new project of key members of the Labour leadership. Crossman argued that it was being pursued as a way out of crisis, by deflecting from underlying problems, as well as helping to outflank the left of the party (p. 349). However, he was also aware of its potency as a solution to this national crisis, capable of providing the party with a strategic direction. By 1967 Tony Benn was commenting that the government was now looking for a solution to its problems from the outside and was persuaded that the common market was the solution (Benn, 1996, p. 171). Pimlott argues that it was a 'gigantic attempt' to distract attention from domestic and foreign policy problems, and to revive the government's 'fighting spirit' (1993, p. 435).

Civil servants were central to persuading the Labour government of the viability of reviving British membership of the Community as a solution to its problems (Young, 1998, pp. 177–90). By 1963 a European 'elite regiment' had emerged and established itself within key administrative offices of government (p. 177). A 'new orthodoxy' was identifiable in the Foreign Office amongst the diplomatic corps who saw both their own and their country's future as being inside Europe. Young, in particular, refers to the role of John Robinson and Sir Con O'Neill, and argues that their appointment to Brussels marked the point at which the Foreign Office's European policy became dominated by men who believed Britain belonged in the Community (pp. 179–80). In the preparatory documents for the October meeting of the Labour Cabinet, O'Neill referred to a country adrift and in decline for 20 years, and how entry into Europe would provide 'a new goal and a new commitment' which would 'crystallise its hopes and energies' (p. 190). The European political vision was presented to the Labour government at a time when its own project was in ruin. Wilson attempted to reignite Labour's idea of the 'technological revolution' by linking it to entry to the Community in the form of a European Technological Community.

After what Wilson believed was a successful meeting with de Gaulle, he returned from the tour of the capitals convinced of the necessity of membership.[7] While the Cabinet was split on the issue, when it came to endorsing the statement of intent to seek membership it was supported by all except Douglas Jay and Dennis Healey, and there were no major battles or resignations (Crossman, 1979, p. 348; Gowland and Turner, 2000a, pp. 165–6). Furthermore, opposition within the party and the trade unions was effectively neutralised by the time of the annual conference in 1967 when the NEC statement favouring entry was accepted by a heavy majority, an outcome indicative of the control the leadership and the centre-right pro-marketeers had at the time (Bilski, 1977, pp. 309–13).

The decision by the Labour party to support membership of the EC was a reaction to a crisis of government coming out of the ruins of the National Plan. As this failure to transform British economy and society became clear, the leadership embraced the Conservative idea of membership as a strategy of contained modernisation and attached the Wilsonian theme of a technological revolution to it. The underlying tenets of this approach remained the same as they were under Macmillan (George, 1990, p. 40; Frey, 1968, pp. 205–6). There was no conversion to the project of European integration: the aims of membership were to stop British economic decline and maintain a semblance of world power status. The policy was firmly couched within the language of British high politics. In Wilson's speeches on the issue he underplayed the integrationist project and emphasised the Anglo-American partnership and Britain's more global ambitions for the Community (see Frey, 1968, pp. 203–4). The issue can be seen as part of the Wilson government's, and in particular Wilson's, attempt to recreate itself after the failure of its modernisation programme as the party of national responsibility (Nairn, 1973, p. 50).

Considering the weakness of the British economy at the time, the distinct limitations of EC membership as a strategy of economic revival and modernisation were overshadowed by the need for political momentum and a continued belief in an external free trade solution to Britain's economic problems. Crossman's reflections on the deliberations about whether to apply for membership at the October 1966 meeting are pertinent in this respect:

> To my great surprise he [Sir William Armstrong, Joint Permanent Secretary at the Treasury] admitted under questioning that entry in 1968 (which all the papers took as a working assumption) was now a bit too early in view of the time it would take to restore the economy to a state healthy enough for entry. This remarkable discussion stimulated a long discussion of the timetable. Some officials suggested it would take two years of the slow growth we must now expect before we got the economy right and then another two years to prove

---

7 Wilson appeared to have exaggerated his influence on de Gaulle and then overstated the possibility that the General would support membership (Crossman 1979, p. 355; Young 1998, p. 194; Gowland and Turner 2000a, pp. 164–5).

that when growth started we wouldn't have inflation. I could see George Brown getting angrier and angrier at this point. The trouble about the morning session was that the Ministers present were determined to use the officials mainly to supply information confirming their own personal point of view. (1979, pp. 260–61)

Any doubts about a shift in economic strategy towards the EC had disappeared by spring 1967, when British industry in the shape of the CBI overwhelmingly came out in support of British membership, despite the immediate effect it might have on the balance of payments (Frey, 1968, p. 218). Many large multi-national companies supported membership, as did the City (p. 219). This support cannot be separated from the intensification of capitalist internationalisation and, in particular, the continued penetration of American-dominated international capital into the European market (Miliband, 1973, pp. 14–15), a trend that was noticeably extreme in the British case where by 1970 all the top 100 manufacturing companies were multinationals (Gamble, 1994, p. 110). In a Cabinet meeting of April 1967 discussing the economic implications of membership, Wilson stated that three principal US car companies (General Motors, Ford and Chrysler) had based themselves in the UK on the expectation, indeed specific pledges in some cases, that Britain would join the EC (Wall, 2013, p. 176). The fear was that incoming foreign direct investment would gradually shift to the rest of Europe if the UK stayed out.

In May 1967 the vote in the House of Commons on applying to the EC was won by the government, with the largest majority seen in the House of Commons in the twentieth century, with 487 voting for and only 26 against (Wall, 2013, p. 202). In retrospect this represented the high point of a governing elite consensus on membership that was endorsed by political parties, interest groups and by the wider public. In the event, the second application for membership was comprehensively rejected by de Gaulle in November 1967 on the grounds that Britain remained insufficiently European. Underlying de Gaulle's veto was his continued concern that Britain's entry would undermine the possibility of an independent Europe, alongside the threat that Britain posed to French national interests, particularly agriculture, once inside the Community. In addition, Schenk argues that the continued international role of sterling, combined with its weakness on the foreign exchanges, was a particular cause for concern for all the member states (2002, p. 366). There was a genuine fear that the Community would be called on to bail out the British economy if it faced another sterling crisis. Even if this was not the case, the volatility of sterling as an international currency left Britain extremely dependent on the United States. These concerns were significant barriers to British membership in 1967.[8]

---

8 These problems seemed to have abated after a reduced role for the pound was accepted after 1968. Nevertheless, the fundamental orientation of British monetary policy did not move in a European direction.

Nevertheless, the indications of support for membership from across the member-states meant that when de Gaulle was replaced by Pompidou in 1969, membership became a real possibility. Early in 1970 the Cabinet endorsed a White Paper favouring membership. However, the Labour government was defeated in an election 12 days before negotiations were about to start. Wall argues that there is no evidence that 'anti-European' feeling contributed directly to Labour's defeat, yet the negative balance of payment figures published during polling week undermined Labour's claim to have strengthened the economy and it was clear by this point that membership would make them worse (2013, p. 360). The negative economic impact of membership, notably the possible rise in food prices, became a particular focus for Eurosceptic attacks.

What had occurred by the end of the sixties was the establishment of considerable support across the political class for membership. It was the stated policy objective of both major parties and had strong support within business circles and across powerful sections of Whitehall. Frey argued that the move towards Europe seemed to reflect a real transformation in the consciousness of the political class (1968, p. 230). Entry into the EC was now held up as a long term economic panacea and as a new arena for British leadership that would restore world power status. However, as with the Macmillan regime, the Labour government emphasised continuity through national renewal inside the EC and remained circumspect on political integration.

At the point at which the elite consensus on membership appeared to have been consolidated, we also begin to see the first significant wave of British Eurosceptic mobilisation. A Eurosceptic politics whereby EC membership was constituted as a threat both economically and politically became increasingly prevalent. There was a clear growth of anti-Community feeling within the country by the end of the decade; an opinion poll early in 1970 found 72 per cent of those questioned to be against membership (Wall, 2013, p. 353). Members of the governing elite began to break ranks and publicly questioned British membership, acting as leaders to Eurosceptics on the backbenches in parliament and the wider party. In 1969 Enoch Powell had declared his opposition to British membership on the basis that it was incompatible with parliamentary sovereignty and, as such, represented a threat to the continuation of the British nation[9] (see Powell, 1971). In March 1970, Peter Shore, a Minister without Portfolio in the Wilson government, made a speech critical of entry, arguing that the decision should not simply be made by politicians but should become a matter of public debate (Crossman, 1979, p. 699). Shore was a leading sceptic at the time, whose position on Europe was that of a left-wing populist nationalism.[10] At the same time we see the extra-parliamentary

---

9   As a popular figure whose nationalism appealed to voters across the party, Powell is credited with being a key factor in the Conservative's surprise victory in the 1970 election.

10   Crossman described it as a 'remarkable' speech particularly in the sense that Shore gave no prior warning to the Prime Minister or the Foreign Secretary of what he intended to say (1979, p. 700).

mobilisation of Eurosceptic interest and campaign groups. In 1969 a number of Eurosceptic groupings came together to form the cross-party coalition Campaign for an Independent Britain. It included the right leaning Anti-Common Market League that had been formed at the time of the first application and, in 1970, the Labour Euro-Safeguards Campaign that brought together Eurosceptics on the left.

Against the background of increased scepticism, the European policy of the Conservative party under Heath was in fact played down during the election campaign. The party only committed to negotiate with the Community; 'no more, no less' (The Conservative Party, 1970). In May 1970, Heath argued that the EC could only be enlarged with the 'full hearted consent of the peoples and parliaments' of the applicant states, implying that a referendum could be necessary alongside parliamentary approval. Nevertheless, once in power it was clear that membership was central to its governing agenda, to the point where neither the compromises that had to be made during the negotiations nor the growing scepticism in the country, were going to prevent it from taking place.

Entry into the Community

With Pompidou replacing de Gaulle and the election of Willy Brandt as Chancellor of West Germany, a re-launch of the EC was possible. This took place at a Summit at The Hague in 1969, and the proceedings included a commitment to enlargement that opened the way for British membership. In June 1970 the Conservatives under Heath won the general election. Heath's[11] life story was that of a committed European (George, 1990, p. 49; Young, 1998, pp. 216–22) and he had led the negotiations on entry under Macmillan. When the first bid for entry came to end with de Gaulle's veto, Heath's concluding speech restated in the clearest terms Britain's commitment to Europe: 'the end of the negotiations is a blow to the cause of the wider European unity for which we have been striving. We are a part of Europe, by geography, history, culture, tradition and civilisation ...' (Heath, 1998, p. 235). Heath articulated a British-European vision that was consistent with that of the Macmillan government within which he had served. The fundamental aim was the same: membership would finally secure Britain's place as a leading European capitalist nation-state and provide the basis for its post-imperial renewal as a world power.

In his Godkin lectures of 1967 Heath (1970) outlined his European vision. He argued that the forms of international cooperation that took place in organisations such as the OECD were insufficient, and he argued for an active European Commission (Lord, 1993, p. 38). He put forward the possibility of a European

---

11 He had been strongly influenced by Churchill's powerful proclamations for a United States of Europe made in the aftermath of the war and, in his maiden speech in June 1950, he criticised the government's failure to become involved in the Schuman Plan (Heath 1998, pp. 145–6).

defence system and suggested the pooling of French and British nuclear weapons (Young, 1998, p. 221; Heath, 1998, p. 361). In effect he proposed putting Europe at the centre of British foreign policy, above either the Commonwealth or the United States (Heath, 1998, p. 361). It was a strategy that distinguished committed European politicians not only from the traditionalists, but also from the opportunists. Nevertheless, it was a British post-imperial vision of transformation that implied continuity. Heath argued that the Community was structured in a similar fashion to the British state. It had institutions that were pragmatic and open, and in which there was no need to 'specify end states or theological principles of arrangement' (Lord, 1993, p. 39). On sovereignty, he said that effective state sovereignty would be improved as membership of the Community increased the range of choices open to the British state (p. 37).

A major feature of the Heathite strategy on Europe was the belief in its contribution to economic renewal. Europe was a defining plank of the government's modernisation programme (George, 1990, p. 49; Morris, 1996, p. 129; Turner, 2000, p. 64). Turner thus refers to membership of the EC 'as the external arm of the Party's domestic Selsdon strategy' (2000, p. 64): the free market policy agenda that was seen to emerge from the Conservative Shadow Cabinet's meeting at the Selsdon Park Hotel in Surrey. This economic strategy was designed to increase the competitiveness of the British economy by removing some of the constraints on economic management and allowing industry to resolve its own problems (Gamble, 1994, p. 123). The exposure of the British economy to European competition would, it was believed, keep down inflation, producing an influx of foreign capital which would help to finance new investment and eventually reduce the balance of payments deficits (Lord, 1993, p. 23). The urgency of this new economic strategy was reinforced by the crisis in the US economy. By 1968 it was running an overall deficit on its balance of payments. By 1971 there was a renewed dollar crisis and a shift towards more protectionist policies. These developments unleashed an international economic crisis, as the US appeared to be withdrawing from its role as the world banker. For British large-scale capital dependent on the Eurodollar market and on overseas investment, the collapse of the international economy under US hegemony was particularly difficult (Nairn, 1973, pp. 25–6; Overbeek, 1990, p. 127). In the context of the continued chronic problems of the domestic economy and the crisis of the international order, outward-looking British capitalists opted for Europe (Nairn, 1973, p. 26). While pro-European politicians saw in Europe the opportunity for a market-led strategy of national economic modernisation, powerful elements of British transnationalised capital supported entry into the EC in order to secure their foothold within the international economy. These economic pre-conditions therefore reinforced the urgency of implementing the government's European policy.

By the time that membership had become a real possibility for the UK, London was, according to *The Economist*, emerging as the 'financial growth pole of Europe' (Nairn, 1973, p. 28). This had been encouraged by the government's deregulation of the City, with the removal of the ceilings on bank lending under the policy known as Competition and Credit Control (CCC).[12] Conversely, the impact of EC membership for UK-centric business was likely to be negative (Haack, 1972, p. 151). The fear was that for a weak economy, in which growth was often artificially manufactured through policy instruments, membership of the EC would contribute to balance of payments problems, and domestic industry would not be rationalised but out-competed and taken over. Nevertheless, what was emphasised in the official documents at the time were the advantages of the dynamic effects on the economy that would offset any negative consequences (p. 143). The economic justification for membership of the EC was increasingly expressed in terms of a competitiveness discourse, which claimed that exposure to the pressures of new markets would help modernise the UK economy. At the time Haack described the presentation of these as 'rather vague' and 'mysterious'; in addition, he noted that they were not quantified despite being 'the most important economic justifications for entry' (p. 143).

The negotiations on British membership lasted for 18 months, and concerned the position of sterling as an international reserve currency, Commonwealth trade, agriculture and fishing, and the British budgetary contribution (George, 1990, p. 50). When the negotiations reached a particularly difficult stage in spring 1971, it was unclear to the British whether the French were looking for a way of preventing British entry (George, 1990, p. 54). The situation was resolved by a summit between Pompidou and Heath. Pompidou appeared to want a gesture on the part of the British that it was fully committed to a European future and a historic shift in its place in the world. Heath was able to successfully reassure the President. In addition, Heath endorsed the French intergovernmentalist approach to Community institutions and the implied right to protect vital national interests. He also committed Britain to full participation in economic and monetary cooperation, which included the gradual reduction in the sterling balances (Wall, 2013, pp. 402–3).

Heath convinced Pompidou that the special relationship with the US was over, as Britain 'was a quarter of the size of the other' and now recognised that, like France, Britain could only continue its 'world vocation' in partnership with its European partners (Heath, 1998, p. 370). It was, however, made against a background of a general loss of confidence in the international hegemonic rule of the United States and, thus, a loss of confidence in the special relationship (George, 1990, p. 45). Nevertheless, membership would secure an important strategic role for Britain vis-à-vis the US and the EC, as a gateway for US multinational companies to enter the European market. In addition, it secured the City's position in the Eurodollar market, which itself had seen a dramatic invasion of US banks during the 1960s (Strange, 1971, p. 234). This interdependence of US and British economic interests both necessitated and problematised Britain's role as an intermediary between the US and the EC. Evidently the formal breakdown of Bretton Woods in 1973 and the end of the sterling area lessened the importance

---

12   However quantitative controls were reintroduced in 1973 (known as the Corset) in response to the overheating of the economy.

of the pound as an international currency, so that it was no longer a significant barrier to British membership. However, it did not necessarily alter the underlying structural interrelationship between the British and US economies and, in particular, financial capital. Nowhere was this more evident than in Britain's position as a chronic international debtor nation particularly dependent for credit directly from the US, as well as the US-dominated IMF (Strange, 1971).

In the end, the British accepted the Common Agricultural Policy (CAP) and negotiated special arrangements for Caribbean sugar and New Zealand dairy produce, but they were forced to make concessions on their budgetary contribution (Young, 1998, pp. 231–2). The British budgetary contribution was particularly contentious because the country's relatively small agricultural sector meant it would receive little back from the CAP and it was projected that by 1981 Britain would be the largest net contributor of any member-state (Wall, 2013, p. 384). The final agreement saw limitations placed on initial British contributions until 1979.

The Heath government appeared to pursue entry into the European Community on the understanding that it represented a historical shift in the identity of the British political order. In fact it was a compromised and constrained position that reflected the tensions that had been evident in the earlier strategy of the Macmillan government, as well as a deepening of the problems of legitimation. The negotiations avoided the 'deep, existential meaning' of Britain's relationship to Europe, the relationship of Britain to the future of the integrationist project or the question of sovereignty (Young, 1998, p. 238). They were effectively a technocratic exercise interrupted by some high politics designed to reassure the French. Despite Heath's opposition commitment to 'full consent', the issue was not presented to the public in terms of a fundamental change for 'the British people'. As Young points out, 'Heath was talking cost of living, not cost of nationhood' (p. 240). This was a conservative vision of national renewal through membership of the EC that emphasised continuity through change, a vision that was evident in the Heath White Paper on membership. It claimed that sovereignty would not be eroded and what was being proposed was an 'enlargement and sharing' of sovereignty (p. 246). Young argued that in the Commons debate on the European Communities Bill to ratify membership, the political implications were disguised (pp. 247–51). In bringing the debate to a close, he claimed that Heath was 'as soporific as could be' referring to a commitment which 'involves our sovereignty' but from which 'we are also gaining an opportunity' (p. 247). The focus was thus on the economic benefits, and not on what would change but on what would stay the same (pp. 250–51). The government failed to articulate its vision of the future of Europe (p. 254). Heath's view is predictably different. He argued that the 'public information campaign on the outcome of negotiations was the most comprehensive ever by a post-war government' and that this campaign focused on both the political and economic issues (Heath, 1998, p. 378). In defence of the comprehensiveness of the political debate, he cited Lord Douglas Home's (Foreign Secretary) speech in 1971 to the Conservative Group for Europe, which emphasised that the application for entry was of 'the utmost political significance'

(p. 378). Heath claimed this was 'perfectly clear' in his closing statement on the Commons debate: 'I want Britain as a member of a Europe which is united politically, and which will enjoy lasting peace and the greater security which will ensue' (p. 380).

If anything, this was a secondary discourse that was subordinated to a more depoliticised emphasis on economic benefits, and on continuity and stability through membership. In fact, Heath's position on integration was not entirely coherent. Although he viewed the Community as a unique political entity, he had little time for supranationalism or federalism, as is evident from his comments on the 1972 Paris summit commitment to the formation of a European Union:

> I had argued that European Union was an admirable objective which could only be achieved by pragmatic steps. The European Union has always developed *sui-generis* ... When the European Union reaches the end of its development, it will remain *sui generis*. I believed, therefore, that there was little point in debating theoretical arguments about federalism. What we are concerned with was making a success of the European Community, and the word 'Union' allowed us to do just that. (pp. 391–2)

What exactly 'sui-generis' meant in this context can only be assumed to be some notion of pooled sovereignty of states, which Heath had referred to in his Godkin lectures and in other speeches and statements. As far as it is possible to identify the position of the Heath government, it saw the Community primarily as an intergovernmentalist arena for the pursuit of British interests (Morris, 1996, p. 129). In the negotiations on entry the government defended the veto and was identifiably 'Gaullist' in its approach to the Community (Butler, 1986, p. 118, 159). This conservatism became evident in the reluctance of the government to constructively engage with the attempts to renew the project of European integration that were occurring from 1969 onwards. The Conservative government was viewed as resistant to progress towards economic and monetary union[13] when it refused to allow sterling to re-enter the 'snake' system of tied exchange rates unless the German government was prepared to underwrite its value (George, 1991, p. 52; Gowland and Turner, 2000a, p. 179). This was not acceptable to the Germans without wider policy coordination. Meanwhile the government vigorously pursued its national interest arguing the case for a European Regional Development Fund, which it was believed would compensate for the perceived unfairness in the budgetary settlement. In this regard, however, the British government was not behaving differently from any other member-state at a point when national interests were dominant and the EC was struggling to establish a common voice.

In a clear irony membership of the EC under the Heath government was a monumental event, yet underlying it was a strategy designed to rescue the British

---

13 Although it should be noted that Heath came out strongly in favour of economic and monetary union and saw it as a part of the solution to the dollar crisis.

state from decline and crisis, which implied continuity within change. There remained the belief that Europe could replace Empire and restore British influence and power. Significantly Heath's vision of the relationship between Britain and the Community gained ascendancy in the context of the failure and exhaustion of alternative bases for renewal, including the special relationship with the United States. At a time of international economic crisis, class conflict and civil strife in Northern Ireland, Europe became the 'essential instrument' for achieving a degree of unity across the political class (Nairn, 1973, p. 36). Nairn points out that 'it, and it alone, offered the way out from the pitfalls which seemed to dominate the political landscape of 1970' (p. 36). In particular, it reflected the immediate interests of British internationalised capital. After 1972, it was the only element of the Selsdon strategy still in place, and the only way the government could reassure British capital as inflation rose and the value of sterling declined. Membership was eventually achieved against the background of an unsustainable expansion of the economy, which resulted in a balance of payments crisis for the incoming Labour government, and growing trade union militancy due to the failure of the government to secure trade union reform and wage restraint. The latter was most clearly evident with a large miners' strike and pay claim that eventually led to the fall of the government. The European strategy then became intertwined with crisis management, and the problems the government had in achieving its objectives in the first year of membership contributed to a growing sense of public disillusionment with the idea that Europe was the solution to Britain's problems. In fact the economic benefits were already evident with an increase in investment, both in terms of UK investment in the EC and vice-versa, and a considerable growth in exports (Wall, 2013, p. 492). Nevertheless, the government failed to present the positive case for membership, and opinion poll evidence during 1972 pointed to continued problems of legitimacy.

The weakness of the Heath government's position was evident in the significant European splits emerging within the Conservative party. Heath was faced with extreme opposition to membership by a faction of Conservatives under the leadership of Powell. Opposition within the Conservative party, powerfully influenced by Powellism, had entered a new phase by the early 1970s, and was less concerned with Empire and Commonwealth than with Franco-German domination and its anti-free market policies (Turner, 2000, pp. 62–3). These arguments were to be echoed during the right wing mobilisation against the Community during the 1980s and 1990s. In his opposition to membership, Powell was supported by 40 Conservative MPs and this obliterated the government's majority during the passage of the Bill on accession. The initial vote on membership in October 1971 and the subsequent passage of the European Communities Bill was only secured for the Heath government by support of the pro-European Jenkinsite faction within the Labour party. The seeds were sown for a right wing backlash against the European policy of the Conservative party. In general there was growing scepticism about Heath's enthusiasm for Europe once he retreated on his Selsdon strategy after 1972. This did not mean the Conservative party was to stop being the 'Party of Europe', and by 1975 this was the orthodox position (Grimmond and Neve, 1975, p. 94; Morris, 1996, p. 129). Yet this position was unequivocally subordinated to a renewed conception of a strong British nation-state.

Mobilising Against Membership

By the time entry into the European Community had been secured, cross-party support for membership had fractured. The opposition to the EC on the Tory right was paralleled on the Labour left. This reflected the polarisation of the main political parties as more extreme political forces grew in significance (Leys, 1983, p. 41). Increasingly membership of the EC became a battleground around which national political projects were contested (George, 1990, pp. 76–7). Clearly this was an unintended consequence of the decision to join the Community that governing elites had not foreseen. As crisis conditions intensified and were exacerbated by the growing divisions within the party, the Labour governments' (1974–1979) approach to Europe was subordinated to the needs of party and national unity. Increasingly, the EC was being invoked by significant sections of the political class not as the saviour but as the 'other' of the British nation. A key proposition here is that this populist Eurosceptic discourse infected the British political culture and curtailed attempts to construct a more positive vision of Britain in the EC. As European policies and strategies became harder to legitimate in the face of Eurosceptic opposition, governing elites began to dissociate themselves from the full political implications of membership. Thus the European Community had no place in the attempt and failure by the Wilson government to construct a stable corporatist regime under the aegis of a Social Contract. Furthermore, when the international economic crisis deepened, the solution to the fiscal crisis of the Callaghan government was to be found in the form of the IMF and to emphasise an Atlanticist approach to the global downturn.

During the Labour party's time out of office, between 1970 and 1974, it became increasingly split on the issue of Europe as the party shifted to the left (Bilski, 1977; Benn, 1996, pp. 249–50; Young, 1998, pp. 270–71). The debate on membership 'played a decisive role in the reconstruction of power and ideological balance inside the Labour Party' (Bilski, 1977, p. 316). The left opposed membership, presenting it as a form of 'narrow regional integration' dominated by French nationalism and as a threat to British socialism and to the British nation (Nairn, 1973, pp. 63–7). On the other side, the Jenkinsite faction of pro-Europeans remained firmly committed to a brand of European social democracy and represented the strongest supporters of a European future for Britain to be found across the political spectrum. However, it was the left wing anti-marketeers, in the ascendant at the time, that were indicative of a profound turn around in a party that had historically been dominated by a right-wing leadership. The re-alignment of trade union power with the left in reaction to the attempts to curb their power by the Wilson government was crucial in this respect.

In July 1971, a special conference was held on membership of the Community at which the irreconcilable divisions within the party were clearly visible (Bilski, 1977, p. 319). The left then used the issue in a highly effective manner to mobilise support and increase their power in the party. Nairn argued that the issue became seen as a way out of the crisis of the Labour party after a disappointing period in office:

> In 1970–71 Labourism was suffering from defeat and deep disorientation, and coping very badly with the situation. And its ominous incapacity to find renewal ideologically was demonstrated against the background of rapidly falling membership and militancy, and the marked trend towards embourgeoisement ... This was the state in which the Party confronted the great debate [on EC membership], a declining empire of national socialism, lifeless at the top and increasingly unsure of its old social basis. (1973, p. 81)

The adoption within the Labour party of a populist position towards EC membership was the response to this crisis. The core characteristics of populism that would come to dominate British Eurosceptic politics were therefore evident for the first time in the Labour left's rejection of Britain's European trajectory (Lazer, 1976). There was an explicit appeal to 'the people' particularly evident in the referencing of opinion polls, which by the early 1970s were reflecting a strong anti-European sentiment amongst the general public. Moreover, this was combined with a criticism of elitism, which was directed as much against the right pro-marketeers in the Labour party as it was against the Conservatives. The anti-European Labour politicians saw themselves as reflecting the grassroots of the Labour party, as well as the wider public, against the British establishment. The latter at this time included the generally pro-European press. That public opinion appeared to hold fast against the pressures from elites was taken as evidence of 'the people's' capacity to resist the 'ruling class', as the Labour MP Norman Atkinson expressed in the October 1971 debate on membership:

> I find it most encouraging that the mind-benders have been defeated. This is the first occasion I recall when, after the British people have been subjected to a deluge of propaganda – educational processes, some Hon. Members have called it – the mind-benders have been defeated. That should give us great encouragement in the Socialist movement. (cited in Lazer, 1976, p. 271)

On this view the logical conclusion to the question of British membership was to defer directly to 'the British people', and Labour, as the archetypal party of British mass democracy, was best placed to make this case. A number of key Labour figures argued that membership was such a major constitutional change that it could not be agreed to without consulting 'the British people'; however the normal mechanism for doing this, a general election, posed a number of difficulties. Most significantly it would have meant a large section of the Labour party not supporting the party official line and potentially splitting the party. In an attempt to contain the splits within the party, in 1972 the Labour shadow Cabinet decided to support a proposed amendment to the European Communities Bill by Enoch Powell calling for a referendum, a proposal that Tony Benn had originally put forward in 1970 (Benn, 1996, p. 255). It was a populist stance taken to try and undermine the government in the context of domestic problems, but also had the potential to unite the Labour party. Harold Wilson, Labour leader, dealt with this split by siding with the left and supporting the referendum. However, he was unable to do this without committing the party to a more oppositional stance on Europe, which led to the resignation of the leading pro-European, Roy Jenkins, in April 1972. During 1972 and 1973, the party was just held together by a commitment to opposing the terms of entry negotiated by Heath and supporting a referendum on the issue. This then was the position of the party when it took office in 1974.

The re-negotiations the British Labour government entered into have been characterised as a 'sham', with no suggestion of revising the Treaty of Rome or the Treaty of Accession (Greenwood, 1992, p. 100). The German Chancellor Schmidt described them later as a face-saving, cosmetic operation undertaken for the British government (Young, 1998, p. 283). Nevertheless, a number of concessions were made to the British on issues such as Commonwealth trade and the CAP. By the time of the Dublin Council in March 1975, the two outstanding issues were British budgetary contributions and New Zealand butter. Wilson approached the meeting as 'a St. George figure who knew how to stand up to foreign dragons and would never sell his country short' (George, 1990, p. 86). His populist defence of the interests of the white Commonwealth played to the nationalism of the British public and large sections of the Labour party. Wilson also rejected calls for increased harmonisation, falsely implying that the Commission was about to impose on the British public a 'Euro-loaf' and 'Euro-beer' (p. 87). Wilson was able to sell the renegotiations as a victory for the Labour government and effectively employed a populist nationalism to legitimise continued membership of the Community. It meant eschewing any attempt to link membership of the Community with a broader Europeanised project of British renewal and modernisation.

When Wilson publicly stated his continued support for a referendum in January 1975, he attracted considerable criticism from within a deeply divided party. He nevertheless succeeded in producing a Cabinet majority of 16–7 in favour of membership based on the renegotiated terms and a majority in parliament (Young, 1998, pp. 284–5; Benn, 1996, pp. 313–15). Divisions within the Labour party by this stage were particularly deep and so intense that a parliamentary victory was only achieved with the support of the Conservatives. Six members of the Cabinet dissented from the Cabinet line, including Tony Benn, Barbara Castle, Michael Foot, Peter Shore, Willie Ross and Eric Varley. During the Cabinet debate on the impact of membership on national sovereignty, both the pro and anti-marketeers defended their positions as consistent with the continuation of British parliamentary sovereignty. Both sides presented themselves as the guardians of the British constitution. These persistent divisions within the party were further exposed when the dissenters in the Cabinet began to mobilise the party against continued membership. By the time of a special Labour party conference in April 1975, a large majority voted against membership.

During the referendum it was the 'Britain in Europe' (BIE) campaign grouping that galvanised key sections of the British political classes. Leading establishment figures from business, politics, the media and even the church lined up in support of a *Yes* vote (George, 1990, pp. 94–5). Its endorsement by the Labour leadership was a key factor in the increased support for continued membership (Butler, 1979, p. 154). The *Yes* campaign emphasised the economic case for membership and considerable attention was given to the effects on the cost of withdrawal (George, 1990, p. 94; Young, 1998, p. 291). They presented their case for continued membership as a pragmatic economic necessity and emphasised the control of national governments over European decision making. It was fundamentally a conservative case for British membership that made no mention of any restrictions on British sovereignty as a consequence of membership. There was no engagement with the project of European integration as representing a fundamental transformation of the British state. As Young points out, the *Yes* campaign,

> conformed to the old familiar rule, the golden thread of deceptive reassurance that runs through the history of Britain's relationship with the European Union up to the present day, our entry was essential, our membership is vital, our assistance in the consolidation is imperative – *but nothing you really care about will change*. (1998, p. 293, emphasis mine)

All the confusions of the British European strategy that had been evident at the time of the Macmillan government, and reflected a fundamentally reoriented rather than restructured political order, were therefore being restated. Yet the emphasis was now on the pragmatic economic necessity of membership rather than the revival of world power status that had been so central to the Macmillan approach.

The National Referendum Campaign (NRC) fight for a *No* vote focused more directly on the populist issues of sovereignty and nationhood. This was the position of Powell and those Conservatives who opposed membership. They were joined in their concern over the nation with those on the Labour left such as Shore, Benn and Foot. Shore proclaimed that membership of the EC meant that the 'long and famous history of the British nation and people has ended' (cited in Young, 1998, p. 292). In a letter in to his constituents in December 1974, Benn outlined what was to be his fundamental reason for opposing Britain's membership in the referendum campaign: 'Britain's continuing membership of the Community would mean the end of Britain as a completely self-governing nation and the end of our democratically elected Parliament as the supreme law-making body in the United Kingdom' (Benn, 1974, p. 38).

Benn, therefore, aligned himself with populist left wing nationalism and against the realities of an advanced international capitalism and its political reorganisation. Nairn points out that the left viewed the common market as a 'disease' of capitalism, like high imperialism or fascism, and not as a new post-national stage in bourgeois society, within which there was also the opportunity to strengthen the position of the working class and European socialism (1973, pp. 145–6). Ignoring the realities of international capitalism, and the possibility of crafting a distinctive national-European accumulation strategy, those on the British left continued to perpetuate a socialist utopia of national economic autonomy. They envisaged a dilution of the possibilities for socialism in Britain as a consequence of membership of a capitalist organisation characterised by the politics of consensus and compromise (Castle, 1980, p. 404). The left's defence of the nation meant they found themselves in an unlikely alliance with Powell and his supporters. Powell proclaimed that membership of the Community meant the end of the British parliament and with it national independence (Ritchie, 1978, p. 35). During the battle over the passage of the European Communities Bill, he had argued that membership of the EC would be bitterly opposed:

> If Brussels. Luxembourg and Paris are imagining that the 'English gentleman' will now 'play the game', they will be rudely undeceived. These resentments will intertwine with all the raw issues of British politics, inflation, unemployment, balance of payments, the regions, even immigration, even Northern Ireland, and every one of these issues will be sharpened to the discomfiture of the European Party. (cited in Ritchie, 1978, pp. 43–4)

Thus on both the left and right Europe was invoked as the 'other' of British freedom and national identity, in order to revive the old Westminster system and construct the 'imagined community' of the United Kingdom. The pamphlet distributed by the NRC claimed that the 'the Common Market ... set out by stages to merge Britain with France, Germany and Italy and other countries into a single nation' (cited in Wall, 2013, p. 585). However, as Forster points out, the NRC was not a unified movement, as it drew on a range of groupings from across the left and right (2002, p. 354). Powell was increasingly isolated by the time of the referendum, having left the Conservative party for the Ulster Unionists and urging a vote for Labour in the 1974 election because of its position on Europe. Many Conservatives who had opposed the government during the parliamentary debates on membership did not follow Powell's lead and party loyalty meant they did not actively participate in the NRC.

In the event the final referendum vote was strongly in favour with 67.2 per cent *Yes* vote on a turnout of 64.6 per cent. This was not, however, the endorsement of 'the British people' for the European project but a vote for the status quo in support of the position outlined by their leaders (Butler and Kitzinger, 1976, p. 280; George, 1990, p. 95; Greenwood, 1992, p. 102). The public effectively endorsed the conservatism of the European strategy of the British state. Membership of the Community came to represent a sense of continuity and security at a time of British decline and crisis. Conversely the anti-Europeans were often viewed and represented as political extremists and outsiders. Wilson made the point that a victory for the *No* campaign would have empowered the 'wrong kind of people in Britain: the Benn left and Powell right, who were often extreme nationalists, protectionist, xenophobic and backward-looking' (Wall, 2013, p. 589). However, the authority of the vote was questionable; as Powell pointed out at the time, 'our continued membership will depend on the continuing assent of Parliament' (p. 589). That the arguments for membership had not been convincingly won was indicated by a majority telling Mori in 1978 that they would vote against continued membership (Butler, 1979, p. 151).

The domestic conflicts over Europe during the 1970s were fundamental constraints on British governments adopting a more assertive European strategy and fully engaging with the process of integration as a leading member-state, as had been envisaged by Macmillan and Heath. Evidently, in the context of a post-imperial crisis that now included an intensification of domestic Euroscepticism, to try and turn Britain into a hegemonic European state was unrealistic. That this was so became immediately evident after the referendum, when the Wilson government blocked and disrupted a range of Community policies on energy, pollution controls, transport and the European Regional Development Fund. In effect, increasingly defensive and exclusive articulations of the national interest became central to the legitimation of governing positions on Europe.

The IMF Steps In

The referendum campaign had taken place against the end of the Labour government's Social Contract as a strategy of national renewal and modernisation. There was a rise in inflation to 30 per cent by the summer of 1974, a balance of trade deficit of £3,323 million by the end of 1974 and widespread structural unemployment that had reached over 1 million by October 1975 (Coates, 1980, p. 12; George, 1990, p. 75). The government could only handle the deficit by raising huge international loans that in turn added to the burden of public spending (Coates, 1980, p. 19). The dilemma was that the Social Contract that was designed to stimulate economic growth could only do so by shifting resources away from the greater social wage on which the contract had been constructed (p. 23). After 1975, therefore, the government was forced to try and win trade union support for wage cuts and ending industrial disputes (p. 25). The capacity of the government to achieve a cooperative relationship with a hostile and fragmented labour movement was limited. In effect, the Social Contract became a mechanism for achieving wage controls and any consensus on the social wage that had been achieved began to break down. In March 1976, Wilson resigned and was replaced by Callaghan. The latter took office at a time of worsening economic conditions with continued high inflation, unemployment and a large balance of payments deficit. The record levels of public sector borrowing finally gave rise to a sterling crisis that consumed the Callaghan government for its first nine months. A run on the pound was ended by an IMF loan of £3.5 billion. The main consequence of this loan was that the government's economic policy was subordinated by the deflationary goals demanded by the IMF. This resulted in the largest cut in public spending since 1945 (pp. 39–41). However, by 1977 Britain's financial position had improved as a consequence of an increase in the value of sterling, and there was a fall in the rate of inflation. During 1977 the government was able to re-inflate the economy. Economic conditions improved with unemployment levels stabilising and the economy growing by 3 per cent in 1978 (p. 48). However, the weaknesses in the British manufacturing base meant that imports began to rise and there was growing speculation on sterling (pp. 48–9). The British economy remained trapped in a stop-go cycle, which during the 1970s crisis of international capital was that much harder to escape from. Furthermore, the government had failed to achieve a productive relationship with the trade unions based on a social wage consensus, and on which a more coordinated response to economic problems could have been based (Rhodes, 2000, p. 170).

Whether these problems could have been eased in the short term by pursuing a European course of action remains debatable. However, the government's approach to the global economic crisis was to move in the direction of an Atlanticist solution. As we have seen, such a position was consistent with the direction of British international economic policy since the end of war. However, during the period 1975–1976 the implications of this position were particularly profound due to the rejection of Keynesianism by the Labour government and the subordination of fiscal and monetary policy to the rules imposed by the IMF. In effect, the British government had concluded that the only solution to Britain's problems was to allow the economy to be dictated by international market forces and that domestic conditions had to be favourable to international capital accumulation. Panitch emphasises the significance of the British case in the shift to financially driven flexible accumulation brought about under US hegemony:

> The conditionality attached by the IMF to the British loan of 1976 was a momentous break with Bretton Woods protocol. For it amounted to nothing less than the imposition of financial capital's long-standing preferences for price stability and private investment as the pre-eminent goals of economic policy, upon a major Western state whose people had just voted for public expenditure and full employment. (2000, p. 12)

The Callaghan government rejected a European monetary policy in the form of the European Monetary System (EMS) in favour of solutions to be carried out under the surveillance of the IMF. The EMS was proposed by a German government that believed Washington's approach to international monetary policy, emphasising the role of stronger economies leading the world out of recession, resulted in increased speculation against the deutschmark (Greenwood, 1992, p. 105). Helmut Schmidt, German Chancellor of the time, stated that 'the whole management of the dollar by the American Administration was absolutely intolerable' (cited in Jenkins, 1989, p. 247). The EMS proposed a system of exchange rates fixed to a common

European parity, based on the deutschmark, but with room for movement up and down. There would be substantial short and medium credit facilities available to governments who faced speculative attack. The British government's position in the negotiations on membership was extremely cautious, and in some cases hostile to the whole idea (Jenkins, 1991, pp. 441–6). In the face of opposition within the Labour party and in the City, as well as American doubts about the system, the position of the government was to adopt informal membership. Greenwood comments that this approach to the EMS indicated 'Callaghan's standoffishness towards Europe and the old hankering for a more global approach to economic management' (1992, p. 106). By the late 1970s, the City was arguing for tight monetary policies and domestic control over the money supply as an alternative to European proposals for exchange rate stability (Talani, 2012, p. 40). Allowing the exchange rate to be determined by the international markets was viewed as a way of forcing governments to adopt domestic policies that were conducive to the interests of global finance. Domestic fiscal discipline, alongside the reduction of state intervention and regulation, promoted private investment and consequently, it was believed, would reduce the risks of speculative currency attacks. The IMF announcement, together with the use of monetary weapons such as high interest rates, certainly halted the decline in sterling in 1976 and reassured the markets that Britain could be lent to (Burk and Cairncross, 1992, p. 157). It also signalled the extent to which economic policy was to be geared towards the imposition of domestic fiscal constraints demanded by the representatives of global finance. Panitch goes so far as to argue that the Labour government was not only 'managing the British crisis' but 'explicitly saw themselves as junior partners with the US in managing the international crisis, through policies to accelerate the free flow of capital' (2000, p. 13). From the perspective of this book it was indicative of the extent to which Britain was out of line with a European solution to the end of the post-war boom, despite the commitments to economic and monetary integration it had made both before and upon entry.

Structural change, and the Labour government's response to it, was therefore undermining the importance that had been attached to EC membership for post-imperial renewal by previous administrations, despite the benefits to the economy that were already evident in the first few years of membership. What was notable about the 1974–1979 Labour governments was the importance they attached to the concept of the nation in order to maintain public and party support. By the late 1970s, Warde notes that all that was left to the Labour government was 'patriotic symbolism' (1982, p. 156). Moreover, as we have seen, Europe had by this point been established as a legitimate target against which more exclusive conceptions of the nation, and the national interest, could be constituted. It is from this perspective that we can understand the entrenchment of Britain's 'awkward partner' status under the Callaghan government (George, 1990). In January 1977 the British assumed Presidency of the Council of Ministers for the first time. By this time the government was embroiled in a number of difficulties with the EC over the common fisheries policies as well as the CAP. The approach of the British

Presidency was outlined by Anthony Crosland, Foreign Secretary, at the European Parliament. It was notably 'low-profile' and emphasised 'a cool and realistic appraisal of what was feasible, rather than ... over-ambitious and misleading commitments to rapid integration' (Edwards and Wallace, 1977, p. 284). The Presidency, therefore, was not used as an opportunity to pursue a more active and constructive approach to the Community (p. 286). Further problems arose with the EC over the agreement to implement direct elections to the European Parliament by May 1978. The proposal was inevitably met with considerable opposition within the Labour party. The Green Paper on this issue was initially debated in March 1976, but the eventual Bill was not passed until the government was forced to introduce a guillotine order in January 1978 (Broomhead and Shell, 1977, p. 152). This motion was passed by 314 votes to 147 with considerable cross voting, with nearly half of those voting against emanating from the backbenches (Broomhead and Shell, 1979, p. 17). In the committee stage David Owen, the new Foreign Secretary, proposed that any further increase in the power of the European Parliament would require domestic legislation (p. 17) The government's approach to the EC was constrained by the shift towards the left that had occurred within the party, yet this only reinforced a more general scepticism across the political class. This was particularly evident in the attitude towards direct elections, which were considered to be 'at best irrelevant and at worst a threat to British democracy in the eyes of all but a minority' (H. Wallace, 1981, p. 122). A compromise had been reached in the Labour party by 1977 on membership, yet this was achieved because of the willingness of the leadership to take a more belligerent line within the Community (*The Economist*, 1977, p. 18). Membership was to be tolerated as long as it was firmly subordinated to national interests. This was the clear intention of the position outlined by Callaghan in a letter to the Labour party Secretary, Ron Hayward. He wrote that withdrawal was out of the question because of its impact on relations with the United States and he called for the maintenance of the authority of national governments and parliaments. Employing a Eurosceptic rhetoric, he also warned of the dangers of an 'over-bureaucratised, over-centralised and over-harmonised Community' (George, 1990, p. 126). In effect, Callaghan was setting out the parameters of Britain's involvement within the Community and establishing a European strategy that emphasised the containment of membership and its subordination to Atlanticism.

Conclusion

The achievement of EC membership under Heath took place alongside a fundamental political challenge to the association between British post-imperial renewal and European integration. Indeed, Heath's Europeanised modernisation strategy became a strategy of last resort for the government, played up as other aspects of its political project crumbled. In this sense, European policy became part of a 'crisis of crisis management' (Offe, 1984) that spoke of a wider and deeper legitimacy across the public and the political class, and which was not resolved by the 1975 referendum. This became particularly evident during the Labour administrations of 1974–1979. In the face of the hardening of Euroscepticism within the party, Labour governments approached British membership of the EC in terms of more restrictive conceptions of the national interest. By the 1983 election many pro-Europeans had left the Labour party to form the Social Democratic Party, and the Labour party stood on a platform of withdrawal from the Community.

While the Conservatives were more united and viewed as the 'Party of Europe', the appeal of Powell had sensitised the party to the electoral possibilities of linking together economic liberalism and a populist nationalism. Powell was a consistent opponent of the Heath government and laid the ground for the rise of the New Right within the party, with its emphasis on the free market and the strong state (Gamble, 1994, p. 141). For Powell there was a clear logic in his opposition to British membership of the EC and his political agenda. For him, joining Europe was a direct threat to the British state and a betrayal of the nation by the Conservative party. Powell persistently invoked the nation by his opposition to the Community. However, the Conservatives remained fiercely loyal to the leadership and Powell increasingly alienated himself from the wider party. In contrast, the election of Margaret Thatcher to the leadership in 1975 was a victory for a nationalist neo-liberalism from inside the party. Notably, she reversed the European priority that Heath had imposed on the party.

While other member-states were responding to an international crisis by beginning to contemplate further European integration, British governments were already limiting the parameters of membership. The emerging assault, not only on welfare spending, but also on the principles of collective social welfare, implied a recomposition of the balance of forces within the British political economic order (Hall, 1979, p. 29; Jessop, 1980, p. 82). The change was in favour of an Anglo-American neo-liberal model of economic development that re-asserted the private political power of capital. In a reversal of the principles on which the Keynesian-welfare state ideal had been based, an attack on social and industrial rights was viewed as a legitimate way to increase competitiveness and restore capitalist accumulation. In effect a crisis of global Fordism and the particularities of its British expression saw the Callaghan government resort to neo-liberal policies in line with the US restructuring of the global economy, despite their impact on the domestic social order. Thus, any European strategy was firmly contained within the newly established parameters of the British state and the forces of domestic Euroscepticism.

Chapter 5
Eurosceptic Thatcherism

Introduction

Underpinning the Thatcherite approach to European integration was a growing opposition to the possibility of a European solution to the post-imperial crisis. This chapter argues that the primary purpose of EC membership for the Thatcher governments lay in the opportunities it provided for extending free market policies. The approach to the Community, typified by the leader herself, is one of strident pursuit of the national interest. With the deepening of the process of integration, associated with the moves towards economic and monetary unification advanced by Jacques Delors, a schism emerged in the Conservative party and government over the extent to which Britain should continue along a European trajectory. For Thatcher and her followers this culminated in a move in a profoundly Eurosceptic direction that represented a reversal of the prominence given to Europe by the party since Macmillan. Traditional anti-marketeers were joined by new Thatcherite Eurosceptics, constituting a powerful group in the party that opposed Europe as antithetical to British interests and identities. To begin with these struggles were expressed in the elite of the party; in particular, between Thatcher and her more pragmatic and European-minded ministers. The chapter explores how these splits and divisions emerged and developed over particular policy areas and how they resulted in the resignation of Thatcher as Prime Minister.

Thatcherism

A considerable body of literature explored the political project of the post-1979 Conservative governments, loosely organised around a conceptualisation and analysis of the phenomenon of Thatcherism (Hall, 1979; Hall and Jacques, 1983, p. 1989; Jessop, Bonnett, Bromley and Ling, 1988; Overbeek, 1990; Marsh and Rhodes, 1992; Hay, 1996; Heffernan, 1999). These debates examined the coherence of Thatcherism as a set of ideas and ideologies and the extent to which it represented a fundamental restructuring and transformation of the British state. Such debates are most usefully understood in terms of the extent to which they focus on Thatcherism as project or as process. Hall (1979), for example, conceptualised Thatcherism as a political project characterised by an 'authoritarian populism', able to win over the hearts and minds of ordinary people. It recast an authoritarian moral conservatism, appealing to nationalism, traditional values and law and order. This approach was criticised by Jessop et al. (1988), who argued that the concept of 'authoritarian populism' ignored the complex and differential impact of Thatcherism, presenting it as too monolithic. From this perspective Thatcherism should be located within a wider set of political processes that constrain its full realisation. While the concept can be used too easily as a shorthand for a complex range of developments and shifts in recent British history, we should not lose sight of its capacity for capturing a re-configuration of state and society around a set of hegemonic neo-liberal principles. It is the contention here that we can usefully employ the concept in order to understand political economic changes that emerged as the dominant response to Britain's post-imperial crisis at the end of 1970s.

Thatcherism represented the clearest ideological break yet with the Keynesian-Beveridge settlement, which had placed the extension of the welfare state, full employment and state intervention at the centre of British politics. Significant constraints notwithstanding, it was a successful political project able to redraw the parameters of the British state, enacting what Heffernan refers to as a new political consensus that reflected a new dominant political paradigm:

> The relative success of Thatcherism in helping to engineer a shift in the political landscape of the UK finds reflection in a reordered political agenda; one which lies at the heart of the political change from a social-democratic inspired political world view to one which owes more to neo-liberalism. (Heffernan, 1999, p. 15)

We should be clear, however, that Thatcherism was an attack on the post-war settlement from within the British state and not an attack on the state per se. It reflected the extent to which this settlement had not been underpinned by more comprehensive forms of modernisation and captured the ideological terrain in the context of the post-imperial crisis of failed British Fordism. Thus it is important to conceive of Thatcherism as structurally continuous with some of the core principles of organisation that have underpinned the historical development of the British state (Leys, 1990; Anderson, 1992; Nairn, 1994). As a political project, Thatcherism ideologically repackaged and reasserted elements of the British political order within a favourable international environment.

Thatcherism was an aggressive post-imperial reassertion of a liberal conception of Britain as a free market society. Its guiding principle was the unleashing of individualism and market forces throughout British society. It sought to resolve the problems of modernisation by economic reductionism, in which 'the market was reconstituted as a major ideological force and crucial distinctions between the productive and unproductive, private and public, wealth creating and wealth consuming came to be the yardsticks for judging policy' (Gamble, 1988, p. 182) The underlying aim was to restore the confidence and security of the capitalist class by removing the destructive interference of a state no longer trusted by business and commerce (Leys, 1990). Nevertheless, the neo-liberal economic project went hand in hand with the assertion of a strong state (Gamble, 1988). It was necessary to attack an inadequately corporatised and unpredictable labour movement and to uphold and restore traditional values and standards of individual and family responsibility, which were believed to underpin the free economy and, thereby, a free society. There was a unity between the belief in the force of the market, the assertion of state domination and a conservative conception of the good society. In so doing there was a clear shift towards a form of populist politics, in which there was to be a more direct relationship between the core leadership and the electorate, and a downplaying of the mediating role played by institutions such as parliament, cabinet and party. This was concomitant with traditional conceptions of British statecraft and an emphasis on governing autonomy that was legitimated by the continuation of monarchical sovereignty as central to British state authority.

At its core, the Thatcherite settlement unleashed a form of market-led economic modernisation that had a number of problematic social and political consequences for which it had no remedy. Despite its success in reshaping political agendas, it did not resolve the British problems of political and economic modernisation. The commitment to low inflation, privatisation and globalisation of the economy intensified social and regional inequities and left the British economy particularly vulnerable to external shocks. Furthermore, the broader complexities of the post-imperial crisis, concerning the constitution of the British national order and the politics of citizenship, were largely dealt with by their exclusion from the political agenda. It was illustrative of the extent to which the state relied on market mechanisms and coercion, while the deeper problems of governing a post-imperial, multi-national, pluralist political order remained unresolved (Hirst, 1989). Nevertheless, despite its compromises and confusions, both the strength and weakness of Thatcherism was an ideological certainty that was consistently and ruthlessly realised in policy.

Thatcherism and Globalisation

As an accumulation strategy Thatcherism depended on the favourable external environment that was emerging in the shift towards more flexible forms of accumulation, engineered by the extensive globalisation of finance. Initially, these developments had proved critical for the US, as it found its banks and corporations seeking out quick profits abroad in the face of domestic instability and overproduction (Arrighi, 1994; 2003; Greider, 1997). However, by the late 1970s and early 1980s, the US had turned the situation to its advantage by restricting the flow of dollars, thus ending its role as world banker and re-routing capital back to the US (Arrighi, 2003, p. 66). This involved a major expansion of the US national debt and financial deregulation, giving it a pivotal role in global high finance. The US effectively created a situation in which the competition for capital was intensified, whilst also establishing the rules and mechanisms by which it could be accessed in the form of what became by the 1990s known as the 'Washington consensus'. Financialisation of the global economy firmly under US hegemony was central to reconfiguring the British economy. Notably, deregulation of the

City paved the way for American investment banks, such as Goldman Sachs and Morgan Stanley, to penetrate the headquarters of British capital through their domination of integrated securities and corporate finance (Ingham, 2002, p. 155). This further privileged incomes from foreign investments, internationally tradable services and inward investment from foreign multinationals; 'a *rentier* class was born again through rebuilding very large portfolio investments in North America and in other parts of the non-European world' (Gowan, 1997, p. 102). The upshot of this was to continue the trend whereby Britain's stock of overseas investments was considerably higher than all Western economies, apart from the US, and at the same time Britain extended its role as a 'host country' for foreign investment and multinationals, particularly American and Japanese (Gamble, 1988, p. 20). By the late 1980s and 1990s the already high levels of mutual investment between Britain and the United States had increased dramatically. The degree of aggregate investment in the US by British firms climbed from £43 billion in 1988 to £122 billion in 1998 (Aspinwall, 2003, p. 152). By the mid-1990s it was clear that the British economy had become far more globalised than its competitors (Hirst and Thompson, 2000, p. 343). An examination of Foreign Direct Investment (FDI) shows that these flows had become far more important for the level of domestic investment and capital formation than in most other large economies. In this respect, the UK began to look 'more like a Malaysia or an Indonesia than ... an Italy or even a France' (p. 344). Both in terms of outward and inward foreign investment, Britain benefited from the deregulation of capital markets initiated by the United States and the expansionist fiscal policy of the early Reagan era. Gamble argues that the recovery in the British economy between 1981 and 1987 was particularly fuelled by the budget and trade deficits of the US that followed from this policy shift (1988, p. 98).

In ideological terms, Thatcherism emerged as a particular British variant of an emerging US global project of neo-liberalism that was attempting to reconstitute the world order. The renaissance of free market ideas in Britain during the 1970s had occurred symbiotically with developments on the right in the US. From such a viewpoint, it was believed that the world should move inexorably towards a universal civilisation modelled on US free market capitalism (Gray, 1998). The Thatcher governments signed up to this worldview, and enthusiastically imported policies from the American right on labour market deregulation and low taxation. Underlying this was an Anglo-American nationalism that was central for Thatcher: 'America is unique – in its power, its wealth, its outlook on the world. But its uniqueness has roots, and those roots are essentially English' (Thatcher, 2002, p. 20).

Thatcherism did not so much drive through the reconstruction of the state and economy as adapt elements of the British political tradition to a new set of global economic and political realities. A declining post-imperial regime that was struggling to find its place in the post-war world of global Fordism, suddenly found that the world had come to it, in the form of a renaissance of financially-driven flexible accumulation under US hegemony. The remainder of this chapter explores how this project came to be realised through the struggles within the Conservative party and government and in relation to the second wave of European integration.

Conservative Divisions on Europe

A significant literature explored the splits and crises of the Conservative party over European integration during the 1980s and 1990s (Baker, Ludlam and Gamble, 1993a, 1993b, 1994; Turner, 2000; Baker, Gamble and Seawright, 2002; Alexandre-Collier, 2009). A useful starting point for understanding these disputes within the Conservative party is the framework developed by Baker, Gamble and Ludlam (1993a). Locating European splits and divisions within a broader historical context, they argue that they reflect continued tensions within the political class over Britain's strategic relationship to the world political economy (p. 422). Parallels are drawn with the splits that emerged over the repeal of the Corn Laws in 1846 and those over Tariff Reform in 1903. The advantage of such an approach, and of particular importance in the British case, is that it attempts to integrate external and domestic policy issues (p. 425). Baker et al map the divisions along two axes of sovereignty and interdependence, in terms of external policy and of limited and extended government in the domestic arena (pp. 426–7; see Figure 5.1).

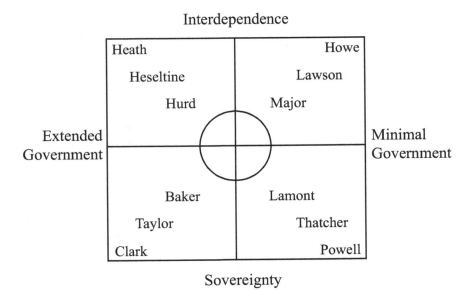

Figure 5.1   Conservative splits on Europe
Source: Baker, Gamble and Ludlam, 1993a, p. 426.

The European split can therefore be understood as follows:

> Thatcher's stance was hard to sustain both because her position was not central and because she separated herself from many of those who had been part of her coalition on other interests. It seems likely that the bulk of Conservative MPs would be placed in the two lower quadrants. But most of the Cabinet Ministers of both the Thatcher and Major governments belong in the two upper quadrants. This is the potential Peelite split. (p. 425)

The European split can be understood as the unfolding of these two splits. Firstly, the split within the governing elite between Thatcher, her supporters and other ministers, and, secondly, as a wider split in the political class between the governing elite and the party during the Major premiership.

This ideological map should be developed and revised in a number of directions. To begin with, the sovereignty/interdependence divide was more complicated than it seemed. The meaning of 'sovereignty' for a post-imperial state should be questioned, as it had become chronically dependent on its relationship to the US both economically and politically. The real issue here is the nature of British post-imperial dependence. At one level the Thatcherite position can be viewed as concerned with national sovereignty, at another it was concerned with consolidating Britain's dependency on the US. What distinguished this from those who favoured interdependence was the extent it was firmly located within an Anglo-American nationalism, often at the expense of a broader internationalism.

Secondly, it is important to emphasise the divisions between those who celebrated British membership of the EC from the perspective of interdependence and extended government and those who supported interdependence alongside minimal government. The first group was committed to European integration as the basis for a broader project of national modernisation and transformation. This project was most clearly articulated by the likes of Michael Heseltine and Chris Patten, both of whom looked to move the Conservative party in a direction that was closer to European Christian democracy. This group can be separated from the European pragmatists who primarily viewed further integration into Europe as a limited project that made a positive contribution to domestic statecraft. They were primarily reformists committed to the Thatcherite revolution but who also recognised the utility of international governance. For political figures such as Geoffrey Howe, a state heritage of conservative modernisation remained important and the European project was viewed as making a significant contribution to this.

In relation to the European issue Thatcherism became an attack on both these forces of modernisation within the Conservative party, in favour of a populist English neo-liberal idealism. It was, in this sense, distinct in its opposition to a politics of accommodation and adaptation to modernity, i.e. conservative modernisation, and instead expressed 'the more radical futurity of reaction' and 'the fervour of a historically purified neo-liberalism' (Osborne, 1996, p. 140). From this perspective, splits in the Conservative party over European integration have been indicative of chronically divergent positions on the politics of modernisation. A further revision is that we have to take into consideration the broader context of these divisions and splits. If, as suggested, we take the hegemony of Thatcherism seriously, its reactionary modernism and concomitant Euroscepticism keeps reasserting itself. In the European struggles within the governing elite Thatcher ultimately lost out, but Thatcherism was rearticulated. The implication was that the European power struggles within the Conservative party and the trajectory of this crisis were framed by the hegemony of Thatcherism.

This framework provides the basis on which to analyse the crisis of the Conservative party over European integration. The initial course of events established a Thatcherite approach to European policy at the expense of more committed Europeans. This was built on a coalition within the senior supporters of Thatcher, bringing together pragmatic Europeans and more radical Thatcherites. It was this coalition that began to unravel in the context of a new wave of European integration. There was a consequent opening up of strategic differences within the governing elite over Britain's relation to the drive for further European economic and political unity that ignited a crisis in the Thatcherite project.

Budgets and Helicopters

As we saw in Chapter 4, under the Callaghan administration there was a clear move away from the priority that membership of the EC had achieved in British strategic thinking since the Macmillan government. This was particularly evident amongst those party leaders who recognised the problems of legitimating a more proactive European policy. It was, however, less evident amongst sections of Whitehall, notably the Foreign Office. The position of the first Thatcher administration towards the EC was therefore closer to that of the previous Labour government than that of the Heath era, in the sense that the EC did not play a fundamental role in its policy proposals for British renewal. Europe was to be conceived as a flexible international arena for the vigorous pursuit of national interest. This strategy was nevertheless pursued alongside a continued commitment to the EC and to the Conservative party as formally the party of Europe. Undoubtedly, however, a key feature of the leader's approach was to resist the constraints imposed by the EC as well as by Europeanists within the state, and to begin to craft a distinctive Thatcherite approach to the Community, and to European cooperation in general, that represented a break with the past. This distinctive approach was evident in relation to two issues: the budget dispute and the Westland Affair.

The issue of the Community budget came back onto the agenda because the initial renegotiation by Wilson had not actually produced any financial results. By 1979 the transitional period was coming to an end, so Britain would have to pay its full contributions (Butler, 1986, p. 94). In addition, Commission figures showed that Britain was likely to overtake Germany as the major net contributor (p. 94). For a government committed to major cuts in public spending, the idea of paying out to the Community an amount that was disproportionate to its economy was abhorrent. When the issue arose at the Dublin Conference in December 1979, Thatcher famously announced her intention 'to get our money back'. The issue was not resolved until the Fontainebleau meeting in June 1984, when Britain received an *ad hoc* refund on its contributions and an annual rebate. It also put in place a new budgetary mechanism. During the budgetary negotiations, the British government had invoked the Luxembourg compromise and Thatcher was quite prepared to use the withholding of British contributions as a negotiating weapon (Butler, 1986, p. 100; Heath, 1998, p. 699). The impact of the British stance towards the budgetary issue on the other Community members should not be underestimated. From interviews with those involved, Ziltener noted that 'the battle cry "I want my money back!" was traumatically imprinted on the memories of many persons who were active in the EC negotiation system at the time' (1997, p. 12).

The budgetary issue both inaugurated and signalled the Thatcherite way of dealing with the Community. The idea of calling to account an overspending bureaucracy fitted neatly with its ideological tenets. Domestically the dispute also enabled the leader to demonstrate her national credentials in a period before the Falklands war when they seemed less certain. The 'confrontational method' adopted meant approaching the Community as an arena in which British interests were either won or lost and in which Thatcher was determined to win (Young, 1998, p. 345). Significantly, the issue also demonstrated an underlying scepticism about the European project. Skidelsky argues that the Prime Minister was in reality questioning the very legitimacy of the Community:

> The quarrel was embittered by Mrs Thatcher's view that the Community did not need a budget at all (apart from one to support its staff) because no continuous cross-border transfers were necessary. Therefore, she concluded, the main function of the budget was political – to provide revenue for a European state. (1993, p. 358)

The issue outraged Heath and led him to write to the Prime Minister outlining his total opposition to any 'act of illegality by HM Government affecting the European Community' (Heath, 1998, p. 699). Thatcher was not only at odds with sections of the party on Europe during the early period of her premiership but also with the pro-European Foreign Office. Owen, Foreign Secretary during the Callaghan administration, claimed that the Foreign Office was dominated by Europeanists who considered Britain's relationship to the Community as their first priority (Owen, 1991, pp. 245–8). Lord Hunt of Tamworth expressed the view that Thatcher did not see the Foreign Office as 'one of us' and 'tended to feel that the Foreign Office was so committed (to Europe) that it wasn't on our side at all' (cited in Young, 1998, p. 316). Thatcher therefore was pitting herself against those who since Macmillan had seen the EC as central to the governing strategy of a post-imperial British state.

These tensions within the political elite also reflected differences emerging over foreign policy, particularly over the relationship with the Reagan administration's increasingly confrontational and unilateralist policy (Overbeek, 1986, pp. 20–21). The inclination of the Thatcher government was to follow the US lead, which was clearly demonstrated by the support given in attacks on Libya. The preference for US military and financial power was evident with the Westland Affair, when the Prime Minister supported an American bid for the British Helicopter firm over a European consortium. Thatcher made a clear strategic choice to support those on the Westland Board, whose primary orientations and connections were with US financial capital (p. 15). The struggles within the government over the decision led to the resignation of Michael Heseltine, the Defence Secretary, who later commented about the failed European bid:

> It is impossible to think of any other country on earth where a defence contractor would be sold to a foreign purchaser with the government refusing even to allow a discussion about the merits of an alternative solution, led by two of its own leading national companies. (2000, p. 312)

Heseltine's position during the Westland Affair reflected a longstanding commitment to a distinctive European industrial strategy that would involve considerable political intervention by European states within the framework of the EC. Moreover, it reflected the belief established since Macmillan that the future of the Atlantic partnership, and British influence, was increasingly dependent on being part of a strong Europe. Thatcherism was emerging as an attack on this establishment position, reflecting an underlying Anglo-American nationalism.

The Single European Act: Thatcherism for Europe

In the run up to the negotiations on establishing the single market, national governments began to outline their vision of the new Europe. George identifies the priority of the Thatcher government, which was 'to turn the direction of discussion towards the practical achievement of a free internal market and away from discussion of institutional reform …' (1990, p. 177). In June 1984 at the Fontainebleau summit, Britain put forward a discussion document entitled 'Europe – The Future', which outlined a distinctively minimalist and free market approach to further integration (p. 175). It did call for closer political cooperation but made no concessions on the issue of institutional reform. It outlined a distinctively pragmatic British conception of Community development that emphasised flexibility and policy exits. This British discussion paper received a lukewarm reception and the summit chose to pursue the Mitterrand line that had been outlined at the European Parliament. Following Fontainebleau, the Dooge Committee was set up with a mandate to look into the possibility of political unity. The majority on the Committee concluded that institutional reform was essential for the achievement of the Community's strategic goals (George, 1990, p. 178). The response of the British government was to vigorously oppose the momentum that was growing for institutional reform and to resist calls for an intergovernmental conference (IGC) to look into the issue, a battle it lost when the Italian Prime-Minister Bettino Craxi called for a vote on an IGC which he won by a majority of seven to three (Young, 1998, p. 333). An IGC was held between September 1985 and February 1986 to negotiate the Single European Act.

Nevertheless, with the focus primarily on economic integration and with few concessions to those who had a more federalist agenda, the eventual outcome of the negotiations over the SEA was viewed as a British victory. In her memoirs Thatcher remarked that,

> I was pleased with what had been achieved. We were on course for the Single Market by 1992. I had to make relatively few compromises as regards wording; I had surrendered no important interest; I had to place a reservation on just one aspect of social policy in the Treaty. (1993, p. 555)

To an extent, these were justified in that it was the drive for the free movement of capital put forward by Sir Geoffrey Howe that formed the basis of the single market project (Gowan, 1997, p. 100). The British government went so far as to trumpet the SEA as 'Thatcherism on a European scale' (Young, 1998, p. 333; Howe, 1995, p. 456). In particular, ministers stressed the benefits that would accrue to the City and Britain's financial service sector in general (Buller, 2000a, pp. 83–4). It was estimated that one third of GDP growth expected from the single market would be the consequence of the expansion of services, and their liberalisation was a key part of the case for the single market outlined in the Cecchini Report (1988).

The SEA appeared to fit neatly into the Thatcherite free market ideology and its programme of flexible economic modernisation. It was a further move in the direction of securing the internationalisation and multi-nationalisation of the British economy. The limitations placed on political integration resonated with the pragmatic British approach to Europe. Moreover, there appeared to be an apparent convergence of economic policy across Europe with that of the British Conservative party, establishing the Thatcher government as a leading player in the Community. Wallace and Wallace commented that,

> By 1986 only a minority of the radicals of the new right retained their earlier suspicions of the European continent, still repeated with diminishing force in parliamentary debate after parliamentary debate. The Prime Minister herself had become the senior member of the European Council, inheriting the status and style of Helmut Schmidt and seeing herself as a central figure in European intergovernmental conversations. The confidence with which the British government approached these European conversations reflected not only its lost fears of the monsters of federalism and corporatism, but also its sense that it was carrying the ideological battle onto the European stage, its policies

on privatization and deregulation being gradually emulated by its continental partners in France, in Spain, even in Germany. (1990, p. 98)

Nevertheless, the states of Western Europe continued to embed market mechanisms within a diversity of national institutional arrangements that can be traced back to earlier phases of political economic modernisation (Crouch, 1993; Hollingsworth and Streeck, 1994; Crouch and Streeck, 1997; Hasse and Leiulfsrud, 2002). In particular, there was no drive to dismantle welfare state regimes or the underlying social contracts that underpinned them (Alber, 1988, p. 463; Pierson, 1991, pp. 173–6; W. Wallace, 1997, p. 38). In contrast, the attacks on organised labour undertaken by the Thatcher government indicated the extent to which the British economy was becoming globalised in far more extreme ways than on the continent. At its core the approach of the Thatcher government remained influenced by developments in the US and, as the Westland Affair demonstrated, it was prepared to align British interests in that direction. The budget dispute, the Westland Affair and the SEA indicated a distinctive Thatcherite approach to dealing with the Community that reflected a British neo-liberal agenda.

In essence the Delors strategy was to use the SEA to create the basis for future spillover initiatives. By playing to Thatcherite neo-liberalism, the British guard was lowered sufficiently to enable suggestions of further integration to be put on the Community agenda. It is possible that Thatcher therefore underestimated the expansionist elements of the SEA because she so firmly believed that her free market agenda had been victorious. Yet at the same time she claims to have been aware of the shifts in power that were occurring in Europe around the time of the SEA:

In the two years of European politicking that led up to the Single European Act, I had witnessed a profound shift in how European policy was conducted – and therefore in the kind of Europe that was taking shape. A Franco-German bloc with its own agenda had re-emerged to set the direction of the Community. The European Commission, which had always had a yen for centralised power, was now led by a tough, talented European federalist, whose philosophy justified centralism. (Thatcher, 1993, p. 559)

The danger was that any withdrawal from European developments meant losing out on the political resources and economic opportunities that were available in the EC and were not forthcoming from other areas (Bulmer, 1992, pp. 18–19). Not least of these was the continued attractiveness of Britain as a centre for international investment within the EC. The British Europeans' case for continued and active engagement with the processes of European integration remained strong. The mid 1980s therefore reflected a large degree of consensus on European policy that reflected long standing foreign policy commitments and an emerging neo-liberal hegemony. In this context, the real tensions between the British state and the second wave of integration remained obscured.

These underlying conflicts of interest and identity began to open up as the full implications of the Delors project became explicit. In particular, for many Thatcherites its emerging programme of economic and political integration was viewed as fundamentally antithetical to its own programme of neo-liberal reform, as well as representing a more fundamental attack on British sovereignty. This was exacerbated by the fracturing of the West as the US began to pursue a more unilateralist and nationalist foreign and economic policy agenda as the Cold War came to an end. The underlying and unresolved strategic dilemmas concerning the role of the post-imperial British state within the global order began to resurface in the form of acute divisions within the governing elite over the relationship to the European project. Thatcher herself was central to the emerging split in the Conservative party as she increasingly attacked Conservative Europeanism as complicit with the Delors project and fundamentally questioned Britain's post-imperial European trajectory. As Gamble notes,

> The depth of the split in the Party was a direct result of Thatcher's leadership. She legitimated opposition to Europe in a way which the leadership had hitherto successfully avoided. She suggested that there was an alternative – continuing to give priority to Britain's Atlantic over its European links, pursuing an open-seas, open-trade policy, which cultivated Britain's connections with all parts of the world economy, rather than being exclusively preoccupied with Europe. She pointed to the trade deficit Britain had with the EU and to the location of the bulk of Britain's overseas investments in countries outside the EU. True internationalism, she argued, meant avoiding entanglement with a protectionist, inward looking, interventionist, high-cost continental economy. (1995, p. 23)

Such a position may not have been fully worked out until Thatcher left office, but it was being devised in collaboration with an inner circle of advisers and supporters during her time as Prime Minister. Her commitment to entrenching an Anglo-American neo-liberal project within the British state led her into a collision course with other members of her government, and to a rejection of the European compromises that had been central to the Conservative party since Macmillan. It was an attack on the forces of conservative modernisation that had viewed accommodation to the European project as central to post-imperial restructuring. Initially, these conflicts arose over Britain's participation within the Exchange Rate Mechanism (ERM) and the proposals for European Monetary Union (EMU).

Governing Elites Divide over Europe

Since the breakdown of the Bretton Woods system, a major factor in economic instability was fluctuating exchange rates and the considerable power this had given to financial markets to influence the course of fiscal and monetary policy. The ERM had initially been established to counter these developments by locking

European currencies into a system of exchange rates that were anchored to the deutschmark. British Chancellors, Geoffrey Howe and Nigel Lawson, were convinced by the merits of the system and increasingly concerned about the impact fluctuating exchange rates were having on the British economy (Lawson, 1992, pp. 647–57; Stephens, 1996, pp. 24–5; Howe, 1995, pp. 111, 448).

The significance of support for ERM membership by those of the governing elite within the Thatcher administrations was that it represented a clear break with monetarist doctrine. In the 1970s, Thatcher and close colleagues had become disciples of monetarism. They believed that the British disease of high inflation could be controlled by restricting the amount of money in circulation. This had an instinctive appeal to Thatcher, who saw 'no reason why the nation's finances should not be managed on the same basis as those of a prudent household or corner shop' (Stephens, 1996, p. 8). As Bonefield and Burnham note,

> Exchange rate problems and balance of payments deficits were seen as pseudo-problems, disguising the real problem of inefficient use of resources caused particularly be wage inflation and labour market inflexibility due to trade union distortion of labour market self-regulation. (1996, p. 9)

Monetarists therefore believed that if governments concentrated on controlling the public spending and removing distortions within the labour market, exchange rates would reach equilibrium. This translated into Conservative government policy in 1980 in the form of the Medium Term Financial Strategy drafted by Nigel Lawson. This set growth rates for the amount of money circulating in the economy known as Sterling M3. The overall aim was to decrease inflationary pressures for pay demands within the economy (Stephens, 1996, p. 13). However, establishing a reliable relationship between the monetary supply and inflation proved unproductive (Buller, 2000b, p. 321). In particular, this policy was at odds with the liberalisation of the financial markets that occurred in 1979, when the government removed the controls on foreign exchange transactions and the abolition of internal credit controls (Hutton, 1995, pp. 64–6; Stephens, 1996, pp. 13–14; Buller, 2000b, p. 321) and in 1986 with the Big Bang which revolutionised City practices by substantial deregulation. Talani argues that the opening of the City during the 1980s resulted in the 'definitive submission of productive to financial capital' and 'the prevalence of short-term considerations over long-term ones in the management of the British productive sector' (2012, pp. 62–3).

A significant domestic consequence of these developments was the dramatic increase of credit, and with it private debt, and the rise of City incomes that precipitated the housing boom of the 1980s. The government's attempts to control public debt and to control the money supply made little sense alongside an economy that was being expanded by cheap credit. The value of sterling did not reflect the government's monetarist targets but the decisions of the financial markets. Control of interest rates was the main instrument available to government to influence the exchange rate and reduce inflation. When Geoffrey Howe raised interest rates in

1981 to counter the devaluation of the pound, it represented the beginning of the end for monetarism and a return to fiscal economic management (Stephens, 1996, p. 24). Nevertheless, the government continued to set unsuccessful monetary targets until 1985 when Nigel Lawson dropped the M3 sterling target (p. 46). In a ministerial meeting on 13 November 1985, Lawson made the case for membership of the ERM as the best way of securing the government's anti-inflationary strategy (p. 49). This was strongly supported by those who attended the meeting (pp. 49–50).

However, it was not supported by Thatcher, who, with the advice of Alan Walters and Brian Griffiths (Head of the No. 10 Policy Unit), listed a number of objections (Stephens, 1996, p. 50). Thatcher regarded the policy as an abandonment of monetarism, as it was no longer the control of the money supply that was being made central to maintaining economic stability but the exchange rate (Thatcher, 1993, pp. 689–90). For her fixing the exchange rate would allow other economic indicators to be ignored for the goal of exchange rate stability and the economy could get out of control. As she said, 'the only effective way to control inflation is by using interest rates to control the money supply. If, on the contrary, you set interest rates in order to stick to a particular exchange rate you are steering by a different and potentially more wayward star' (p. 690). Conversely, the realignments within the ERM were a matter of 'political horse-trading rather than the workings of the market – and the market does a better job' (p. 693). Stephens points out that when Thatcher refused to consider entry into the ERM in 1985, it was the only time during her premiership when she stood alone against the will of her most senior ministers on a crucial aspect of policy (1996, p. 51). She not only held out against the advice of her top ministers but undermined them by looking to personal advisers. It was a radical assertion of the powers of the Prime Minister's office and the clique of supporters and advisers who constituted it.

Despite Thatcher's opposition, Lawson began to pursue informal membership of the ERM when he introduced a policy of shadowing the deutschmark, as a way out of the sterling crisis of 1986 when the value of pound fell by 12.5 per cent (Lawson, 1992, p. 647). This crisis occurred as a consequence of the fall in the price of oil and the depreciation in the value of the pound, because of the financial markets' perception of it as a petrocurrency. Lawson's policy of shadowing the deutschmark and securing the Bundesbank's support for sterling was therefore an attempt to find a European solution to this economic crisis. In effect the underlying strength of the German economy and the deutschmark were being used to stabilise sterling and a volatile British economy. The belief was that this could be sustained because of the improved competitiveness of the British economy, which in turn would be helped by a stabilised exchange rate and low inflation. Lawson believed that the markets had got it wrong and exaggerated the continued dependency of the British economy on North Sea oil (Lawson, 1992, pp. 648–9). This policy worked and took some pressure off the pound. At this stage it was a short-term measure; however, in March 1987, after the Louvre Accord when agreement was reached by finance ministers to stabilise international exchange rates, it became policy; a policy shift that Thatcher claimed not to have known anything about (1992, p. 701).

Lawson was clearly pursuing an approach to monetary policy that favoured forms of international economic governance as part of the solution to domestic instability. His self-styled approach to Europe was that of a pragmatist: 'I am neither a Europhobe, nor a Eurofanatic and had no wish to ingratiate myself with either group' (1992, p. 912). Yet this masks the fact that Lawson was clearly far more influenced by European models of economic development than his leader. He evidently believed that a new industrial competitiveness could replace the reliance on North Sea oil revenues, and this would be underpinned by a stable and competitive exchange rate anchored inside the ERM. Stephens notes that 'Lawson's model was West Germany, the deutschmark had been strong throughout the post-war period, but remained competitive because of the country's strong inflation and productivity performance' (Stephens, 1996, p. 55). Nevertheless, as a strategy of long-term economic reform, ERM membership was problematic in the British context.

The period from 1987 to 1990 saw an intensification of economic problems for the third Thatcher administration. The expansion of demand that had occurred during 1987 was triggered by the deregulation of the financial markets, which led to a massive reflation of the economy (Hutton, 1995, p. 71). This was further fuelled by cuts in direct taxation. The economy quickly overheated and in 1989 it began to enter recession. There was a record balance of payments deficit, rising inflation and two million unemployed. A consequent rise of interest rates to counter inflation saw them reach 15 per cent by May 1989. In effect, the globalisation of the British economy had been pursued without any broader strategy designed to support the domestic economy and maintain long term stability. By this point, ERM membership was less a long term strategy to achieve economic stability following the failure of monetarism than a short term measure designed to restore confidence in the economic policies of the government. The City had become critical of Lawson's chancellorship, blaming tax cuts and increases in public spending for increased inflation, and saw the external rules offered by the ERM as a potential solution (Talani, 2012, pp. 69–70).

Thus the EC offered political opportunities, particularly as an external policy discipline, at a point at which the economy appeared increasingly difficult to control and Thatcherism looked to have run its course. Predictably, as the economic indicators worsened, the Prime Minister came under increasing pressure to join the ERM. By this time the Labour party had also dropped its opposition to the European Community, and its European policy now endorsed membership of the ERM and the Delors Report. Meanwhile, the Prime Minister's opposition to ERM membership was hardened by the Delors Report, which linked entry into the ERM as stage one of EMU and, ultimately, she believed to the derogation of British self-government:

> The ERM was seen by the European Commission and others as a path to EMU – and this subtly changed the former's purpose. But EMU itself – which

> involves the loss of the power to issue your own currency and acceptance of one European currency, one central bank and one set of interest rates – means the end of a country's economic independence thus the increasing irrelevance of its parliamentary democracy. Control of its economy is transferred from the elected government answerable to Parliament and the electorate, to unaccountable supra-national institutions. (Thatcher, 1993, p. 691)

By representing ERM membership as a fundamental threat to the British state, Thatcher set herself apart from the pragmatic Europeanism of Howe and Lawson and opened up a strategic split in the governing elite. Despite the fact that Lawson shared Thatcher's opposition to EMU, she believed that his policy of shadowing the deutschmark had 'so undermined confidence in my government that EMU was brought so much nearer' (p. 691). In May 1989, Thatcher publicly blamed Lawson's policy of shadowing the deutschmark for the rising inflation seen during the late 1980s (p. 710). After the June European elections in 1989, Lawson continued to press for membership of the ERM and, to questions in a House of Commons Select Committee on the Delors Report, responded that 'it would reduce rate fluctuation and we would be able to use it to assist us in our anti-inflationary policy' (Lawson, 1992, p. 923).

The matter came to a head in the immediate run up to the Madrid Council in June 1989. During the weeks beforehand, Lawson and Howe attempted to obtain a commitment from the Prime Minister that Britain would enter the ERM by the end of 1992. They also wanted commitment on moves towards EMU, while arguing that there would be no moves towards stage three 'until further work was done on what it entailed, including notably its political implications' (p. 929). Thatcher responded with a number of reasons for delaying even further Britain's entry into the ERM for four years or more based on a number of conditions outlined to her by her economic adviser Alan Walters (Thatcher, 1993, p. 709). When Lawson and Howe met with her on 25 June, Thatcher again refused to adopt a specific date for entry to the ERM and instead said she would continue to pursue a policy of 'when the time is right' based on Walter's conditions. The meeting ended with both Howe and Lawson threatening to resign (Lawson, 1992, p. 933). A profound split had emerged in the governing elite that threatened the government and forced Thatcher to take a more conciliatory tone at the Madrid Council at the end of June. However, the consequence of the deterioration in the relations between Thatcher and Howe in the run up to Madrid led to his dismissal from the Foreign Office. Nor were the relations between Lawson and Thatcher to improve. When the pound began to fall during 1989, Lawson found that his policy of trying to hold its value against the 'psychologically important' DM3 level was undermined by the increasingly public pronouncements of Thatcher and Walter's that the pound 'should find its own level' (pp. 949–50). Eventually Lawson considered his position as increasingly untenable and eventually resigned when Thatcher refused to remove Alan Walters as her economic adviser.

Euroscepticism: Renewing Thatcherism?

For Thatcher, engagement with an increasingly organised European political order became diametrically opposed to a project that was rooted in a neo-liberal Anglo-American nationalism. The Thatcherite attack on the second wave of integration lay the foundation for a revived right wing Euroscepticism, which was to become entrenched within the Conservative party and the wider political culture. European integration began to be constituted as the 'other' of British national interests and identity. While it led to Thatcher's eventual downfall, it can be seen as an attack on the established governing position from within the state that emerged as a populist right wing movement determined to break with Conservative Europeanism.

Thatcher's concerns about the direction of the Community had been confirmed by the launch of proposals for a European social space to be formalised in a European Social Charter, which became a particular *bête noire* of Thatcherite Eurosceptics. It was rejected by Thatcher at the Madrid summit and the British government went on to obstruct any proposals coming out of the Community's Social Action Programme that followed the signing of the Charter. Delors had chosen the British TUC conference of 1988 to outline a vision of a Social Europe: 'the internal market should be designed to benefit each and every citizen of the Community. It is therefore necessary to improve workers' living and working conditions, and to provide better protection for their health and safety at work' (cited in George, 1990, p. 193). Before this speech he told the European Parliament that within ten years 80 per cent of economic and possibly fiscal and social legislation would be coming from Brussels. In her memoirs, Thatcher describes her growing distrust of Delors and his 'expansionist' aims and her belief that this would not be acceptable to British public. In her memoirs she refers to her decision to oppose integration:

> By the summer of 1988 he [Delors] had altogether slipped his leash as a functionnaire and become a fully fledged political spokesman for federalism. The blurring of the roles of civil servants and elected representatives was more in the continental tradition than in ours. It proceeded from the widespread distrust which their voters had for politicians in countries like France and Italy. That same distrust also fuelled the federalist express. If you have no real confidence in the political system or political leaders of your own country you are bound to be more tolerant of foreigners of manifest intelligence, ability and integrity like M. Delors telling you how to run your affairs. Or to put it more bluntly, if I were Italian I might prefer rule from Brussels too. But the mood in Britain was different. I sensed it. More than that, I shared it and I decided that the time had come to strike out against what I saw as the erosion of democracy by centralisation and bureaucracy, and to set out an alternative view of Europe's future. (1993, p. 742)

In framing her opposition to integration in terms of the superiority of the British political tradition, Thatcher's position was increasingly populist. In the summer of 1988, she commissioned a paper from an official which spelt out to her how the Commission was 'pushing forward the frontiers of its competence' and had 'misemployed treaty articles' in order to get directives past under qualified majority voting (p. 743). She went on to ask,

> Were British democracy, parliamentary sovereignty, the common law, our traditional sense of fairness, our ability to run our own affairs in our own way to be subordinated to the demands of a remote European bureaucracy, resting on very different traditions? I had by now heard about as much of the European 'ideal' as I could take; I suspected that many others had too. In the name of this ideal, waste, corruption and abuse of power were reaching levels which no one who supported, as I had done, entry to the European Economic Community could have seen. Because Britain was the most stable and developed democracy in Europe we had perhaps the most to lose from these developments. (pp. 743–4)

Thatcher rounded on Delors and his conception of the Community in a speech at Bruges delivered in September, only weeks after Delors had addressed the TUC. In the speech she outlined an alternative vision of a Europe of nation-states:

> Let Europe be a family of nations, understanding each other better, appreciating each other more, doing more together, but relishing our national identity no less than our common European endeavour. Let us have a Europe which plays its full part in the wider world, which looks outward not inward, and which preserves that Atlantic Community – that Europe on both sides of the Atlantic – which is our noblest inheritance and our greatest strength. (p. 745)

This speech indicated that Thatcher believed that Europe was more than an economic area and she saw it as a defender of freedom within an 'Atlantic Community' (Young, 1998, p. 357). It was not the basis for a new strategy towards European integration that could find favour across the member-states, but was designed as an attack on those 'enemies of freedom' she had identified in the Community. As she pointed out, 'we have not successfully rolled back the frontiers of the state in Britain only to see them reimposed at a European level, with a European super-state exercising a new dominance from Brussels' (Thatcher, 1993, pp. 744–5). This was a far from veiled attack on the Commission and the centralising French socialist who headed it. But the Commission was not the only target. A draft of the speech, which the Foreign Office insisted was toned down, had also contained a reference to Britain having saved Europe from being united 'under Prussian domination' and Britain as the only successful European imperial power (Young, 1998, p. 348). A strong element of Thatcher's growing Euroscepticism was her distrust of Germany. During the sterling crisis of 1986 when the Bundesbank had refused to directly support sterling, Lawson recollected Thatcher 'was furious that the Germans were not being more helpful, and went into her gut anti-German mode, which was never far from below the surface' (Lawson, 1992, p. 656).

It was the Bruges speech that marked the clear break with the legacy of Heath. It was a powerful Anglo-American assertion of state power and free markets, and a populist ideological expression of British exceptionalism that clearly reflected the continued influence of Powell. It contained a number of themes that were to be replayed by Eurosceptics in their opposition to further British involvement in the integrationist project in the 1990s and beyond. It was constructed around a number of oppositions between Britain and Europe, including European bureaucracy and political formalism versus British pragmatism and democracy; British free trade liberalism versus European protectionism; British globalism versus narrow Europeanism and British political stability versus European instability. It was aimed at the Delors project but also at an established governing position that saw accommodation to European integration as an inevitable feature of Britain's post-imperial trajectory.

For Thatcherite Eurosceptics the combination of a Europe economically dominated by Germany and an expansionist Commission headed by a French Catholic socialist meant that the second wave of integration was increasingly conceived as a project of Franco-German state building. These fears were exacerbated by proposals for German unification in the wake of the fall of the Berlin wall, a development that Thatcher opposed. While the Heath government had seen Europe as the only way back to some sort of power in the world, Thatcher could claim to have achieved this by reasserting the special relationship. She had put herself at the centre of super power relations and reasserted British claims to global leadership.

By 1989, Thatcher linked opposition to European integration to a wider electoral strategy in the face of the growing unpopularity of the government. A populist Euroscepticism was embraced in the run up to the European elections: 'the overall strategy was simple. It was to bring Conservative voters – so many of whom were thoroughly disillusioned with the Community – out to vote' (Thatcher, 1993, p. 749). Lawson described the campaign as a crude and embarrassing anti-Europeanism that was encapsulated in the poster: 'Do you want to live on a diet of Brussels?' (Lawson, 1992, p. 922). He records he 'suddenly realised, with a shiver of apprehension, that she saw the Euro-campaign as a trial run for the next general election campaign; and that, with the short term economic outlook unpromising, she saw a crude populist anti-Europeanism as her winning strategy' (p. 922).

The campaign further opened up the splits in the party. Thatcher complained of the 'Heathism' of many Conservative MEPs who were at odds with her anti-European line and undermined the campaign (Thatcher, 1993, p. 749; Lawson, 1992, p. 922). Support for Thatcher's Euroscepticism was evident with the formation of the Bruges Group and the parliamentary 'Friends of Bruges' in 1989. The press also supported a revival of anti- Europeanism that culminated in a series of attacks on Delors in *The Sun* during 1990 (Wilkes and Wring, 1998, p. 197). Meanwhile, during the European election campaign, Heath launched attacks on Thatcher in Brussels and in the media (George, 1994, p. 215; Heath, 1998, p. 710). The message was that Britain would be left behind and become a second-class member of the Community. The result of the election was that the Conservative share of the vote dropped from 40.8 per cent to 34.7 per cent. Conversely, the Labour party pursued its most unified pro-European campaign in its history.

The End of Thatcher

With the resignation of Lawson and the demotion of Howe, Thatcher's position had been severely weakened. Moreover, she was beginning to be viewed as an electoral liability and the cause of the government's unpopularity. The possibility seemed to emerge of a revisionist Thatcherism centred on a renewed coalition of committed and pragmatic Europeans within the governing elite. The alliance of Douglas Hurd, as Foreign Secretary, and John Major, as Chancellor, forced the Prime Minister to accept British ERM membership in 1990. Hurd was a classic Tory European; he was, as Young says, 'a Foreign Office man to his roots, trained there as an embryonic mandarin, embraced there as Heath's private secretary when the 1971 negotiation took place' (1998, 362). Major was to all appearances a Thatcherite, but his views on Europe took shape while he was Foreign Secretary and Chancellor (p. 363). While at the Foreign Office he became more positive about the EC and began to develop good relationships with his European counterparts (Seldon, 1998, p. 95). In a speech to the Conservative party conference in October 1989 he restated Britain's commitment to membership of the Community, and in private he expressed reservations about Thatcher's oppositional line. As Chancellor, he was committed to membership of the ERM as the only way of countering inflation (Major, 1999, p. 138).

When, in the summer of 1990, Thatcher lost Nicholas Ridley from the Cabinet because of his anti-German comments in *The Spectator*, she lost what she referred to as 'almost my only ally in the Cabinet' (Thatcher, 1993, p. 722). With John Major replacing Lawson as Chancellor her position was so weakened that she was unable to hold out any longer against membership and Britain eventually joined on 5 October 1990. As she recalled, 'although the terms that I had laid down had not been met, I had too few allies to continue to resist and win the day' (Thatcher, 1993, p. 722). Nevertheless, her Euroscepticism had not abated and was on display at the Rome summit in the same month. She attacked the plans for EMU as 'cloud-cuckoo land' and promised to block anything that was not in Britain's interest (Young, 1998, p. 367). On her statement to the Commons she rounded on Delors and the Commission, referring to it as trying to 'extinguish democracy' and create a federal Europe: '"no ... no ... no", she bawled, her eye seemingly directed to the fields and seas, the hills and the landing grounds, where the island people would never surrender' (p. 368). It was at this point that Geoffrey Howe made his decision to resign, and his resignation speech that followed secured Thatcher's downfall. This speech was a powerful defence of the Tory Europeanism of Macmillan and Heath. He referred to the necessity of facing the 'realities of power' as Macmillan had done and not to 'retreat into a ghetto of sentimentality about our past' (*Hansard*, Vol. 180, Col. 2, 13). It succinctly defended this political project and portrayed Thatcher as its enemy:

> The tragedy is – as it is for me personally, for my party, for our whole people and for my right hon. friend herself a very real tragedy – that the Prime Minister's perceived attitude towards Europe is running an increasingly serious risk for the future of our nation. It risks minimising our influence and maximising our chance of being once again shut out. We have paid heavily in the past for late starts and squandered opportunities in Europe. We dare not let it happen again. If we detach ourselves completely, as a party or a nation, from the middle ground of Europe, the effects will be incalculable and very hard to correct. (*Hansard*, Vol. 180, Col. 2)

Howe argued that the Community should be seen 'as an active process which we can shape, often decisively, provided that we allow ourselves to be fully engaged in it with confidence, with enthusiasm and in good faith'. In contrast he referred to Thatcher as viewing the continent as 'teeming with ill-intentioned people, scheming, in her words to "extinguish democracy"'. Howe emphasised the negative consequences of becoming marginalised from European developments and defended the 'middle way', which was neither a federal Europe nor a Europe of sovereign nation-states. He termed Thatcher's view that there were only these polar opposite positions 'a false antithesis, a bogus dilemma'. It was a characteristic reassertion of the British governing position on Europe. The Community was an arena in which Britain could pursue its national interest in free markets and 'maximise its sovereign power' within an increasingly interdependent world (Howe, 1990, p. 687).

Howe's speech confirmed to many Tory MPs that Thatcher was now too out of step with the mainstream. The first challenge to her leadership came from Sir Anthony Meyer in 1989, whose motivations were directly related to Thatcher's anti-Europeanism (Young, 1998, p. 370). He received 60 votes, indicating that her leadership was weakened. However, it was Michael Heseltine's challenge, that emerged after Howe's resignation speech, that finally brought about her downfall. At this stage, as John Major recalls, 'the backbench rats began to desert the Prime Minister' and 'malcontents stalked the parliamentary lobbies' (1999, p. 179). Heseltine succeeded in achieving 152 votes to Thatcher's 204, forcing a second ballot. This was to be the fatal wound that destroyed her political authority and led to her resignation. The implications of Thatcher's defeat at the hands of Conservative Europeans was to have far reaching consequences for the Conservative party and for the overall trajectory of British Euroscepticism.

What Kind of a Victory?

The splits in the leadership and the party over the ERM and EMU represented fundamental strategic divisions within the Conservative party. Since the end of the 1970s, Britain had been on a particular trajectory that emphasised the defence of a strong and unitary state, as well as a particular form of flexible economic modernisation that prioritised a global free market strategy. European policy had been subordinated to these wider objectives. By the beginning of the 1990s continuing to engage with the process of integration, as many pro-Europeans claimed was essential, potentially compromised this trajectory.

The choices regarding the nature of post-imperial dependence determined the overall trajectory and structure of the British political order. The question arises as to whether the downfall of Thatcher represented a fundamental shift away from a neo-liberal Anglo-American trajectory in favour of a politically and economically integrated Europe. Were these strategic choices clearly articulated within the factions of the Conservative party? To answer in the affirmative is to understate the significance of the Thatcherite settlement and the complexity of the divisions within the political class over European integration and the politics of modernisation. The Thatcher years had entrenched British dependence on the US and provided a short term solution to the British problems of economic modernisation by the re-assertion of *rentier* capitalism. The post-imperial crisis appeared to have been resolved in favour of globalisation, which offered an alternative to further integration into a European regulatory regime, a position articulated by Thatcher once out of office:

> the European Community's relative importance as regards both world trade and Britain's global trading opportunities is diminishing and will continue to diminish. Our politicians should become less concerned with European markets, whose most dramatic expansion has probably been achieved and more interested in the new opportunities emerging in the Far East, Latin America and the North American Free Trade Area. (Thatcher, 1995, p. 498)

While the removal of Thatcher seemed to represent the defeat of Euroscepticism, the election of the right wing pragmatist, John Major, to the leadership of the Conservative party was not necessarily a success for pro-Europeans. Major was viewed as a party manager, whose role was clearly to unite the various factions and constitute a viable European policy. A Heseltine victory would have brought the party 'much nearer to a fatal split on Europe' (Turner, 2000, p. 136). In contrast, the election of Major was therefore primarily about the consolidation of the Thatcherite settlement. This was most clearly seen in Major's strategic decision to try and keep the right of the party on board in key policy decisions. As we will see, the attempt to square this with a viable European policy that could positively engage with the second wave of European integration created a distinctive and unresolved European crisis for the Conservative party and the British state.

Conclusion

During the course of the three Conservative governments of the 1980s, Thatcherism emerged as a significant ideological challenge to the established governing elite position that accommodation to Europe was essential to Britain's post-imperial trajectory. The context for this was the second wave of European integration and the growing unpopularity of the third Conservative government. Thatcher's Euroscepticism was a populist reassertion of a British exceptionalism that located national interests and identity in a purified conception of the sovereign state and the free market. It was firmly believed by a growing number of those on the right that Britain could and should be re-imagined in opposition to Europe. It was left to John Major to try to accommodate the Thatcherite settlement with proposals for a European Union.

Chapter 6
A European Crisis of the British State

Introduction

As a new Prime Minister and party leader, John Major was faced with an economic recession, the growing electoral unpopularity of the Conservatives and significant divisions within the party over Europe. In forging a post-Thatcher agenda on Europe, the Major government set itself the task of rebuilding relationships on the continent and re-engaging with the integration process. A new constructive European policy, including a commitment to ERM membership, was to be a central plank of the Major administration's governing agenda. However, the attempt to establish a revisionist Thatcherism that could accommodate a constructive European strategy quickly unravelled. Initially, the government's European crisis emerged in the form of a humiliating ejection of sterling from the ERM. It culminated in an extraordinary attack on the governing elite by a populist Eurosceptic movement during the attempts to ratify the Maastricht Treaty (1992) and in its aftermath. This chapter explores the unfolding of this crisis, its aftermath and its implications for the arguments developed in the course of this book. I shall show that these events are central to understanding the continued construction of Eurosceptic Britain.

Majorism: The Missing Political Strategy

'Majorism' did not exist as a distinct political project but was primarily an attempt to consolidate the Thatcher legacy (Marquand, 1991, p. 41; Riddell, 1992, pp. 428–9; Hay, 1996, p. 163; Seldon, 1998, pp. 742–3). Nevertheless, a key reason for the electoral success of the Conservative party in 1992 was that it presented itself as less ideologically doctrinaire than it had been during the 1980s. It referenced the One Nation tradition that had served the party so well under mass democracy and, in this respect, committed to protecting and improving public service provision. A significant intellectual force behind this new focus was Chris Patten, Chairman of the Conservative party (1990–1992), who advocated a social market philosophy along the lines of the German Christian Democrats (Riddell, 1992, p. 427). Alongside Patten, David Willetts attempted to articulate modern conservatism as a combination of Thatcherite free trade radicalism and a belief in community that was rooted in a long tradition of Conservative nation building:

> This preoccupation with linking communities and markets is part of a continuing Conservative concern with national integration. Disraeli's two nations,

> Salisbury's fears of national disintegration, the One Nation Group, John Major's opportunity society – all address the question of how to ensure that all British citizens feel that they participate in national life. (1992, p. 420)

Therefore, the Major administration initially looked to a more inclusive conservatism in order to distinguish its policy agenda. Major's apparently emollient and conciliatory nature seemed to fit with this mood and had been important in securing his leadership bid. Nevertheless, this was clearly not a radical agenda for modernisation but a pragmatic Thatcherism tempered by English social liberalism. Noting the underlying vacuity of this strategy, Marquand commented,

> The end of Thatcherism has, however, left a vacuum which nobody had yet rushed in to fill. Majorism is not a project in the sense that Thatcherism was a project. It is a sort of ragout of old style Tory paternalism and new-style Thatcherite entrepreneurialism, laced with upward social mobility and palpable personal decency of its author ... There is no evidence that it offers any solution whatever – good, bad or indifferent – to the long-drawn-out crisis of maladaptation which grips the British state. (1991, p. 41)

The Major government remained strongly attached to a traditional conception of British sovereignty and it did not consider redrawing the existing constitutional settlement. Apart from Northern Ireland, the sensitive and contentious position of the non-English nations was ignored. There was no resolution of what Hirst had referred to as the 'constitutional crisis' that continued to challenge Britain's homogeneity as a nation-state (1989, p. 40). While the organisation of political authority across European states became more decentralised and neo-corporatist (Crook, Pakulski, Waters 1992, pp. 97–104; Offe, 1996, p. 65), what was notable about the British case was the extent to which this was primarily associated with privatisation and marketisation of state functions. The losses of power faced by organised labour in Britain during the 1980s and 1990s meant that Britain was not going to engage in the kinds of modification of institutionalised class compromises that other European states began to embark on (Grote and Schmitter, 1999; Rhodes, 2000, pp. 162–3).

Continuity with Thatcherism and political survival became the hallmarks of the Major governments. A programme of privatisation was continued in the areas of coal (1994) and rail (1996–1997). There was a radical shake up of Whitehall, with the extension of compulsory competitive tendering and contracting out to central government (Riddell, 1992, p. 428). Thatcherite welfare reforms were continued, such as the opting out of schools from local authority control and the extension of the quasi-market in the health sector. While the government began to grapple with the politics of the welfare state, it did so by reinforcing the status of the individual consumer in the shape of proposals such as the Citizen's Charter. Increasingly, the power of centralised government combined with the language of consumerism was used to justify increased surveillance over public services and the intensification of the 'audit culture'. The key focus here was on finding performance indicators for the producers of public goods and to maximise efficiency and competitiveness. After 1993 this programme was underpinned by economic policies designed to ensure British economic stability once ERM membership had been ruled out. Kenneth Clarke, as Chancellor (1993–1997), put in place a more transparent process of decision making, which gave increased power to the Bank of England in the setting of interest rates (Stephens, 1996, pp. 292–3). Gamble and Kelly argued that it represented a significant reform of infrastructure of domestic economic policymaking that contributed to an impressive macro-economic performance between 1993 and 1999 (2000, p. 19). Despite the reform of the institutions of monetary policy, the emphasis on economic stability did not represent any commitment to a long term industrial strategy. Indeed, fixed investment per year in manufacturing in Britain between 1992 and 1994 was lower than 1961–1973, while imports had reached 33 per cent by 1990, compared to 21 per cent in 1970 (Northcott, 1995, pp. 202–3). In comparison, by 1994 London accounted for 44 per cent of European equity markets, which represented three times as much as Paris or Frankfurt (p. 202). There was a continued emphasis on the stability and attractiveness of Britain for mobile capital, largely at the expense of social cohesion and a productive economy (Hirst and Thompson, 2000, p. 354). The approach was one of national neo-liberalism occurring in the absence of participation in European Monetary Union, a position that aligned with a City fearful of European regulation.

It was in the area of European policy that the Major government faced its severest test, when it attempted to move beyond the increasingly Eurosceptic agenda set out by the former Prime Minister. Initially, the Major government saw its commitment to the ERM and to a more constructive European policy as the basis for distinguishing it from the later Thatcher governments, and as part of a bid to revive electoral fortunes and outflank an increasingly popular pro-European Labour party. Yet, Major's attempt to stake the national prestige of the government on a revived Europeanism proved to be an unmitigated disaster that split the Conservative party and destroyed the credibility of the government. While it might be argued that this was a product of a particular set of circumstances, it was the way in which these events reinforced and made manifest persistent structural tensions between British politics and the process of integration that is central to the argument of this book.

Three key factors emerged during the period of 1990–1993, undermining the government's policy and firmly establishing Britain as a Eurosceptic state. Firstly, the government's policy proved at odds with the extensive nature of the second wave of European integration. Bulpitt notes that from 1988 the Community could no longer be confined to,

> a common external tariff, the CAP, and internal tariff reductions – EFTA with knobs on. On this level the Community threatened to become an 'association' possessing that capacity for continuous, comprehensive and public penetration

of British governing, which, Conservative leaders had always tried to avoid. (1992, p. 266)

The government's claim that the Maastricht negotiations were a British victory and that the extensiveness of integration could be contained proved unsustainable. In the domestic arena the British government was faced with having to publicly defend a European agreement in which they were not only awkward but increasingly marginal participants. Secondly, the government's attempt to craft a European monetary policy based on membership of the ERM proved unsustainable, in the context of a classic British recession that demonstrated continued weaknesses in the domestic economy. Furthermore, the government's reaction after ERM withdrawal was to further undermine the possibility of participation in EMU and to advocate national solutions to monetary problems that reflected the dominance of financial interests. Finally, and most significantly, these two developments exacerbated and provoked a comprehensive Eurosceptic mobilisation, particularly on the right of the Conservative party, which launched one of the most devastating attacks on a British government in the twentieth century. The combination of these three factors was to further distance the government from European developments and move it in the direction of an explicitly Eurosceptic Thatcherite approach to the EU. It is to the history of this European crisis of the British state between 1990 and 1993 that we now turn.

At the Heart of Europe

The conditions in the country in 1990–1991 appeared favourable to a more pro-European stance. The Eurosceptic forces in the Conservative parliamentary party had been temporarily muted by the downfall of Thatcher. There was growing public support for a pro-European position, with a two to one majority believing Europe was a good thing for Britain in 1991, the highest level of support since the 1975 referendum (Northcott, 1995, pp. 330–31). The continued membership of the ERM had become the central plank of the Major administration's economic policy. Europe appeared to be fundamental to the government's attempts to revise the Thatcher settlement and symbolised a modification of some of its less palatable elements. In this context, Major proposed to place Britain at the 'heart of Europe'.

A key feature of the initial approach of the Major government to the EC was to rebuild relations and secure those alliances with European politicians and governments that had been alienated by Thatcher. The main figures behind this strategy were Chris Patten and the Foreign Secretary, Douglas Hurd (Forster, 1999, pp. 32–3). A central aim of the Hurd-Patten strategy was to place British Conservatives in the mainstream of European politics. Patten already had considerable contacts with European Christian Democratic parties from the time when he was Head of the Conservative Research Department. When he became Party Chairman, he aimed to have British Conservative MEPs join the Christian

Democratic centre-right group in the European Parliament. He believed this would lead to Major attending Christian Democratic leaders' meetings, where many European bargains were struck. The main focus, however, was to improve relations with Germany and Major set about building a strong alliance with the Christian Democratic government in Bonn. Forster argues that behind this was the aim of exploiting German concerns over Jacques Delors' proposals for monetary union. The close relationship built up between Major and Kohl was in marked contrast to Thatcher's lukewarm meetings with the German Chancellor. In his memoirs, Major emphasised his friendship with Kohl, as well as with other leaders, and claims that 'he had no hang ups about Germany' (1999, pp. 265–7). Unsurprisingly, therefore, Bonn was chosen for a keynote speech by Major in March 1991, in which he emphasised the differences between his government and that of his predecessor to the European Community. In the speech Major stated that 'my aim for Britain in the Community can be simply stated. I want us to be where we belong. At the very heart of Europe. Working with our partners building the future' (p. 269). This new cooperative approach within the Community was concomitant with an economic policy that placed ERM membership at its centre.

For domestic Eurosceptic forces the speech was a cryptic statement of federalist intentions; in fact, it largely reasserted a conservative governing position, as the summary by his advisers at the time demonstrates:

> Europe, John Major said, should develop by evolution, not some treaty-based revolution provoking disunity in the cause of unity. It must keep its Atlantic ties strong. Britain had not, by playing its part in the transformation of Europe, 'abandoned our history or our ties with the Commonwealth and the United States'. But there were limits to the notion of a common foreign and security policy for European countries; NATO must remain paramount. So far as monetary union was concerned, 'we think it best to reserve judgement', and 'we accept its imposition'. Co-operation – already a code word for a way of doing business outside of the Brussels institutions – was the way forward for members of the Community. (Hogg and Hill, 1995, p. 78)

Above all, Major emphasised that 'Europe was made up of nation-states' and that a right balance had to be found between 'closer cooperation and a proper respect for national institutions and traditions' (p. 78). Moreover, this was to proceed alongside the overarching aim of advancing a free trade Europe. Major therefore re-emphasised what he saw as the limitations of the European project. From the outset the government's position was unconvincing. It combined a clear statement of constructive engagement with the second wave of integration, even reviving the idea of a leadership role for Britain in that process, yet re-affirming a fundamentally Thatcherite set of principles focused on free markets and state power. The consequence of the latter was that the government increasingly looked for policy exits and appeared sceptical about the new multi-level institutional architecture that was taking shape. The Commission, under the leadership of Delors, and many member-states, were moving towards an overtly supranationalist agenda. Thus the idea that the Community could be reduced to a common market firmly under the control of states appeared out of date, and out of step with the direction of the integrationist project. As the largely negative and obstructive goals of the British government for the Maastricht Council began to emerge, the ambition to put Britain at 'the heart of Europe' looked increasingly problematic.

The Maastricht Negotiations: A Roman Triumph?

The position of the British government during the Maastricht negotiations has been comprehensively documented (Blair, 1999; Forster, 1999). The government's objectives during the negotiations were to pursue selective opt-outs in the areas of monetary union and social policy, and to put forward proposals designed to obstruct the more ambitious objectives of the other member-states. Both Blair and Forster emphasise that this negotiating strategy was largely determined by domestic circumstances and, in particular, the need to maintain Conservative party unity (Blair, 1999, p. 219; Forster, 1999, p. 177). Forster notes that by September 1991, 'the problem of Eurosceptic dissent was an increasing preoccupation for John Major' and he was forced 'to abandon his Party Chairman's attempt to chart a new intellectual path for the party' (p. 88). Yet, at the same time, the government was committed to continuing to engage with European developments and, as Major later protested, 'engage in the argument' and 'argue the British case' (cited in Seldon, 1998, p. 167).

The bargaining position of the Major government during the Maastricht negotiations reflected Britain's European dilemma. More specifically, it reflected the impossibility that a government operating within the paradigm of Thatcherism could engage with a process of deepening European integration. Therefore, it proved increasingly difficult for the government to defend its policy against the Eurosceptic right of the party. The attacks on Major's policy followed immediately after his 'heart of Europe' speech. In an interview in the US, Thatcher railed against German domination of Europe and the idea of European unity. In June of 1991, *The Daily Telegraph* gave prominent coverage to a publication by the Bruges Group, which effectively accused Major of supporting a federal Europe (Major, 1999, p. 269). This right wing pressure group had become the 'rallying point' for sceptics and opponents of further integration across the party, and by 1990 had 132 Tory backbenchers as members as well as prominent right wing academics such as Patrick Mitford, Norman Stone and Kenneth Minogue (Seldon, 1998, p. 164). However, arguably more significant in shaping the direction of the government's approach to Europe during the run up to the Maastricht negotiations was the influence of Eurosceptic ministers (Blair, 1999, pp. 203–4). Major's consensual style of leadership and Thatcherite sympathies increased the power of these ministers who held portfolios directly relevant to the IGC. As Blair notes, 'the Eurosceptic quartet of Baker, Howard, Lamont and to a lesser extent Lilley, led government departments influential in the formation of British European policy' (p. 204). In effect what Major did was to successfully buy off the support of these ministers while still putting together a realistic bargaining position. He did this by holding firm on the opt-outs over EMU and the Social Chapter. This was evident in the Commons debate that took place before the IGC. Major recalled that 'the debate worked well. I set out our negotiating aims with great care. No federalism. No commitment to a single currency. No Social Chapter. No Community competence on foreign and home affairs or defence' (Major, 1999, p. 274).

By emphasising these negative goals and objectives, the Major government was able to resist Eurosceptic pressure for a British veto to be exercised over EMU and new treaty agreements on political integration. In effect, the British government's position at the Maastricht Council (December 1991) was to try and prevent moves towards further integration without having to veto the Treaty. It indicated the extent to which the structure of British politics prevented any British European strategy becoming part of a broader European Christian Democratic project, as politicians such as Patten and Hurd may have wanted. The overriding concerns at the Maastricht Council were increasingly those of domestic politics and Conservative party unity (Forster, 1999; Blair, 1999). Once Major had won over Eurosceptics to his negotiating position, it became possible for the government to make concessions, such as strengthening the European Parliament to include co-decision making powers. Such areas remained under the tight control of the foreign policy executive (Hurd and Major) and it was made difficult for more Eurosceptic ministers to challenge such decisions (Blair, 1999, p. 204). On EMU, the government's negotiating position was to seek a general opt out for all governments and to continue to pursue the alternative of a hard European Currency Unit (ECU) as a parallel European currency. The latter was designed to halt the move towards monetary union. This was pursued alongside attempts to separate the French from the Germans by playing on differences over the speed towards monetary union (Forster, 1999, p. 59). The British government failed to achieve these objectives and underestimated the momentum for EMU amongst the other member states: 'London was left to determine the terms and conditions of its own self exclusion and negotiators concentrated on securing a UK opt out and the important right to reverse the initial position at a later date' (p. 72). A particular problem for the government was that it had failed in the negotiations to address the growing concerns of the City that EMU would threaten London's competitiveness and dominance in European financial markets, thus facing potential regulation and domination by a German-dominated European Central Bank set up in Frankfurt (Talani, 2012, p. 88).

The opt-out over the single currency was relatively easy to achieve, as it allowed the other member states to negotiate the details of EMU without the risk of a British veto. In contrast, the British opt out of the Social Chapter was a matter of intense political bargaining during the final stages of the negotiations. A compromise agreement on social policy circulated by Ruud Lubbers, President of the European

Council, was rejected by Major when Michael Howard, Employment Secretary, threatened to resign (Forster, 1999, p. 92; Blair, 1999, p. 113). The conclusion to this was the negotiation of a separate protocol by the other 11 member states that inevitably weakened the development of the social dimensions that had been so central to the Delors project.

The pursuit of selective opt-outs and the negative negotiating position adopted by the Major government was the only viable position that the government could hold in the face of a divided party and cabinet. It enabled Major to avoid the political ramifications of the moves towards EMU and the Social Chapter without having to veto the entire Treaty. However, the degree to which the government had been pressured into adopting a hard-line and negative stance towards the Treaty meant that the attempt to place Britain, and the Conservative party, at the 'heart of Europe' was shattered. In effect the British government had contributed to the emergence of a two speed Europe in which Britain would be in the second lane; the very thing it had argued against.

The scepticism shown towards European developments contrasted with the government's continued support for American global power, most clearly evident in the extent of British support for the First Gulf War. In marked contrast to the divisions over Europe, Major reflected in his autobiography on the cross-party support for the war and British involvement; 'here was a nation working together. It was an enriching experience' (Major, 1999, p. 237). Thus, behind the rhetoric of the new relationship with European partners remained a strong attachment to an Anglo-American conception of the global order. As William Wallace noted, the Gulf War was welcomed by commentators on the right as the re-emergence of an Anglo-Saxon partnership:

> Pride in the past, pride in Britain as a military power, seeking to regain and reassert a status which marked us off from the defeated nations across the Channel; contrasting – to use Peregrine Worsthorne's graphic revealing language – the 'selfless even self-sacrificing idealism' of Britain's response with the flabbiness of a European Community dominated by a lobotomised German economic giant, psychologically unable to spill blood even in a good cause. (1991, p. 30)

This Anglo-American nationalism remained at the heart of the Conservative party and the Major government. Patten's attempt to construct a project of British Christian Democracy that fitted with mainstream European developments was an exceptional attempt to shift the trajectory of Eurosceptic Britain. The undermining of the Maastricht Treaty and Britain's marginalisation from the integration process was viewed as a success for Major both in the party and sections of the press. Major described it as the 'modern equivalent of a Roman triumph' (1999, p. 288). Nevertheless, it was a hollow victory, as Major had signed up to a Treaty that involved institutional developments that would not be acceptable in the longer run to Eurosceptics. This was the dangerous consequence of the salvage operation on

European policy carried by pro-European politicians such as Hurd, Heseltine and Clarke, who remained at the core of the governing elite.

For a short period Major had united the party and helped secure the election victory of 1992. In retrospect, however, the truce within the Conservative party was inherently fragile because the Maastricht Treaty had deepened integration and the British had failed to prevent the moves towards EMU. In early 1992, Delors told the European Parliament that the Maastricht Treaty was a significant move in the direction of further integration (Turner, 2000, p. 155). Despite the limitations of the Treaty, this was certainly the case and it contradicted Major's claim that he had halted the drive for further integration. Thus, the Major government entered into a highly dangerous political game with its own party as it attempted to ratify the Treaty in parliament and secure legitimacy for its Maastricht deal. What stood out was the extent to which loyalty to both party and leader began to breakdown during the ratification process. For an administration already weakened by a small majority of 21 after the 1992 election, the European issue was to result in a crisis that derailed the government to such an extent that it was unable to recover. Yet, before exploring more fully the Maastricht rebellion, we should note that the ferocity of this attack on the government became increasingly evident with the failure to Europeanise economic policy.

'Black' or 'White' Wednesday?

As we have seen a central plank of the Major government's economic policy was membership of the ERM, as Chancellor Major had persuaded Thatcher to enter the system. At a time of recession ERM membership was viewed as fundamental to keeping inflation under control and bringing interest rates down (Hogg and Hill, 1995). Membership was seen to give the government's economic policy credibility in the eyes of the financial markets and thereby avoid destabilising speculations on the pound. It was a policy designed to break the stop-go cycle of the British economy by facilitating stable growth alongside low inflation (Stephens, 1996, p. 198). The value of sterling once again became the guiding principle of British economic policy. A questionable form of financial management was equated with a broader project of modernisation.

The difficulty for the government was the nature and depth of the recession of the early 1990s. The bank base rate had risen to 15 per cent in 1989 to take the heat out of the housing market, with the result that house prices collapsed in 1990. Between the first and second halves of the same year, GDP fell by 2 per cent and manufacturing output fell by 9 per cent in nine months. Both consumers and companies faced problems of debt, stopped spending and unemployment began to rise sharply. Underlying these problems was the continued structural weakness of the British economy, already evidenced by a current account deficit of 20 billion pounds in 1989 (p. 175). Therefore, the concern was that 'unless demands for higher pay could be resisted, and productivity increased, then rising inflation would lead to sustained pressure on the pound' (Bonefield and Burnham, 1996, p. 14). The government entered the ERM at the relatively high rate of DM 2.95 in order to help bring down inflation, and believed this rate could be sustained by the underlying competitiveness of the British economy rather than devaluation (Hogg and Hill, 1995, p. 175). This strategy was thought to form the basis for a sustained recovery and ward off speculative pressure. However, the British economy nosedived into a recession characterised by low output and disinflation, alongside an overvalued currency.

The real problems for the overvalued pound began to emerge once the ERM was discredited, in the aftermath of the Danish *No* vote on the Maastricht Treaty. The result of the Danish poll had shaken confidence in EMU and financial markets began to question the existing ERM parities. Furthermore, these problems were exacerbated by a German refusal to cut its interest rates, as Stephens notes:

> The deutschmark was the anchor for the system, but Germany was sailing in the opposite direction to its European partners. Its domestic economy demanded high interest rates to stifle inflationary pressures caused by reunification; elsewhere in Europe governments were struggling to pull their economies from recession and inflation was subdued. As long as interest rates in Germany remained high, its partners could not cut their own borrowing costs to stimulate economic expansion. (1996, p. 194)

The ERM increasingly became the target for those attacking the government's economic policy. The government, however, stuck to its chosen course and, in a speech to the European Policy Forum on 10 July 1992, Norman Lamont ruled out either a cut in interest rates or leaving the mechanism (Seldon, 1998, p. 298). Although the economy required lower interest rates, it was believed that these were more likely to be delivered inside the ERM and that devaluation would ultimately lead to higher borrowing costs (Stephens, 1996, pp. 209–10). The argument was that a devaluation of the pound would undermine confidence in sterling and lead to depreciations which could only be halted by high interest rates. The Treasury believed that the consequence of a devalued pound would be similar to the 1980s, when a weak currency had resulted in rising inflation (pp. 210–11). Following Lamont's speech, Major told the House of Commons that the government's commitment to the ERM was '100 per cent' (p. 214). In late July, Major went so far as to state at a dinner hosted by *The Sunday Times* that he believed that sterling would become one of the world's strongest currencies, possibly stronger than the deutschmark (Stephens, 1996, p. 219; Seldon, 1998, p. 298; Major, 1999, p. 317). This led to headlines in *The Sunday Times*, emphasising the extent to which the ERM policy had now become a symbol of 'national pride' for the Major government (Stephens, 1996, p. 219).

As the government defended its ERM policy, the extent of the British recession became clearly visible. Between 1990 and 1991, unemployment increased by 700,000, business failures ran at 930 a week, and house repossessions climbed continuously (Bonefield and Burnham, 1996, pp. 20–21). The second quarter of 1992 saw Britain's GDP fall 3.6 per cent from its 1990 level whilst other EC member states experienced a rise of 2.8 per cent, and industrial production began to fall, culminating in a balance of payments deficit of £13,680 million in 1992. In effect, the British economy remained too weak to ride out a global recession. This was compounded by the depth of the US downturn and a weak dollar, which made British exports uncompetitive. The pound continued to fall against the deutschmark during 1992, while it rose against the falling dollar (Stephens, 1996, p. 221). Meanwhile at a meeting of European finance ministers at the beginning of September, Lamont criticised German economic policy for the growing turmoil within the exchange markets because of its refusal to cut interests. This outraged the Bundesbank President, Helmut Schlesinger, and was indicative of the extent to which the Treasury had not become Europeanised. As Stephens argues,

> Britain's membership of the ERM was not followed by a coordinated attempt to make friends among those upon whom the government might well have to rely. In the summer of 1992 an imperious manner could not disguise the absence of reliable allies. As one Treasury official was to lament, 'We were never much good with foreigners'. (1996, p. 233)

When Schlesinger announced only a small cut in German interest rates of 0.25 per cent in response to an Italian devaluation, the markets began to put increased pressure on sterling. On Tuesday 15th September 1992, the Governor of the Bank of England sought approval to step up the scale of intervention to stabilise the value of the pound. The following day saw sterling driven out of the ERM by financial speculators. The extent of the speculation on sterling meant that intervention by central banks was ineffective. Indeed, the Bank of England's holdings on foreign exchange amounted to just over 10 per cent of the average £300 billion in the average daily turnover of the London markets (p. 249). Despite what was evidently the largest intervention into the currency markets ever seen by the Bank of England,[1] and raising interest rates to 15 per cent, the government was unable to halt the massive speculation, and by the end of the day the pound was forced to leave the ERM.

The government was overwhelmed by the events of Black Wednesday, which it considered to be largely out of its control. In the Commons debate that followed, Major reported that sterling was forced out of the mechanism by events worldwide and the severity of the attack by the markets (*Hansard*, Vol. 212, Col. 2). He implied that if responsibility lay anywhere it was with the Bundesbank, which had encouraged the markets with 'injudicious comments about realignment that should never have been made'. There was no official apology or acceptance of responsibility by the government and no inquiry followed (Stephens, 1996, pp. 255–6; Seldon, 1998, p. 323). Certainly, there were flaws with a system that

---

1 This had the consequence of effectively exhausting the reserves (see Stephens, 1996, p. 254).

depended so heavily on one anchor currency and this was evident once the German economy diverged from the rest of Europe as a consequence of unification. The British difficulties with the ERM, however, also reflected deeper political and institutional problems that were primarily of a domestic nature. The economic policy was inherently paradoxical. On the one hand, it was believed that an economic policy that focused on a stable exchange rate would secure stable growth without leading to high inflation. It was viewed as an essential political instrument for the economic modernisation of a weak economy. On the other hand, this policy was only viable because a strong and stable exchange rate reflected the supposed underlying competitiveness of the British economy. In this sense it was considered to be symbolic of the new found strength of the British economy. The exchange rate became both a cause and an effect of British economic renewal. When the extent of the recession was evident in 1992, it was clear that maintaining a high exchange rate was damaging the economy, and the eventual fall in the pound reflected the reality of the British economy. As Stephens notes,

> Sterling's steady depreciation over several decades had been a symptom as much as a cause of economic failure. Fixing the exchange rate would not solve the more fundamental structural problems besetting the economy – a weak manufacturing base, a large current-account deficit, low investment, poor education and training among them. (1996, p. 259)

In a similar vein Bonefield and Burnham pointed out that 'the continued comparative decline of British competitiveness made an eventual devaluation of the pound inevitable, in spite of the ERM' (1996, p. 29). What compounded the problem for Major was the fact that the exchange rate had been made into a symbol of national pride, particularly evident when he claimed that sterling would come to rival the deutschmark. According to an editorial in *The Independent on Sunday* (1992), the failure of this policy represented an end of another British delusion akin to the Suez crisis of 1956. This also meant that it was not prepared to take actions that could have kept sterling in the ERM, such as devaluing or raising interest rates earlier. This left the markets sceptical of the underlying commitment of the British government to the policy, which was compounded by its non-participation in EMU.

The government seemed to lack any economic policy once blown off course by forced withdrawal from the ERM, a situation exposed by John Smith, as opposition leader, who picked up on Major's earlier comments that sterling could rival the deutschmark:

> To claim that the German economic miracle had been surpassed and then in the middle of the recession, to go on to foresee the pound replacing the deutschmark takes a certain detachment from reality of which Walter Mitty would have been proud. The real lesson to be drawn from a comparison between the British and German economies is that, before one can have a strong economy we need consistent investment, a recognition of the vital importance of manufacturing as

the basic wealth creator, a strategy of training, for innovation and technology and for regional development. In short, an industrial strategy. (*Hansard*, Vol. 212, Col. 13)

In a devastating attack Smith stated that with its ERM policy blown apart, any claim to economic competence by the Conservative party had been destroyed. Nevertheless, the ERM debacle was not simply a verdict on the government. The crisis reflected the general vulnerability of a globalised British economy and the underlying weakness of British economic governance. Yet the Labour party did not call for the end of the pound, which was at the time the logical conclusion to be drawn from the events of Black Wednesday.

The withdrawal from the ERM allowed the Major government to rethink its European strategy in the light of wider European developments and domestic political problems. The role of ERM membership was reduced to a policy designed to curb inflation and was no longer part of a broader 'heart of Europe' strategy (Major, 1999, p. 340). The withdrawal from the ERM was rewritten as an opportunity to push Europe further in a British direction, as Major told the Commons during the ERM debate:

We have the chance to build in our time, in our generation, the sort of Europe for which we have always longed for; the sort of Europe I believe its citizens want; a secure Europe of nation-states co-operating freely for the common good; a prosperous Europe, generating new wealth within the biggest free trade area in the world; a free trade Europe in which Brussels is kept off industry's back. (*Hansard*, Vol. 212, Col. 11)

In many of the member states, the problems and eventual collapse of the ERM only highlighted the weaknesses of the current arrangements and the need to press ahead with full EMU. It had proved the case for more extensive forms of economic governance beyond the nation-state to resist the autonomy of the financial markets. However, the British government and Eurosceptics began to see the crisis over the European project as a validation of their different positions. For the Major administration, the viability of the whole EMU project was considered to be even more problematic, and the government's focus shifted further away from European monetary arrangements towards domestic reform of monetary policy. In effect, the capacity of the global financial markets to judge economic policy by speculating on a currency was accepted and the possibility of long term stability within a European set of arrangements was questioned. The possibility of giving up a debased currency chronically exposed to financial speculation was clearly not on the agenda. For Eurosceptics, 'White Wednesday' as they called it was validation of the crisis of legitimation at the heart of the European project, and had proved that the Maastricht Treaty was fundamentally flawed and had to be defeated. Thus, the ERM debacle fuelled the emerging crisis over Maastricht ratification that was facing the Major government.

The Rise of the Eurosceptic Right

As a number of commentators have shown, the Eurosceptic groups that emerged during the Maastricht ratification crossed the party divide and often consisted of disparate political positions and motives (Norton, 1996; Berrington and Hague, 1998; Forster, 2002). Young described Conservative Eurosceptics as,

> A confederacy of zealots and lurchers, with the latter amply outnumbering, often outreaching, the former. One might venture some conclusions from their history. Some were moved by disappointment born of failed ambition. They resented their exclusion from office sufficiently to allow an embryonic scepticism, hitherto suppressed, to prepare them for full rebellion. Others were pushed by personal loyalty to Mrs Thatcher, over an edge they had already spent some time looking across. (1998, p. 387)

As a starting point, a chronological distinction can be made between those implacable marketers, Young's zealots, who had been opposed to Britain's initial membership of the Community under Heath in 1972, and those who became later converts to the cause. In the first group were politicians such as Teddy Taylor, John Biffen and Richard Body. This group consistently attacked the Community as primarily a political project that represented a profound attack on the British nation. As we saw in Chapter 4, the exemplar of this tradition had been Enoch Powell. There was also a second small group that came to prominence during the Thatcher years and who opposed the Single European Act. Notably, this group included Enoch Powell's successor in Wolverhampton, Nicholas Budgen, but also the former party Chairman, Edward Du Cann. The Single European Act separates the latter two groups from those politicians who became increasingly sceptical of the benefits of integration and aligned with Thatcher's growing opposition to the Community. This group included Bill Cash, a leading Eurosceptic politician during the Major government, who had been a supporter of both British entry in 1972 and the SEA in 1986. There were, however, different variants of Euroscepticism that further separated out the groupings. As Baker, Gamble and Ludlam note (1994), some such as Cash could be described as constitutionalists whose primary concern was the federalist intentions of the Community and its impact on parliamentary sovereignty. Others were English nationalists motivated by anti-German and anti-French sentiment. Forster points out that the key unifying moment for Eurosceptics was Thatcher's Bruges speech, which saw these disparate groupings come together as a right wing Eurosceptic movement that increasingly broadened its membership to include academics and journalists (Forster, 2002, p. 166).

Out of office Thatcher became a prominent spokesperson for the Eurosceptic cause and she began to articulate an alternative free market vision of European integration. In May 1992 she made a speech at The Hague where she called for a decentralised Community in 'which the model should be a market – not only a market of individuals and companies, but also a market in which the players are governments' (Thatcher, 1995, p. 489). In this national neo-liberal scenario governments would compete with each other for foreign investment, top management and high earners through lower taxes and lower regulation. She went on to call for a multi-track Europe and argued that 'we have to face up to the fact that a united Germany was a problem' (pp. 489– 491). The extent of Thatcher's personal involvement in supporting the Eurosceptic cause was recalled by Major:

> It was a unique occurrence in our party's history, a former prime minister openly encouraging backbenchers in her own party, many of whom revered her, to overturn the policy of her successor – a policy that had been a manifesto commitment in an election held less than six months before. It was Margaret's support for the defeat of the Maastricht legislation which helped turn a difficult task for our whips into an almost impossible one. Beyond this she began to cast around to see how the party could be moved to a more Eurosceptic position. By the early autumn of 1993 she was telling friends that she hoped for a leadership contest a year before the next election, and for Michael Portillo to win it. (Major, 1999, pp. 350–51)

Thatcher's speech at The Hague was made ten days after the Bill had gone through parliament to implement the Maastricht Treaty. Major made the decision not to try and force the Bill through quickly but to allow time for a full debate on the Treaty. It successfully went through its first and second readings then, as Major put it, 'all hell broke loose' (1999, 347). The cause of this was the Danish *No* vote on the Treaty. The government made the decision not to proceed with the Committee stage of the Bill as they believed this would reignite the divisions over Europe (p. 349). However, this decision gave the Eurosceptics time to fully mobilise against the Treaty. The day after the Danish referendum result, an Early Day Motion was signed by 69 MPs calling for a new approach on Europe.

At Prime Minister's Questions on 3 June 1993, Major defended his European stance: 'the Maastricht Treaty began to build the kind of European Community that we wish to see. It introduced the concept of intergovernmental cooperation outside of the Treaty of Rome. It established the principle of subsidiarity rather than centralism. It established financial and other controls over the Commission' (*Hansard*, Vol. 208, Col. 827). Major consistently emphasised the themes of subsidiarity, enlargement and intergovernmentalism as the guiding principles of the Maastricht Treaty. He presented the Treaty as a British victory for a decentralised Europe, contradicting the interpretation of the Treaty that was presented by Delors and Mitterrand. Thus, the Maastricht Treaty was sold to the Conservative party as a victory for Eurosceptic Britain. In the debate, Major's version of the Treaty came under heavy criticism from Eurosceptics such as Bill Cash:

> In the light of my right hon. friend's insistence on decentralisation in Europe, with which we all agree in principle, how is it that there is in the common provisions in title 1 of the Treaty an insistence that we comply as an obligation

with the single institutional framework which implies centralisation together with those provisions that deal with the union, which imply that we will be citizens of a union with duties imposed on us, and as a result of which we shall be moving into a centralised Europe? (*Hansard*, Vol. 208, Col. 831)

The central demand of the Eurosceptics and of the Liberal Democrats was for a referendum, which Major refused to grant them. The statement to the House on the Danish result represented a turning point in the Conservative party. As a Foreign Office official recalled, 'behind him there were rows of sullen faces. He had virtually no support. Suddenly, we had the sense that whatever goodwill and pro-European feeling there had once been, was gone, and that the atmosphere from then on was going to be ugly' (Michael Jay cited in Seldon, 1998, p. 294).

The Eurosceptic cause found continued support within sections of the British press. Two of the three most powerful press proprietors, Rupert Murdoch and Conrad Black, questioned Britain's European involvement and both of them had appointed editors with similar views (Major, 1999, p. 358; Turner, 2000, p. 158). Notably, 'both proprietors and their editors maintained close relations with Mrs Thatcher and her circle, and filled their columns with contributions from intellectuals she had encouraged' (W. Wallace, 1994, p. 286). The Murdoch-owned *Times* and *Sunday Times* took a strongly anti-European line, while *The Sun* and *The News of the World* became increasingly nationalistic and xenophobic in their attacks on European institutions and partners. Meanwhile, *The Daily Telegraph*, *The Sunday Telegraph* and *The Spectator* took the side of the rebels against the government's policy; in particular, opposition to Europe and admiration for the United States were persistent themes of these publications (W. Wallace, 1994, p. 286).

The problem for the Major government, therefore, was that it did not only face a small group of zealous Eurosceptics within the parliamentary Conservative party, but that this was part of a broad-based mobilisation of anti-Europeanism that reached across key sections of the Conservative press, as well as the higher echelons of the party and the government itself. This was a particularly British variant of a broader crisis of legitimation for European unity, which was evident in the narrow *Yes* vote for Maastricht in France and the growing concern over monetary union in Germany. Its full impact, however, was not felt until the Maastricht Treaty finally came to parliament to be ratified at the end of 1992.

Maastricht Ratification and Eurosceptic Mobilisation

The Eurosceptic campaign in parliament during the process of ratification of the Maastricht Treaty represented one of the most significant rebellions in parliamentary history and, alongside the ERM debacle, helped destroy the credibility of the Major government. It was a profound attack on the governing elite by a Eurosceptic movement. It undermined the legitimacy of the government's strategy on Europe, exposed the contradictions on which British policy towards European integration had been based since Macmillan and, significantly, contributed to a potentially fatal split in the Conservative party. Indeed it was a powerful reassertion of the extensive nature of Euroscepticism at the heart of the British state and intensified the uncertainties about Britain's European future. A discussion of the dramatic events surrounding ratification will demonstrate the extensive opposition faced by the Major government.

The ratification of Maastricht was rescheduled to begin again in the autumn of 1992. In the wake of the ERM crisis, the Major government came to the conclusion that it was a way for the government to regain the initiative on the European issue and to reassure its European partners of its commitment to the Treaty (Seldon, 1998, p. 326). The decision to press ahead immediately led to attacks on the government at the Tory party conference in October. The former Party Chairman, Norman Tebbitt, made a powerful speech that ignited the conference floor. He called on Major to 'raise the flags of patriots of all the states of Europe' and that the conference wanted to see 'policies for Britain first, Britain second and Britain third' (p. 327). In response, Hurd, as Foreign Secretary, defended a traditional Tory pragmatic policy on Europe and that going back on Maastricht would destroy Britain's future in Europe. However, further attacks on the government came from Thatcher, who argued in an article for *The European* newspaper that Maastricht was a 'ruinous straitjacket' damaging Britain's 'constitutional freedoms' (p. 328). It was evident from the number of Eurosceptic motions submitted to the conference that there was strong grassroots opposition to Maastricht within the party and this became crucial for legitimating the Eurosceptics' causes within parliament (Turner, 2000, p. 162). Major made a speech that was sympathetic to Eurosceptic concerns but restated his commitment to the government's policy of ratifying the Maastricht Treaty.

During the Maastricht rebellion it is possible to identify three objectives adopted by the rebels in their bid to undermine the government (Baker et al., 1994, p. 38). Firstly, they aimed to delay the Bill, hoping that it would be made invalid by external events such as another *No* vote in a second Danish referendum. Secondly, they campaigned for a referendum as they increasingly believed they had considerable public support. Thirdly, they put forward and supported Treaty amendments that they considered fatal to the Treaty and would force the government to abandon ratification. This added up to an extraordinary attack on the governing elite from within the ruling party.

The first test for the government was the paving motion introduced in November 1992. In the debate, Major defended the government's conception of the Community: 'we can develop as a centralist institution, as some might want, or we can develop as a free-market, free trade, wider European Community more responsive to its citizens' (*Hansard*, Vol. 213, Col. 284). He expressed a Thatcherite conception of the Community but also reiterated traditional conservative fears of the negative consequence of marginalisation from core European developments. Although the government won the paving motion, it did so by a small margin (319–16) and Eurosceptics were successful in forcing a promise from the government that the third reading of the Bill would be delayed until after the Danish referendum (Seldon, 1998, p. 342). After the problems over the paving motion, some of the initiative appeared to return to the government with a successful European summit for Major in Edinburgh in December. Under the British Presidency agreements on Denmark, enlargement of the Community and the European budget were reached. Furthermore, there was a stronger commitment to the principle of subsidiarity that had been incorporated into the Maastricht Treaty. Major was credited with having patched-up Maastricht, while avoiding further moves along the road of political integration. With a second Danish referendum agreed to take place on 18 May 1993, the committee stage of the Maastricht Bill began in December 1992. The rebels continued to attempt to delay the Bill in order to demonstrate the intensity of British Euroscepticism and hopefully contribute to another Danish rejection of the Treaty (Baker et al., 1994, p. 39). By the time of the third reading of the Bill, there had been 210 hours of debate and over 600 amendments. It was now recognised by the government that the rebels were un-whippable and had become a separate organised faction within the party with their own offices, unofficial whips and 'briefing books' (Seldon, 1998, p. 369). The rebels proved successful in defeating the government on the method for selecting UK members of the Committee of the Regions proposed at Maastricht. However, this did not stop ratification of the Treaty and the Bill continued its passage through the Commons. Alongside delaying ratification, the rebels kept up their pressure on the government to hold a national referendum. This came to a head on 21 April when the rebel Richard Shepherd called on the government to 'trust the people' and stated that the Bill had no mandate as the public had been denied a choice on Maastricht during the election of 1992 (*Hansard* Vol. 223 Col. 383–4). Major had already stated his opposition to a referendum in the June debate following the Danish referendum when he defended parliamentary sovereignty in a reply to Tony Benn. The rebels' referendum amendment was defeated by the government but only with the support of the opposition.

With the defeat of the referendum amendment, the Bill had finally passed through the Committee stage proceedings. Major celebrated with an upbeat speech to the Conservative Group for Europe that underlined the economic importance of Europe and claimed that the Community was heading in Britain's direction (White, 1993, p. 1). The extent to which the party was now moving in Major's direction was, however, another question, as a *Guardian* editorial noted:

> The speech did not tell the Conservative party things it does not know. But it tells the party many things which large parts of it still prefer to ignore. Recent surveys have implied, not always convincingly, that the rank and file Tories are not only unhappy with the rows over Maastricht but are moving towards a more Thatcherite position on Europe. (*The Guardian*, 1993c, p.19)

The Maastricht crisis was already adding to the depth of the growing disillusionment with the Major government that was evident since ERM withdrawal. At the beginning of May during the local elections and the Newbury by-election, the Conservative party faced heavy defeats. The Conservatives lost 500 seats in county councils across the country and Newbury was its worst by-election defeat since 1979 with a 28.4 per cent swing from the Conservatives to the Liberal Democrats.

The government eventually secured the passage of the Bill through the committee stage and it was eventually ratified on 20 May, two days after a positive vote in the Danish referendum. Yet the rebellion had not subsided and the number voting against the third reading of the Bill had risen to 41 with 5 deliberate abstentions, up from 22 and 6 abstentions during the second reading in May 1992. The Bill then went to the House of Lords where Thatcher led the attack, claiming she would never have signed the Treaty and calling for a referendum (Seldon, 1998, p. 384). In the Commons the government's problems were not yet over as they had to concede to a special vote on the Social Chapter. The rebels had joined with the Labour opposition in supporting the restoration of the Social Chapter, believing that Major would not proceed with the Bill if the opt-out was not included. There was considerable confusion over whether a vote on the Social Chapter could kill off the Bill or whether the government could circumvent a defeat on the opt-out using the Crown prerogative (Baker et al., 1994, p. 41). Douglas Hurd confirmed that this was a possibility when he announced that 'there was no question of our ratifying a treaty other than the one we negotiated' (*The Guardian*, 1993a, p. 20). The role of parliament in ratifying the Treaty became increasingly unclear.

In April, the government accepted the opposition's clause 75 calling for a debate on the Social Chapter but it was delayed until after the Bill had been ratified. The government continued to intimate that even if there was a majority vote for the Social Chapter they would not be bound by the vote (*The Guardian*, 1993b, p. 24). On 22 July it faced two votes: the first on Labour's amendment on the Social Chapter; and a second on the government's motion noting the opt-out. The first vote was won by a margin of one vote while on the second vote the government was defeated by 8 votes (324–316). Twenty-two rebels had resisted the government and voted with the opposition. Baker et al. described it as the most damaging Commons defeat for a Tory government in the twentieth century (1994, p. 47). Those rebels who went back to supporting the government only did so after they extracted government statements stating there would be no re-entry into the ERM or moves towards joining a single currency. On 23 July the government was forced to call a confidence motion on its policy on the Social Chapter and, only with the threat of a general election, which the Conservatives looked destined to lose, did the rebels support the government. It was a 'pyrrhic victory' for the government that had needed to resort to various deals and compromises with opposition parties, bullying of its own MPs and threats to use the Crown's prerogative. In effect there had been such a profound attack on the governing elite that only the full exploitation of the power at the disposal of the British executive secured ratification, and only when Major threatened a general election did the rebels come back on board. In contrast the rebels' victory was considerable as 'they had imposed longer-term constraints on the European stance of the government that would certainly not dare to bring any new treaty before parliament that furthered European integration. ERM re-entry was off the agenda even before the collapse' (p. 47). In particular, the problems that emerged over Maastricht indicated 'the nature and depth of penetration of the Thatcherite revolution in the party' (Baker et al., 1994, p. 57).

A National Movement for Eurosceptic Britain

When Major was interviewed about the Eurosceptic rebellions within the Conservative party, he referred to the rebels as 'a tiny minority' (Seldon, 1998, p. 389). However, the real sociological dilemma for the Major government was that by the July vote the Eurosceptics had become a significant right wing movement. They drew strength from the extensive extra-parliamentary support that was emerging for their cause. Increasingly their refusal to accept the government whip suggested that their primary loyalty was to the anti-European cause and not to the Conservative government under John Major. We should note that in comparison to many other political movements, the Eurosceptics were able to exert considerable power because they had access to, and were part of, the centre of British political authority. It was only when a general election threatened to remove this influence that they sided with the government. Rather than viewing it as a fragmented or marginal political movement, it should be seen as the manifestation and reassertion of macro-ideological norms within the British political order, primarily centred on the populist articulation of Eurosceptic Britain.

Extra-parliamentary Mobilisation

The extent of Euroscepticism as a national movement had been evident in the sustained attack on the government's attempts to ratify the Maastricht Treaty. They had become organised into a number of cross-cutting alliances and groupings both inside and outside parliament. Indeed, some 27 separate groups had been created in the 18 months following the December 1991 Maastricht Council (Forster 2002, p. 200). Notably the Fresh Start Group, set up after the debate on the Danish referendum, provided the organisational dynamism for opposing the government's European policy and became the dominant parliamentary grouping. Its radical opposition to government legislation and fundraising activities outside the party dramatically altered the rule of political conduct (Young, 1998, p. 366). Forster describes its impact as follows:

> Until its creation, sceptics had been rather like individual fish who had been swimming in the same general direction. Fresh Start offered a sense of community and purpose, transforming the sceptics into a shoal of fish synchronising their activities with a shared objective, opposition to the ratification of the Maastricht

Treaty. Thanks to the Fresh Start Group, Euroscepticism thus matured rapidly within the parliamentary Conservative Party. (2002, pp. 199–200)

Alongside growing parliamentary organisation and support, Eurosceptics found that they could look to the press, the wider party and public opinion for support. Significant sections of the press continued to provide substantial backing for the cause. *The Sunday Telegraph* and the Murdoch press all supported the call for a referendum (Baker et al., 1994, p. 46). The Newbury by-election defeat led to vicious attacks in the Murdoch press on Major's leadership, which culminated in a notorious article by Lord Rees Mogg on how 'Major fails the leadership test' (p. 46). Support was also evident across all sections of the Conservative party. A survey of 4,000 grassroots Conservative supporters by the Conservative Political Centre, made public during April 1993, indicated widespread disaffection with the Maastricht Bill and significant support for a referendum (Bates, 1993, p. 3). This trend was confirmed by surveys that showed a significant shift to the right on European issues amongst Conservative supporters between 1991 and 1996 (Turner, 2000, p. 175). Furthermore, there was significant financial support for the rebels' Maastricht referendum campaign (Marc) from traditional Tory business fundraising channels and overseas supporters (Baker et al., 1994, p. 46). In terms of public opinion, polls demonstrated that there was widespread support for a referendum, alongside growing disillusionment with the process of European integration since the Maastricht summit of 1991. A vivid expression of this new movement was the founding of the European Foundation in October 1993, headed by Bill Cash. The European Foundation became an important vehicle for developing a more sophisticated Eurosceptic case than had been seen in the past, providing the evidence and arguments to attack both the Government's European policy and the European Union in general. It also introduced a significant figure into the European debate in 'Jimmy Goldsmith, its biggest patron, a man of gigantic wealth who had the quixotic idea of using some of it to promote the anti-EU cause in Britain' (Young, 1998, p. 407). Goldsmith went on to form the Referendum party and fight the 1997 general election, attracting 811,827 votes, the best ever showing by a minority party (Carter, Evans, Alderman and Gorham, 1998, p. 483).

The Discourse of Euroscepticism

A populist right wing movement had therefore begun to emerge that had minimal loyalty to the Conservative government and successfully re-asserted Eurosceptic Britain. The most influential alliances and arguments developed by Eurosceptics were on the Thatcherite right of the Conservative party. These included significant Eurosceptics in the Major Cabinet (Lilley, Redwood and Portillo) and vocal ex-ministers from the Thatcher and Major administrations (Tebbitt, Baker and Lamont). The most prominent backbench rebel during the Maastricht crisis,

Cash, was essentially a Thatcherite, as were the most prominent of the 1992 intake of MPs such as Iain Duncan Smith and Bernard Jenkin (Forster, 2002, p. 247).

The conflict over Maastricht consolidated a shift to the right by the Conservative party that placed Euroscepticism at the centre of the defence of Thatcher's legacy (Berrington and Hague, 1998, p. 54). In particular, with the Maastricht Treaty the Eurosceptics had a clear object on which to focus their critique and begin to apply many of the arguments Thatcher had already developed in her Bruges speech (Forster, 2002, p. 207). However, what was notable was the extent to which Euroscepticism was fashioned as a populist reassertion of British independence and self-government in opposition to Europe. A key feature of the right wing Eurosceptic discourse during the Maastricht debate was that they presented themselves as the representatives of 'the people' and the guardians of national sovereignty. For instance, in the debate following the Danish *No* vote, Tony Marlow, MP for Northampton North, enquired of the Prime Minister,

> Would my right hon. Friend suggest to Monsieur Napoleon Delors who today rather than showing humility, seems to be showing his customary arrogance that, henceforth 2nd June should be a public holiday throughout Europe, to be known as the day of the people, the day of democracy or, even better, the day of the nation-state? (*Hansard*, Vol. 208, Col. 835)

The argument was that 'the people' of Europe, and in particular 'the British people', did not want the kind of Europe that had been envisaged at Maastricht. The freedom of 'the people' was posited against a centralising European state. As the former Home Secretary, Kenneth Baker, stated,

> the Danish and French referenda have shown vividly in the past six months that there is a movement across Europe which is not anti-Europe but anti-bureaucratic and against a centralised and bossy Europe. That is what I believe the no-votes in France and Denmark were saying and what many people in Britain feel. (*Hansard*, Vol. 212, Col. 56)

Although the Eurosceptics aligned themselves with 'the people' of Europe, they articulated a conception of popular sovereignty that claimed to be rooted in the everyday lives and concerns of British people. The MP John Butcher claimed that 'our people have always been in favour of a Europe-wide free trading area. They have never been in favour of the gradual and surreptitious building of a European state' (*Hansard*, Vol. 208, Col. 838). A distinctive feature of the Eurosceptic position was that the governing elites could no longer be trusted on Europe and had led 'the British people' into a European state against their will. In the early Committee stages of the Maastricht Bill, Cash made the point that Heath, when Prime Minister, had misled parliament and 'the people' in a government White Paper claiming that Britain would retain its essential sovereignty on membership.

Cash went onto argue 'that it is the basis on which the process has tended to move, and I believe that the same thing is happening with the present treaty, too. The British people are not being told the truth; they are not being told exactly what is involved' (*Hansard*, Vol. 215, Col. 214). Cash proved a tenacious opponent of the government. He tabled 240 amendments to the Bill and voted 47 times against the government when a three line whip was in place (Young, 1998, p. 395). Crucially, he set out to prove that the Treaty was not the decentralising document that the government claimed. He claimed that 'the bottom line is that the treaty creates a legally binding union within Europe, which is quite different from the treaties that are normally transacted among countries' (*Hansard*, Vol. 215, Col. 205). Essentially Cash argued that the government's interpretation of the Treaty was misleading and different from the other member-states:

> the Government, in their booklet 'Britain in Europe', say that they do not want and will not have a united states of Europe, but that is the objective to which the German Chancellor has been moving ... The problem is that on European union we are at loggerheads with the Germans, as we are with other member-states. (*Hansard*, Vol. 215, Col. 210)

The fear that Britain was being incorporated into a European state was compounded by the imbalance of power within the European Union. In particular, Cash highlighted concerns over German domination: 'we must contain Germany by a balance of power and not by a spurious, academic, theoretical, theological attempt to contain it by pieces of paper. I remember Munich at least I remember that it was the waving of a piece of paper' (*Hansard*, Vol. 215, Col. 222). This echoed Thatcher's comments in May 1992 in which she had argued that Maastricht and its federal agenda augmented German power rather than contained it (Thatcher, 1995, p. 491). While Eurosceptics appeared to recognise and fear a revived nationalism emerging from the process of European integration, they also seemed to welcome and incite these developments as evidence of the rightness of their cause.

A further theme of the Eurosceptic discourse was the underlying instability of Europe. The folly of the Maastricht Treaty was that it continued the European trend of centralised state-building that had created the problems in Europe in the first place. European political modernisation was in essence flawed, fundamentally anti-British and potentially aggressive. With regard to the latter, Cash warned the House of Commons of what he saw as some of the less explicit implications of the formation of a European Union:

> What is the most important function, or certainly one of the prime functions, of a legal entity of the kind that this European union is to be? It is the call to arms. That is the direction in which this is going, to a common defence policy. What is the first requirement, the first duty to be imposed on citizens? It is that they may be conscripted. (*Hansard*, Vol. 215, Col. 227)

Another key argument was that the other member-states and the Commission effectively wanted to impose socialist policies on Europe. This was an argument that was central to Thatcherite Euroscepticism and drew on the arguments set out in Thatcher's Bruges speech. Teresa Gorman, MP for Billericay, restated this 'threat' when she claimed that this was the intention of the establishment of a social cohesion fund: 'Is not the cohesion fund the essence of a communist ideal of taking from the people to redistribute to the people? Is not that socialism, the tooth and claw?' (*Hansard*, Vol. 215, Col. 225). Thus, the Maastricht Treaty and, in particular EMU, represented an attack on the principles of free trade. It was an argument taken up once more by Cash who argued that the original free market agenda of the Community had been thwarted by the desire for political integration: 'they want to have fixed exchange rates not only to get a greater degree of control over the currencies but also to create one country' (*Hansard*, Vol. 231, Col. 222).

From this discussion, it is evident that key aspects of the Eurosceptic discourse were centred on a call for the reassertion of a powerful, sovereign Britain and a free market economy. The second wave of European integration was seen to represent the antithesis of this. In particular, the parliamentary debate over Maastricht reflected the continued political currency of the arguments made by Thatcher in her Bruges speech. Moreover, in its claims to represent and defend the will of 'the people', Euroscepticism was fundamentally populist, employing simple messages and emotive language. It was populism more than anything else that provided an important ideological unity to Euroscepticism, as it brought together disparate figures in the campaign for a referendum and a defence of 'the British people'. It was also ideologically powerful as it exposed the problems of legitimacy and democratic accountability that were undoubtedly features of the supranational elitism that was driving integration. For Eurosceptics the Major government was part of this drive and its claims to the contrary were increasingly viewed with incredulity and as misleading 'the people'. Cash, for example, dissected the Treaty and exposed the extent to which the Major government had signed up to further political integration. That the government had attempted to force this through parliament and would not agree to a referendum, demonstrated that the British governing elites could not be trusted and the people's democratic rights were being ignored and given away. While Cash's arguments centred on a defence of British parliamentarianism and democracy, these were not incompatible with a Thatcherite belief in a strong and exceptional British state that was aligned with global capital interests, represented by the likes of Murdoch and Goldsmith. This was what Thatcherism had claimed to be at the core of British national identities and interests, and was fundamentally threatened by the European project.

British Euroscepticism emerges as a populist movement of the right challenging the existing governing position on Europe. It developed an exclusive discourse that constituted Europe as essentially the 'other' of British society. Young characterises it as follows:

> Even where unanimity was required, the EU had its own momentum. It couldn't be stopped without a massive, perhaps destructive, effort. All these features rendered it an unlovely, sometimes highly dangerous, menace to the British way of life and government. Above all, perhaps, it was not British. As the years passed, a critique developed which asserted that the differences between island and mainland were written into history; were unalterable, were, sadly, part of the ineluctable order of things. (1998, p. 403)

This populist articulation of British exceptionalism and European 'otherness' was possible because it reflected the underlying continuities in a post-imperial state, a state in which post-war modernisation had proved inextricably and chronically constrained. The hold of this rigid and exclusive discourse over the Conservative party left the Major government little room for more constructive statecraft on Europe. In relation to European policy, the Maastricht rebellion and the extensive nature of Eurosceptic mobilisation was to further push the Major government in a more confrontational direction. Its impact can be demonstrated by the exploration of policy shifts that took place in the aftermath of the rebellion, and as the government adjusted to sustained pressure from Eurosceptic forces.

The Aftermath of the Crisis: Major's Euroscepticism

Initially the 'heart of Europe' strategy was an attempt at a revisionist Thatcherism designed to reinforce the distinctiveness of Major's leadership and secure conservative Europeanism. From the start of his premiership, however, Major's position on Europe was ambiguous because his key objective was to maintain party unity and appeal to both Europeanists and Eurosceptics. Major reflected the impossible compromise at the heart of his European policy, at times appearing as the heir of Heath, while at other times claiming to be on the side of the Eurosceptics. However, in the long run the Major government responded to its European dilemma by trying to placate Eurosceptics and in so doing moved to the right. The government increasingly adopted an obstructivist, Thatcherite approach to the European Union that left it marginalised and damaged.

In the wake of the Maastricht rebellion, in an article in *The Economist* in September 1993, Major fleshed out what was to be the focus of government European policy for the next four years. Here, Major came out as overtly hostile to the European project, claiming that 'we take some convincing on any proposal from Brussels' (1993 p. 29). He effectively dismissed the Delors project and argued that 'the new mood in Europe demands a new approach'. As for this new approach, it can be read as a restatement of Thatcher's Bruges address:

> It is for nations to build Europe, not for Europe to attempt to supersede nations. I want to see the Community become a wide union, embracing the whole of the democratic Europe, in a single market and with common security arrangements

> firmly linked to NATO. I want to see a competitive and confident Europe, generating jobs for its citizens and choice for its consumers. A community which ceases to nibble at national freedoms, and so commands the enthusiasm of its member-states. (p. 29)

Major emphasised a vision of the European Community as one of independent nation-states within a single market. In particular, he questioned the legitimacy of the EMU project:

> I hope my fellow heads of government will resist the temptation to recite the mantra of full economic and monetary union as if nothing had changed. If they do recite it, it will have all the quaintness of a rain dance and about the same potency. (p.29)

This reflected the belief within the government that the problems of Maastricht ratification across the EU and the collapse of the ERM in 1993 meant that the drive for integration was over. The British government viewed this as an opportunity for it to pursue a more neo-liberal agenda. A British 'exceptionalism' was to be the driving force behind the construction of a residualised European market society overseen by competing sovereign states. Indeed, there was a growing belief that the EU was now heading in a British direction. This was the position that Douglas Hurd, as Foreign Secretary, was increasingly advocating, as Young comments:

> He developed the conceit that Europe was 'moving our way'. Those who called on him heard these words often. So did the Cabinet. They were a way of arguing that, if you took the long view, the problem between, say, Portillo and a pro-Europe man like Michael Heseltine might be said not really to exist. For Britain's objectives were coming about anyway. 'The climate is changing', Hurd told me on several occasions between 1992 and 1996. The Commission, repeatedly, was said to have got the message about subsidiarity. So had Delors and Mitterrand personally. There was now a new stream of higher wisdom percolating through the Community from its source-bed in London. Ideas that had once been regarded as 'heresies, eccentricities of British thought' were now beginning to prevail, a development that made it 'not sensible to back off into noisy and destructive isolation'. (1998, pp. 450–51)

The immediate post-Maastricht period was characterised by uncertainty about the integration project. There were tensions between Paris and Bonn over enlargement and the future of a single currency policy. The commitment to monetary union locked governments into an anti-inflationary policy that, during a recession, increasingly seemed to be at the expense of growth and jobs. Further problems emerged over the institutional reform of the Union in order to rectify the so-called 'democratic deficit' and make way for enlargement. For the remainder of its time in office, the Major government was not able to constructively exploit these differences. Instead it was pursuing a more aggressive and oppositional Thatcherite approach in response to Eurosceptic mobilisation. On a number of issues, most notably over voting arrangements in the Council of Ministers after enlargement, and on the non-cooperation policy during the beef crisis, the British government was isolated and obstructive. The government increasingly turned issues of Community business into totemic struggles over the preservation of national independence and identity.

The most significant problem for the government was over EMU, which, despite the predictions of the British government, was continuing to go ahead. The government, while sticking to its opt-out position negotiated at Maastricht, refused to rule out the possibility of membership. The Eurosceptics increasingly demanded that the government did so. In an attempt to placate its opponents, the government promised a referendum on the issue and that if it did go ahead, which it considered unlikely, then Britain would not be part of the first wave. It was further evidence of how little room was left for manoeuvre for the Major government in continuing to engage with European developments.

Conclusion

In conclusion, we can say that the Major administration was primarily a Thatcherite government and its European policy came to reflect Thatcherism's underlying Euroscepticism. In an attempt to resolve the chronic problems of modernisation that continued to haunt the British state, Conservative Europeans used the crisis of Thatcherism at the end of the 1980s to try and push the party and government in a more constructive European direction. However, this was clearly at odds with the overall general direction of Eurosceptic Britain. The Europeanisation of British political identity and political economy was fundamentally contested by a right wing Eurosceptic movement. Euroscepticism became a way of consolidating and reinforcing the Thatcherite legacy and securing its grip over the Conservative party. As it remained committed to continued EU membership, the only viable strategy for the government was to try and push the EU towards its worldview. This meant pursuing an agenda that was characterised by economic reductionism and policy exit. The main difference between the government's position and the Eurosceptics was that the government continued to claim that the EU could be moved in a British direction and that it was necessary to stay in the game. Thus, it remained nominally consistent with the post-imperial governing code on Europe. However, arguments of an emerging Anglo-Europe failed to convince Eurosceptics and the government could not unite a bitterly divided Conservative party around a common European strategy. The Eurosceptics increasingly envisaged more radical forms of exit from the EU, albeit without necessarily proposing complete withdrawal, and questioned the economic basis for Britain's involvement in the integration process.

In this intensely contested political terrain, Eurosceptic Britain was once again reproduced against the European project. The political basis for the incorporation of British citizens within a European political order remained chronically undermined. Rather than reflecting the exaggerated influence of a political faction or part of the subversion of national liberal traditions, Euroscepticism should be seen as continuous with the post-imperial re-articulation of Britain as a fundamentally Eurosceptic political order. This left the Major government without either the inclination or political resources to engage constructively with the process of integration as a project of political and economic modernisation. Instead, the British government became a force for disintegration.

Chapter 7

Labour in Power: The Rise and Fall of Anglo-Europe

Introduction

The election of Labour in 1997 put into power a party that had undergone considerable Europeanisation since it had fought the 1983 election on a platform of rejection of British membership. It was only with the 1988 policy review exercise under Neil Kinnock following the 1987 election defeat that a more positive position was set out. For the leadership, it took on significant importance for re-establishing Labour as a credible party of government. Moreover, as the Conservative party moved in a Eurosceptic direction, Labour was able to present itself as the pro-European party of the middle ground. The 1990s witnessed growing support for the EU's economic and social agenda, including membership of the single currency (Gamble and Kelly, 2000; Fella, 2006a). On entering office, the contrast with the Conservatives was immediately apparent when the government successfully negotiated the Treaty of Amsterdam, including opting in to the Social Chapter. What is more, Tony Blair was viewed as the most pro-European prime minister since Heath, clearly comfortable on the European stage. As will be shown in this chapter, New Labour combined its British modernisation agenda with a commitment to Europe with some significant success, and promoted a distinctive Anglo-European vision consistent with its approach to globalisation. However, this vision proved difficult to sustain in the face of British policy deviation from the European core on issues such as Iraq and the single currency, and persistent domestic Eurosceptic opposition. It will be argued that there were structural limitations to Labour's Europeanism, and this became more apparent the longer it was in power. The key point is that British Euroscepticism emerges as integral to, rather than a deviation from, its European strategy. Finally, it is argued that the financial and Eurozone crises unfold in such a way that they further distanced Britain from the EU and reinforced Eurosceptic Britain.

New Labour, Modernisation and Europe

New Labour's modernising agenda appeared to represent a genuine shift away from the British political tradition of centralised, majoritarian rule and towards a system of multi-level governance. There were to be devolved authorities, the incorporation of the European Convention on Human Rights, the adoption of proportional representation in regional and European elections, and the introduction of a directly elected London Mayor. This commitment to devolving power downwards was concomitant with a principled support for the institutions of global governance. Antony Giddens' Third Way (1998) provided an important intellectual rationale for the New Labour project that was rooted in an analysis of globalisation. A central claim of the Third Way was that the nation-state alone could not meet the challenges of an interdependent world and must embrace the complexity of global governance. Once this position was established, it enabled Labour, once in power, to normalise relations within the EU without being compromised on a matter of fundamental political principle.

What therefore marked out the Labour government, especially in its first term of office, was an approach to European affairs that was constructive in terms of what could be achieved. It emphasised good working relations between British ministers, civil servants and other European member-states and European institutions, and saw an 'impressive investment of British politicians in all the European institutions' (Elisabeth Gigou cited in Baker, 2003, p. 237). Of particular symbolic importance was Blair's 1998 speech in French to the National Assembly, which was heralded as a triumph and a new beginning in Britain's relationship with Europe. On a number of issues, the Labour government placed itself in the mainstream of European policy-making and aspired to a leadership role in areas such as crime, immigration, defence and foreign policy.

Blair emphasised the importance of good relations with both the US and EU to British interests, arguing that a choice between the two was unnecessary. Instead he proposed that Britain was the 'bridge between the US and Europe' (Blair, 1997). Positioning Europe alongside the US as a central pillar of British foreign policy implied a different emphasis from the Anglo-American nationalism of Conservative governments and the constraints it had imposed on European cooperation. This approach was given substance in 1998 by the Anglo-French St Malo Declaration, which set out the initial framework for a common European security and defence policy.[1] The role of transatlantic intermediary was most effectively realised by Blair when he built a coalition in support of humanitarian intervention in Kosovo in 1999 and, initially at least, in legitimising the 'war on terror' after the 9/11 attacks in 2001.

Overall, Europe was a fundamental element of New Labour's agenda for modernising Britain. Daddow documents how Blair and Brown 'argued the case for Europe on the grounds of a fresh idea about Europe, a new understanding of Britishness, "enlightened patriotism" the EU as international actor and a re-rendering of British and European history' (2011, p. 12). In so doing they looked to change public opinion and to challenge the British Eurosceptic political

---

1 The pursuit of a common European defence policy, including military capacity, was consistently attacked by British Eurosceptics as a threat to NATO. The Conservatives, under Hague, committed to pulling out.

culture. This modernising Europeanism was then contrasted with a reactionary Euroscepticism, as Blair recalled in his memoirs:

> I regarded anti-European feeling as hopelessly, absurdly out of date and unrealistic. It was also the product of a dangerous insularity, a myopia about the world that I thought affected adversely the whole psychology of the country. It was a kind of post-empire delusion. (2011, p. 533)

Labour's position on Europe was thus presented as realistic and rational, aligned with the direction and demands of the modern world and with new generations for whom 'Europe is a fact' (p. 96).

Labour contrasted their approach with 'wild eyed anti-Europeans' in an out of date and out of touch Conservative party (p. 236). This worked well for Labour in a context in which the Conservatives under William Hague were unsuccessful in establishing a populist Euroscepticism as a viable electoral strategy. Initially buoyed by success in the 1999 European elections, Hague supported a number of negative, populist campaigns on Europe, law and order, asylum seekers and homosexuality. As Reyes (2005) argued, this was an attempt to reconnect Conservatism with the British electorate by the articulation of a populist Conservatism focused on the construction of the 'mainstream majority' against established liberal elites:

> The people are British, tax-payers, married couples (with children), home-owners, car owners, (small) business people, farmers, private-sector workers, pensioners and patients. And they are dismayed by red-tape, higher taxes, regulation, bureaucracy, interference, excess paperwork, waste, centralising decisions and political correctness – all of which are imposed upon them by politicians, quangos, government and unelected EU bureaucrats in Brussels. (p. 109)

On the surface, Europe represented only one issue amongst many, yet Hague's populism was principally conceived with Europe in mind and it remained pivotal to its articulation: 'the only party that speaks to the mainstream view of the British people of this country. The only party that wants to be in Europe, not run by Europe ... It's our approach to Europe, because it's our approach to everything' (cited in Reyes, 2005, p. 110). This was confirmed by the 2001 Conservative election strategy, which was dominated by the party's populist campaign to 'Keep the Pound'. In the end, a combination of internal and external opposition successfully labelled Hague's Conservative populism as extremist, hence its position on Europe became associated with hard-line policies on gay people, asylum seekers and criminals. The strategy therefore backfired, as to identify with the 'mainstream majority' was to align with a party defined by its hatred of others and obsessed with Europe. Nevertheless, Hague had shifted the Conservative leadership further in a direction that many Eurosceptics had wanted to see since Maastricht, which was to configure Thatcherism as populist Euroscepticism.

Conversely, the modernisation of the Labour party undertaken from Kinnock to Blair reformed what was by the 1980s a hard Eurosceptic party, opposed to the British establishment approach to Europe, into a party of government that had accommodated to the governing position on Europe. In certain key respects it went further than previous elites in presenting the case that Britain's post-imperial national interests had to be firmly anchored within Europe, and that this did not threaten national identity but was in fact indicative of an enlightened patriotism. Hence, it not only endorsed the position established since Macmillan but reclaimed it as a new modernised approach in opposition to what was presented as the isolationism and indecision of the past (Daddow, 2011, p. 197). The Labour government domestically legitimated its pro-Europe stance by opposing their position to Eurosceptic 'extremists', presented as out of touch with the reality of contemporary Britain (p. 161). On this basis the Conservative party was attacked; however, it also allowed the government to appear more pro-European than was actually borne out in practice. As we have seen, governing elite constructions of the national interest and identity have never been clearly and unambiguously pro-European but have adapted traditional conceptions in order to legitimise Britain's relationship with Europe.

Britain: A Beacon for Europe

More than anything else, a decisive commitment by the Labour government to joining the single currency would have demonstrated a significant shift in a pro-European direction. In October 1997, Brown made it clear that Britain would not join in the first wave from 1999 and set out five economic tests for entry: a convergence between Britain and the Eurozone's economic cycles and suitable interest rates; the flexibility within the system to cope with economic change; the implications for investment of EMU membership; the impact on the City and, finally, on employment. If the government recommended joining, a referendum would then follow.[2] In the run up to the 2001 election, Blair announced that if elected the government would conduct a full review within two years. The result was a comprehensive assessment by the Treasury that included 18 background documents and a final report of nearly 2,000 pages (Buller and Gamble, 2008, p. 260). In June 2003 Brown concluded that the tests on convergence and flexibility had not been met, which in turn had implications for those on employment and investment. The economic tests laid down by Brown have been viewed as a fudge – a product of the Blair-Brown split (Seldon, 2005, pp. 639–40), wresting the decision from the Prime Minister and putting it in the hands of the Treasury, or to depoliticise the issue and the damaging prospect of a referendum defeat (Aspinwall, 2004, p. 170). This, however, understates the extent to which the

---

2 Blair had matched the Conservative commitment to a referendum on the single currency in the run up to the 1997 election.

decision was based on economics and, in this regard, the assessment of EMU membership was shared by Brown and Blair:[3] 'unless it was economically plain that it would be good for Britain, it was simply not politically sellable, i.e. the political problem was economics. The trouble was the economic case was at best ambiguous and certainly not beyond doubt' (Blair, 2011, p. 537). By the time of the 2003 assessment, the concern was that inside the single currency Britain would lack the necessary flexibility over monetary policy, putting at risk New Labour's reputation for economic stability and competence. The premise for this was that if Britain had joined in the first wave it would have been forced to adopt lower interest rates than were necessary for the economy, thus fuelling the housing market, inflation and risking a boom-bust cycle (Elliott, 2003).

By 2003 the British economy was in a period of stable and consistent growth, which seemed to demonstrate the success of the Brown model of political economy. At the Labour party Conference in Bournemouth, Brown claimed that,

> while America and Japan have been in recession – while half of Europe is still in recession, Britain with a Labour Government pursuing Labour policies has achieved economic growth in every year, indeed in every quarter of every year, for the whole six and a half years of this Labour Government. (Brown, 2003b)

The principles on which the Brown model was based were a combination of fiscal rules and monetary flexibility. The former included the 'golden rule' that government borrowing should only be for investment, not to fuel public consumption, and the 'sustainable investment rule' that public sector net debt would be kept below 40 per cent of the national income. In terms of monetary policy, the decision to grant independence to the Bank of England gave responsibility for setting interest rates to the Bank's Monetary Policy Committee (MPC), which was expected to make adjustments in order to meet the government's target of 2 per cent inflation. As the British model of economic governance was consolidated, a 'subtle policy of retrenchment' towards the Eurozone and its institutions took hold at the Treasury (Buller and Gamble, 2008, p. 261). There was particular concern over the amount of power that had been ceded to the European Central Bank in that, in comparison to the Bank of England, it had 'goal' as well as 'operational' independence, meaning it could set its own inflation rate at which interest rate adjustments may be necessary. In comparison, the British government retained control over the target, which was symmetrical so that intervention was required to address deflation as well as inflation. In addition, by setting the parameters of fiscal targets over the full length of the economic cycle the government retained sufficient autonomy to overshoot when growth was lower than expected and to undershoot during the 'good' times (Strange 2013). Conversely, EMU was

---

[3] The difference between the Prime Minister and the Chancellor seemed to concern presentation and Brown's more negative public statements on the Euro (Blair, 2011, p. 537); also see Wall's assessment (2008, p. 170).

considered to lock governments into annual debt targets that considerably reduced their room to manoeuvre.

The debate on the Euro seemed to combine a realistic assessment of the differences between the British economy and the Eurozone with a belief in the superiority of the British approach. Brown's assessment of the single currency tests took place at a high point in his chancellorship, having established credibility with the financial markets alongside relatively high levels of public trust. A key argument that Brown was making in 2003 was that, while other countries were facing the consequences of an economic downturn and recession, the British economy under his stewardship was able to buck the trend and remain stable and growing. Hence, he claimed that the British success story offered a model of economic governance from which other states could learn:

> Britain can be more than a bridge between Europe and America: our British values -what we say and do marrying enterprise and fairness, and about public services and the need to relieve poverty, can and should, in time, make Britain a model, a beacon for Europe, America and the rest of the world. (Brown, 2003b)

There was in this globalised nationalism an implicit rejection of the progressive left argument for EMU, which had viewed it as a way of regaining economic control in a context of globalisation, a position that had been supported by the British Labour movement since the end of the 1980s (Strange, 2006, p. 209). The established argument was that social democratic projects were fundamentally threatened by the capacity of global financial markets to veto national policies by currency speculation and capital flight. From this perspective, EMU provided the macroeconomic leverage and protection against market turmoil that was no longer available to individual states. By the point that the decision was made not to join the single currency, it appears that the Labour leadership had concluded that globalisation could be made to work for the nation-state in such a way that it provided stable growth and sufficient income to fund public services and, consequently, did not have to be underpinned by regional monetary integration. In many respects, the Labour government's opposition to the single currency hardened at the point at which the 'neo-liberal' self-limitations of EMU were being challenged and subject to significant reform, including the suspension of the Stability and Growth Pact in November 2003 (Buller and Gamble, 2008, p. 265; Strange, 2012, p. 261). Nevertheless, Labour's position under Brown was to firmly position Britain outside of the Eurozone, offering a model to be followed rather than working alongside as a potential participant.

There remained, however, underlying problems with Brown's global-national approach to the British economy. Britain was not outperforming other economies to the point where there was a clear advantage. Hirst and Thompson argued that 'far from being ahead, the UK is just more exposed' (2000, p. 354). This exposure was especially problematic because Britain was increasingly dependent on the financial sector for its external income, with growth linked to the financialisation of the domestic economy. The clearest example of this was the British housing market, cited by Brown as a barrier to EMU membership, where the City and the financial service industry had engineered a speculative boom. The capacity to generate profits from speculation on asset values dramatically increased during the 1990s, as the profit margins from industry were squeezed by the intensification of global competition, particularly with the rise of China (Harvey, 2010, p. 29). Moreover, the deregulation of finance created a shadow banking system of increasingly complex and opaque financial instruments designed not only to manage risks but to turn them into profit. The dramatic rise in liquidity, fictitiously leveraged, fuelled house prices and the overextension of the property market.[4] From this perspective, the Labour boom was not rooted in any new productivist settlement and industrial competitiveness, but in London's pivotal role in global finance and the peculiarities of the British housing market. In 2003, the IMF warned that 'domestic demand is being sustained by high and increasing levels of household debt, fuelled by house price inflation and low interest rates, which increases vulnerability to potential adverse shocks' and called for 'heightened vigilance to these risks by the authorities, especially regarding the possible existence of a housing price bubble' (cited in Lee, 2009, pp. 23–4). Crouch (2009, p. 390) refers to this system as one of privatised Keynesianism in which the economy is expanded by private debt created by the extraordinary growth in mortgages, credit cards and bank loans, enabling people to borrow easily and cheaply often against the value of their homes. In turn, Labour maintained its social democratic credentials by rises in public spending that were increasingly dependent upon tax revenues from the financial sector (Darling, 2011, p. 22).

At the centre of this 'virtuous cycle' was the City, lauded by Brown as a model for the whole economy:

> The City of London – and our financial services industry – has learnt faster, more intensively and more successfully than others the significance of globalisation: that you succeed best not by sheltering your share of a small protected national market; but by striving for a greater and greater share of the growing global market; and that stability, adaptability, innovation and openness to new ideas and to global trading opportunities – great British assets and advantages – matter even more today than ever. And what you have achieved for the financial services sector, we as a country now aspire to achieve for the whole of the British economy. (Brown, 2004)

In taking advantage of globalisation, finance was viewed as the most successful sector in the country. In this regard the City was seen to have successfully adapted to the euro; by the turn of century it was handling more international

---

4 Mortgage debt was 129.1 per cent of disposable income in the UK in 2006 compared to 70.9 in Germany (Crouch, 2009, p. 391).

euro-denominated transactions than Frankfurt and Paris combined (Kynaston, 2002, p. 785). As Ed Balls, as City Minister, pointed out,

> A few years ago there were many who feared that in not joining the first wave of monetary union, London would be excluded from euro-based financial markets. Yet since the launch of the euro in 1999, London has established a pre-eminent position in euro-denominated international transactions, consolidating its position as Europe's financial gateway to the rest of the world and the world's gateway to Europe. (2007, p. 11)

It was widely believed that innovation and openness enabled the City to manage risk and sustain economic stability while external regulation was considered a potential threat to its global competitiveness;[5] the consensus across the political spectrum was that any regulation should be 'light touch' (Darling, 2011, p. 24). As such, the Labour government saw its role in Europe as one of resisting attempts by the Commission to regulate financial services and harmonise legislation across the EU, ensuring that there was 'no unnecessary and burdensome gold-plating' (Balls, 2006).

New Labour asserted national economic governance with a proactive globalism that was rooted in the historical structure of the British economy. From this perspective, the European social model was not to be imitated but argued against and, if possible, reformed in line with the requirements of globalisation. In the European context, as in the domestic one, it 'defined itself through its opposition to traditional social democratic concerns such as centralised wage bargaining, neo-corporatist approach to policy formation, higher marginal rates of taxation, extensions of economic democracy, or an increasing ratio of public expenditure to GDP' (Gamble and Kelly, 2000, p. 22). It proselytised for an Anglo-American form of capitalism, which was pressed on its European partners as providing the preeminent way to create a stable and prosperous economy (Callaghan, 2000, p. 127; Gamble, 2003, p. 106). This was evident from the outset: while signing up to the Social Chapter at Amsterdam, the Blair Government rejected French plans for interventionist policies on growth and employment. Moreover, further measures under the Social Chapter were rejected, as was any extension of Qualified Majority Voting to social policy. The focus was to be on flexible labour markets, supply side economics and openness to global markets as the driver of economic success and the basis for public investment. On this agenda Britain was well placed to lead; because the economy deregulated 'much further, much faster, much earlier' than any other EU state, it 'simply absorbed EU related policies without substantially changing its own policies or institutional arrangements' (Schmidt, 2006, pp. 16–17). By the Lisbon Summit of March 2000, the Labour Government

---

5 In his 2004 Mansion House Speech Brown promised to subject Financial Services Authority rules to scrutiny by the competition authorities and to examine the impact of regulation on competition, alongside resisting the 'unnecessary' 'red tape' coming out of Europe.

was already leading the agenda for European economic liberalisation in the face of French opposition (Black, 2000). In and out of office, European social democrats took inspiration from the Blair and Clinton governments (Ryner, 2010, p. 510) and this gave the British government considerable influence in the EU, even in the absence of EMU membership. In selling to Europe the benefits of the Third Way's combination of economic liberalisation with an 'enabling' welfare state, Lisbon was the highpoint for New Labour in Europe. The agreement signalled the end of any attempt to renew the Delors vision of a more interventionist European Union in terms of growth and employment. At the summit's conclusion, Blair claimed that 'there is now a new direction for Europe, away from the social regulation agenda of the 80s and instead a direction of enterprise, innovation, competition and employment' (Black, 2000). The Lisbon Agenda that followed centred on turning Europe in to a dynamic knowledge economy based on supply side reform and including proposals for the liberalisation of financial services, such as eliminating barriers to investment in private pensions.

In this narrative, finance was presented as an exemplar of a global industry, when in practice it turned out to be the highly unstable mechanism underpinning the entire model. Nevertheless, a consensus amongst European elites had emerged by the turn of the century that liberalised and integrated financial markets were a positive development. Lisbon was the impetus for the 2001 Lamfulussy Report on the EU financial markets. The outcome of this was the Lamfulussy Process, which devolved considerable responsibility for regulation to the European Securities Committee made up a group of financial officials and experts from the member-states (Macartney and Moran, 2008, pp. 328–9). Its main impact was to further secure the interests of transnational finance by enacting legislation that reduced barriers to competition. Notably, the Market in Financial Instruments Directive, which came out of the Financial Services Action Plan agreed at Lisbon, established the principle of maximum harmonisation, limiting the capacity of national governments to augment European legislation with their own rules. Nevertheless, as Macartney and Moran point out, tensions continued to exist between Anglo-American and French/Italian elites over price transparency clauses designed to reduce any competitive advantages of transnational capital (2008, p. 332).

New Labour's political economy was highly influential in establishing European policy agendas by the turn of the century. However, in this we can also begin to see the paradoxes of its Europeanism. British influence and European credentials were increasingly dependent on maintaining and promulgating British success and distinctiveness. Hence, despite a broad neo-liberal consensus within the European Union, Labour often accentuated and essentialised the differences between Britain and Europe. In this regard, Gordon Brown was particularly vocal and fully prepared to adopt the language of Euroscepticism. 'Europe' was characterised by having 'old flawed assumptions' about inexorable moves towards federalism (Brown, 2003c). Thus, an Anglo-European nationalism began to take shape, enabling the government to continue to present Europe as fundamental to Britain's post-imperial trajectory yet rooted in traditional constructions of British exceptionalism:

> British values have much to offer, persuading a global Europe that the only way forward is inter-governmental, not federal; mutual recognition not one-size-fits-all central rules; tax competition, not tax harmonisation, with proper political accountability and subsidiarity, not a superstate. (Brown, 2003c)

> ... a consensus can be built in Britain and Europe for a new vision for Europe, that, as a trading bloc, Europe is superseded by the Europe of the global era, Europe's institutions are having to be reshaped in line with long-held British values – internationalism, enterprise, fairness, political accountability. (Brown 2003a)

From this perspective, the non-participation of Britain in EMU alongside the pursuit of opt-outs and 'red-lines' in negotiations was not 'awkwardness' and 'semi-detachment', but the British-European vision in practice. While there were differences in emphasis between Blair and Brown, both adopted an established governing position that Britain could lead and shape the direction of integration from the inside. British 'awkwardness' was thus re-packaged as a new Europeanism underpinned by New Labour's modernisation project. Central to this was Blair's 1998 announcement of a 'step change' in the ways in which British ministers and officials engaged with their European counterparts (Smith, 2005, p. 709). This involved an intensification of bilateral relations in order to ascertain the direction of thinking on European policy in both member and accession states. The approach facilitated good working relations and a reputation for constructive engagement, as well as identifying areas where the British government could gain a strategic advantage (p. 709). Smith describes the British approach as one of 'promiscuous bilateralism', 'working with whichever country or countries had interests that coincided with the UK's on a particular issue' (p. 709). Nevertheless, what became increasingly important were the alliances with centre-right leaders and governments (Blair, 2011, p. 539). This was particularly the case once it was clear that the German Social Democratic Party did not share the British approach to the 'Third Way' (p. 539). Thus, alliances with José Maria Aznar in Spain and Silvio Berlusconi in Italy were crucial to the success of the Lisbon Agenda. Blair therefore found common cause in resisting worker protections and pressing for further liberalisation, alongside the pursuit of a common immigration and asylum policy to strengthen the EU's external borders and take a harder line on illegal migrants. A vision of an Anglo-Europe began to take shape that contrasted with the Franco-German tradition. Yet after 9/11 this became associated with a profound division within the European Union.

Iraq and Anglo-Europe

The normalisation of relations between Britain and the EU under Labour was fundamentally challenged in the crisis in EU-US relations that followed the decision to invade Iraq. The aggressive and unilateralist stance taken by the post-9/11 Bush administration as it embarked on the 'war on terror' opened up a stark ideological divide in international affairs. The US refused to see its actions constrained by either the United Nations or its European allies. In joining the US in Iraq, Britain placed itself in a position that was fundamentally in opposition to the European core, notably the line taken by France and Germany, and to domestic and European public opinion.

The failure to find a strong justification in international law for the invasion particularly compromised the Blair government, as it was seen to have unconditionally adopted the US line. The justification for war on the basis that Iraq held weapons of mass destruction that were a national security threat proved highly contentious. In aligning itself so firmly with the Bush administration, the Blair government nevertheless appeared not only to have undermined its own commitment to international law and the institutions and norms of a multilateral global order, but also to a broader European approach to global affairs. It was not possible to bridge this fundamental difference in international political principles, as the Bush administration placed US sovereignty, interests and security above international law, to the point where its contempt for the United Nations was barely concealed.

The politics of Iraq became Europeanised in the run up to the invasion when the US Defence Secretary, Donald Rumsfeld, caused outrage amongst the leaders of France and Germany by characterising the different positions taken over the use of military force as a divide between 'old' and 'new' Europe.[6] While Rumsfeld's remarks were considered offensive and undiplomatic, the divisions in Europe over Iraq were, at the time, public and real. An Anglo-American Europe appeared to be at odds with the Franco-German core Europe, the driving force behind European integration since the 1950s. The dichotomy was given intellectual force by Jurgen Habermas and Jacques Derrida's unprecedented public intervention into the Iraq debate when they defended a European 'core' vision against the 'hegemonic unilateralism of the United States' (2005, p. 6). This 'Europe' represented an alternative model of the good society, which was viewed as concomitant with an approach to global affairs that should actively counterbalance Anglo-American domination. While recognising what the West had in common, Habermas and Derrida wished to identify a distinctive post-war European consciousness, which through historical experience was radical and progressive in ways not seen elsewhere and certainly not in the United States. This included the privatisation of faith, a different understanding of the relationship between politics and the market, sensitivity to the paradoxes of progress and a belief in the mutual limitation of sovereignty. The experiences of war, revolution, colonialism and the holocaust had therefore shaped a European collective identity that was highly reflexive and a force for good in the world. From this perspective, Europe's duty was to resist a war that lacked strong legitimacy within international law and was driven by

---

6 Answer to a journalist on 22 January 2003.

US unilateralism. The position they outlined ignited the debate not only to do with transatlantic relations but more broadly about Europe's collective identity. A central criticism was that their dichotomising of Europe and the US was analytically problematic and politically suspect. It was not, according to critics, an academic exercise in understanding transatlantic differences but a manifesto that actively constituted a divide to the point where it was viewed as an exercise in anti-Americanism. Krishan Kumar, for instance, criticised this 'construction of a European identity as against America' (2008, p. 91). While acknowledging that Habermas and Derrida's article was 'not, in many respects, a bad summary' of what Europeans 'have come to value', he went on to question the extent that the differences outlined in any way reflected coherent and distinct collective identities (p. 91). With particular reference to Britain, Kumar pointed to significant transatlantic convergences as well as divergences between and within Europe:

> It has been customary in the past, it is true, for the British – or at least the English – to distinguish themselves from 'Europe', a compliment only too readily repaid by many Europeans. But with Britain now firmly part of the European Union that custom seems more than usually quaint. At any rate, what needs to be emphasized more is the variety of European traditions, with contributions from many different sections of Europe, including Britain. (p. 95)

Kumar's defence of a British European tradition had meaning in the context of an enlarged and diverse EU, no longer easily reducible to Franco-German hegemony. On this view, rather than highlighting Britain's marginalisation, the Iraq crisis saw the Blair government act in alliance with a number of member-states, new accession and candidate states that seemed to reflect the emergence of a different kind of Europe. As Stephen Wall explains, it was this emerging Anglo-Europe that was problematic for the French government; in the case of Jacques Chirac, 'it was not just the British action in support of the United States that riled him. It was the fact that Blair could carry with him around half the rest of the membership, including governments of Spain, Italy and Poland' (2008, p. 178). It was the prospect of an Anglo-Europe that Blair set out in his 2003 Warsaw speech to a receptive Polish audience:

> For Poland as with Britain, our strategy should be: get in it, make the most of it, have the confidence to win the debate not be frightened by it. Do we believe that the Europe our people want is a Europe of nations not a federal superstate? Yes. Do we believe Europe must reform economically to succeed? Yes. Do we believe Europe and the USA should be allies? Yes. Are our arguments good ones? Yes. Can we win the debate? It's up to us. But great nations don't hide away or follow along, stragglers at the back. They lead. They win. They have the confidence that comes not from arrogance but from a true understanding of the modern world. The belief that Europe is something done to us, that everyone else spends their time ganging up on us, to do us down, is a belief fit for a nation

with an inferiority complex not a proud nation that knows it can win and has proven its courage and its confidence by its record in history. So: you in Poland, we in Britain are once again contemplating our future in Europe. (Blair, 2003)

The Iraq crisis may have damaged Britain's relations with the core European member-states but it did not fundamentally wreck Britain's European credentials, and the government was determined to remain fully engaged with European developments. This could not be achieved without rebuilding relationships with France and Germany, and in December 2003 the possibility of a trilateralism was reinvigorated when The 'Big Three' met and agreed to cooperate on a common approach to the Constitutional Treaty and to European defence (Smith, 2005, p. 716). While it had limited success, 'the experiment in trilateral partnership with France and Germany was the most prominent example of a consistent effort by the Labour government to put Britain's relationship with her partners on a new footing' (Wall, 2008, p. 176). In general, the profound thickening of relations between Britain and other states evidenced a significant Europeanisation of the British state, in which policy was increasingly being agreed and developed in collaboration with European partners. It was also compatible with a change in style in major negotiations on the part of the Blair leadership that looked to achieve victories through skilled networking and cooperation (Wall, 2008, p. 177). As a consequence of this, the Iraq crisis did not leave Britain isolated but, in certain respects, demonstrated its influence and desire for influence.

The Constitution and the Budget Dispute

Labour accommodated Britain to the reality of European integration but did so in ways that were consistent with traditional British state objectives, acutely sensitive to the perception that British identity and interests could be at risk. It was on this basis that Blair supported the principle of a Constitution for Europe, arguing that 'the driving ideology' was 'a union of nations, not a super-state subsuming national sovereignty and national identity' (cited in Wall, 2008, p. 183). Hence, despite its initial reticence, the British government supported the 2001 Laeken Declaration that committed the EU to becoming more democratic, transparent and efficient, and the creation of a European Convention with the remit of drafting a European constitution. By establishing a Convention, the Constitution process side stepped intergovernmentalism and represented a reassertion of European federalism. The method had already proved successful in drafting a European Charter of Fundamental Rights in December 2000. At that time the British government had argued for a body composed of government representatives but was outflanked by Germany, who secured a Convention made up of elected representatives from both national and the European parliaments. What is more, guarantees that the Charter would only codify existing rights and that its legal status would remain the preserve of national governments proved worthless. When a new Convention was proposed,

Blair made it clear that this would only be acceptable if it produced options to be considered by an Intergovernmental Conference. The British proposed over 100 amendments in an attempt to reduce the more federalist elements of the proposals and to re-assert the control of national governments over the process (Magnette and Nicolaïdis, 2004). Nevertheless, contra the British position, when it first met under the Chair of former French President Valéry Giscard d'Estaing, he announced that,

> the Convention would try to agree on a single text rather than options, that this text would have a "constitutional" shape, that it would include all aspects of EU action even those not mentioned in the Laeken declaration, and that he understood the calendar as an indication more than as an obligation. (p. 389)

The Constitutional process was illustrative of how formal non-state processes could at times drive integration and prove difficult for governments to control. Nevertheless, Blair defended the eventual constitutional package agreed by the IGC as a victory for the nation-state against supranationalism. The British government successfully weakened the status of the Charter of Fundamental Rights in the Constitutional Treaty and trumpeted the retention of unanimous voting in areas including tax, social security, foreign and defence policy (Fella, 2006a, pp. 633–4). Additionally, the acceptance of British proposals for a President of the European Council, and for a European foreign minister under the control of the member-states, was seen as a victory for intergovernmentalism.

Meanwhile, domestic politics proved more difficult. Blair described the Constitution as 'fatally named' (2011, p. 530), creating 'a political whirlwind that blew the Prime Minister into his decision to offer a referendum' (Wall, 2008, p. 207). In the run up to the European elections in 2004, the Conservative party challenged the government over the Constitution, pledging a referendum on the issue and ruling out signing up if it was rejected by the British public. In the end, Blair announced to the House of Commons on 20 April 2004 that the government would support a referendum. This was clearly a tactical decision by a government experiencing declining poll ratings[7] with European elections on the immediate horizon and a general election in the following year. There was vehement opposition from the Eurosceptic British press as the issue grew in prominence on the domestic political scene in 2004 (Wall, 2008, p. 207). The short term promise of a referendum was a way of depoliticising the issue. This *volte face* did not, however, halt Conservative gains in the European elections, and their opposition to the Constitutional Treaty 'played a central part in their manifesto occurring as a leitmotif throughout the document' (Taggart, 2004, p. 4). Yet the election was no outright success for the Conservative party and its share of the vote suffered from the rise of the United Kingdom Independence Party (UKIP), which captured 16 per cent and increased its MEPs from 3 to 12.

---

7 By 2004 there was a marked decline in the support for the invasion of Iraq following the failure to find weapons of mass destruction, undermining the justification for war.

No votes in France and the Netherlands in May and June 2005 put an end to the Constitutional Treaty and, therefore, the British referendum. Blair recounted that 'I knew at once I was off the hook', while Jack Straw, the Foreign Secretary, described it as 'great news' (2011, p. 531). On taking over the Presidency in June 2005, the Blair government saw an opportunity for British leadership emerging out of the crisis over the Constitutional Treaty. In his speech to the European Parliament on 23 June he set out his approach to the Constitution but he also linked this to the ongoing debate and disagreements over the future of the European budget:

> It is time to give ourselves a reality check. To receive the wake-up call. The people are blowing the trumpets round the city walls. Are we listening? Have we the political will to go out and meet them so that they regard our leadership as part of the solution not the problem? That is the context in which the Budget debate should be set. People say: we need the Budget to restore Europe's credibility. Of course we do. But it should be the right Budget. It shouldn't be abstracted from the debate about Europe's crisis. It should be part of the answer to it. (Blair, 2005)

Blair proposed that political leadership within Europe would be brought back in line with people's concerns when it was recognised that their disillusionment was not about the 'idea of Europe' but the changes in their economies and societies: 'traditional communities are broken up, ethnic patterns change, family life is under strain as families struggle to balance work and home'. The solution was not institutional change but to confront the problems that people faced and help them better cope with globalisation, 'embrace its opportunities and avoid its dangers'. The themes were familiar ones: an open, competitive and enlarged EU that cooperated to confront crime, security and immigration. Britain was once again presented as the exemplar of modernisation to be followed with its strong economy, active labour markets and high levels of public investment.

While Blair's speech was well received across Europe, it was overshadowed by the debate over the European budget and the reform of the Common Agricultural Policy. As we have seen, the British contribution to the European budget had been a longstanding and difficult issue for successive governments. What is more, the British rebate secured by Thatcher in 1983 had, in the words of Blair, 'become part of hallowed mythology' (2011, p. 535). The Labour government was faced with a situation where, particularly with enlargement, the British rebate was evidently unfair to other member-states; however, as Blair continued: 'none of this mattered in the UK debate. The rebate was untouchable. To question it was to betray the nation. To analyse the figures was itself to push Britain down the slippery slope' (p. 535).

On the eve of its Presidency of the European Union, the British government found itself isolated when it attempted to defend the rebate. France and Germany were joined in their opposition by the new EU states from Central and Eastern Europe, whose membership Britain had so vigorously supported. Blair's defiant approach culminated in the breakdown of negotiations at the Luxembourg summit in June 2005. It was a position criticised by Robin Cook, the former Foreign Secretary, who sensed that the Prime Minister was trying to appease the forces of domestic Euroscepticism:

> In domestic politics, isolation in Europe fans the flames of Euroscepticism. Anyone who doubts that we are playing with fire has only to look at how the rightwing press gloated over the failure of the summit. The Sun celebrated with a "Hallelujah" (yes, truly) that we are all Eurosceptics now and claimed "it is possible to imagine Britain outside the European Union". Those who would most rejoice if that came about would be the neocons in Washington, for whom preventing the emergence of a united Europe as a rival to US influence is an explicit policy objective. The patriotic agenda that the Sun advocates is an American one, not a British one.(Cook, 2005)

Cook had become increasingly critical of the party leadership approach to Europe, which he saw as a move away from the European social democratic vision that had been central to the party's modernisation (Fella, 2006b).[8] Yet a Eurosceptic nationalism was integral to New Labour's European strategy. It became essential for neutralising the press and maintaining the support of the Murdoch empire. This depended on asserting a vision of an Anglo-Europe, rooted in an Anglo-American approach to globalisation, and with it a revival of British influence and leadership in the EU. During the Constitution process and the budgetary dispute this proved difficult to sustain. On the Constitution, the government was initially outflanked by a more federalist agenda and, in the end, only saved by the French and Dutch *No* votes. On the budgetary issue, the British government was seen to be pursuing a nationalist agenda that left it isolated. When the negotiations were concluded in December 2005, it was forced to concede a reduction in the rebate that was seized upon by the Eurosceptic press. The *Daily Mail* (2005) referred to a 'spectacular European U-turn by surrendering more than £1 billion a year from Britain's rebate'.

The Lisbon Treaty

Following the failure of the Constitutional Treaty, the European Union declared a 'period of reflection'. A consultation process was then initiated under the German Presidency at the start of 2007. The British Minister for Europe, Geoff Hoon, set out the government's approach in December 2006. Echoing Blair's speech to the European Parliament, his opening remarks referred to the need to equip Europeans 'to maximise the opportunities (and minimise the risks) that globalisation presents' (*Hansard*, Vol. 454, Col. 10–11WS). The British focus was to be on delivering practical benefits to citizens based on prosperity and security.

---

8 Also see Clark (2005).

The national interest was presented in terms of Britain's role as a 'strong, confident and influential European power that can help to lead reform and modernisation' (*Hansard*, Vol. 454, Col. 10–11WS). Hoon's statement confirmed the view that the constitutional crisis was viewed as an opportunity to bring the EU agenda back into line with more pragmatic British concerns. The overriding concern of the government was to ensure that any reform process based on the Constitutional Treaty should proceed along traditional intergovernmental lines of an amending treaty (Blair, 2012). The aim was to regain governmental control over the process and to ensure that any new treaty could be presented as a very different being to the Constitutional Treaty, therefore not requiring a referendum. In preparation for his final European Council in June 2007, Blair set out the British 'red lines' for negotiations, including not accepting any changes to British law following from the Charter of Fundamental Rights; any displacement of British control over foreign policy, the common law and judicial and policy systems; and resistance to further moves to qualified majority voting that might impact on the tax and benefit system (Tempest, 2007). Moreover, he made it clear that Europe did not need a constitution or a treaty that resembled a constitution. The British government then allied itself with those countries (Poland and the Czech Republic) who wanted to see a minimalist treaty, setting out a position that was more hard-line than it had adopted over the Constitutional Treaty (Blair, 2012). The German Presidency made it clear that the decision to replace the Constitutional Treaty already represented a major concession considering that it had been ratified by 18 countries. Nevertheless, British demands were sufficiently met to enable Blair to announce to the House of Commons on 25 June that as a consequence of securing its 'opt-outs' no referendum was necessary.

On the 27 June, Brown replaced Blair as Prime Minister. While the position adopted was similar to his predecessor, Brown took some time to agree to the final text, to the point where his fellow Heads of Government grew increasingly impatient with him (Seldon and Lodge, 2011, p. 166). The Brown government finalised the content of the Treaty: all references to EU symbols, such as the flag and the anthem were removed, the Charter of Fundamental Rights was given far less prominence and was not domestically binding, and a right to opt out of justice and home affairs was included. Nevertheless, the Treaty of Lisbon incorporated key aspects of the Constitutional Treaty, notably the establishment of a President of the European Council and a new post of High Representative combining the existing roles of foreign and external affairs. What is more, the power of the European Parliament was increased, placing it on an equal footing with the Council of Ministers, which in turn saw an extension of the use of qualified majority voting.

Despite the clear similarities between the treaties, the British government was determined to present Lisbon as a clean break with the Constitution and close down the domestic debate on the new Treaty. Preceding and during the negotiations, the then Foreign Secretary, Margaret Beckett, maintained virtual public and parliamentary silence on the issue (Blair, 2012). When the new Foreign Secretary, David Miliband, came to give evidence to the House of Commons

European Scrutiny Committee (2007) in October, he made it clear that the 'period of reflection' had brought to an end the debate over whether the EU was developing into a 'super-state' or continuing to be a 'coalition of nation-states': 'It does end that debate in favour of not just the British vision of the future of the EU but other countries as well'.

By the time Brown replaced Blair, the discourse of 'enlightened patriotism' was exhausted. Daddow points out that by his third term Blair had all but given up trying to persuade the country of the case for Europe (2012, p. 15). For Brown the case for Britain in Europe was pragmatic and realist, but also more sharply ideological in a negative sense than was the case for Blair. His willingness to adopt the Eurosceptic language of a dystopian 'European super-state' should be viewed alongside his assertions of Britishness as an expression of liberty, pluralism, and a moral civil society (Lee, 2006). In this endeavour he did not look to the European social democratic tradition but drew moral inspiration from English and Scottish liberalism, and North American conceptions of civil society. Indeed, both Brown and Miliband privileged Anglo-Americanism as central to British political identity; Britain 'was locked in a values-based relationship with the US but it was merely a run-of-the-mill, interest-based member of the EU' (Daddow, 2011, p. 251). Seldon and Lodge point out that Brown did not regard Europe as a 'united entity' but as a 'confederation of individual states', treating it 'as a series of floating alliances on different issues', and 'he doubted even whether the European Commission needed to exist' (2011, pp. 163–4).

The construction of Europe in terms of pragmatic interests was therefore dependent on resisting, if not denying, an EU based on values and identity. On this view, the Lisbon Treaty was firmly in the British interest because it prevented the emergence of a European super-state. Unsurprisingly, Eurosceptics came to precisely the opposite conclusion. The Bruges Group launched a campaign against the Treaty on the basis that it was no different to what had been proposed in the Constitution. With the possibility that Brown might call an election, the Conservative leadership seized the opportunity to rally Eurosceptics. In an article in *The Sun*, Cameron made a clear commitment that a Conservative government would hold a referendum on the Lisbon Treaty:

> Today, I will give this cast-iron guarantee: If I become PM a Conservative government will hold a referendum on any EU treaty that emerges from these negotiations. No treaty should be ratified without consulting the British people in a referendum. (cited in Watt and Wintour, 2009)

The decision of Brown not to call an election in the autumn of 2007 severely damaged the government and left a lasting impression that the Brown government was weak and incapable of controlling the political agenda. This seemed to be confirmed by the European summit in December, when heads of governments gathered to sign the finalised version of the Lisbon Treaty. Brown was the only one who did not attend, delayed for the signing by an appearance at the Parliamentary

Liaison Committee. While initially claiming it was a diary mix-up, members of his team briefed *The Sun* that it was a deliberate snub to other EU leaders (Seldon and Lodge, 2011, p. 169). Once in Lisbon it was clear that Brown was considered to have damaged the reputation of the EU.

Notwithstanding successes in the negotiations, the Constitutional and Lisbon processes were indicative of the continued structural difficulties of the British governing approach to Europe. A powerful drive for further institutional reform, contested by the forces of domestic Euroscepticism, once again challenged the idea that the politics of Europe could be contained by British governing elites.

The Financial Crisis: Saints and Sinners

At the start of Brown's premiership, the global economy began to falter. This initially became apparent in the US housing market when, in the first half of 2007, prices started falling and there were a record numbers of defaults on subprime loans (those with no or poor credit histories). The reasons for this included a sharp rise in interest rates in the US in response to a falling dollar and rising inflation (Hay, 2011, p. 10–11). As subprime mortgages had become part of structured finance worldwide this quickly impacted on the global banking system. Importantly it occurred in a context in which banks were already highly leveraged and dependent on short term funding markets. By August 2007, credit markets were facing severe liquidity problems as the risks of lending increased exponentially. On 10 August the FTSE 100 faced its biggest drop in four years and on 14 and 15 August, the Governor of the Bank England, Mervyn King, and the Chancellor, Alistair Darling, were informed that Northern Rock was in difficulties. By the middle of September, it had asked for emergency assistance from the Bank of England and, when the news broke, customers queued to take their money out of branches. The situation settled down when Darling confirmed that the government would guarantee 100 per cent of deposits, but it was a foretaste of what was to come and signalled the onset of the financial crisis in Britain.

By the beginning of 2008, it was clear that the period of uninterrupted economic growth over which Labour had presided was coming to an end. Alistair Darling describes the approach of the government from this point, as essentially supporting the economy through recession and then to cut the deficit once growth was re-established (2011, p. 71). By August 2008 he told *The Guardian* that the economy was at a 'sixty-year low' and the downturn would be 'more profound and long-lasting' than many had feared (Watt, 2008). By the Autumn the entire British banking system was at risk, as the shockwaves from the collapse of Lehman Brothers began to be felt. Most dramatically, the Royal Bank of Scotland's share price collapsed and dealings in its shares were suspended. It was a pivotal moment, as Darling recalled: 'the game was up. If the markets could give up on RBS, one of the world's largest banks, all bets on Britain's and the world's financial system were off' (2011, p. 225). On 13 October, the Chancellor made a statement to the

House of Commons announcing an emergency rescue plan for the banking system, including recapitalisation of Halifax Bank of Scotland, Lloyds TSB and Royal Bank of Scotland, with the government taking a substantial shareholding in all three. Additionally, the government agreed to provide liquidity to the banking system to £200 billion and to underwrite any borrowing between banks.

The globalisation of the British economy, which had become so central to New Labour's programme, was acutely exposed by the financial crisis. The British government's rescue plan prevented the full scale economic collapse of a national economy that would have had profound global implications. Brown's claims that he had established a successful British model of political economy unravelled in 2008. There was negative growth in the second half of the year, indicating that the economy entered an official recession, the housing market slowed, inflation rose and there were sharp monthly increases in unemployment. The CBI reported a dramatic decline in business confidence to its lowest point since 1980 (Wearden and Seager, 2008). By October, there was 'frantic' selling of sterling as it reached a five year low against the dollar. In a series of interventions in 2008, the influential economist Willem Buiter (2008) argued that Britain was exceptionally vulnerable to financial crisis and that the government should immediately consider entering the Eurozone. Buiter argued that 'it is not much of an exaggeration to describe the UK as a giant hedge fund, a highly leveraged entity borrowing shorter than it lends and invests'. In the absence of a reserve currency, yet with external liabilities of well over 400 per cent of GDP, Britain was at risk of a triple financial crisis: banking, currency and sovereign debt. He drew parallels between it and Iceland in terms of its external exposure and the size of the financial sector. In such a situation financial security for Britain would be best achieved by the protection provided by the Euro because of its role as a reserve currency. His arguments were echoed by Will Hutton (2008) who argued that the Euro may be the only way for Britain to avoid national bankruptcy.

In the end the Euro option was kept off the agenda as a consequence of the timeliness and effectiveness of the government's response. Moreover, in the context of the crisis that was manifestly not contained to Britain, the opportunity arose for the Brown government to reconstruct itself as a global policy entrepreneur. On 12 October, Brown was invited to attend a meeting of the Eurogroup where a concerted action plan was agreed, which was subsequently endorsed at the European Council meeting a few days later. Notwithstanding the considerable degree of national discretion allowed for in the proposals, the British approach was the template (Quaglia, 2009, p. 1080).

The opportunity for global leadership once again arose when it was agreed that London would host the G20 at the beginning of April 2009. In the run up to this meeting, Brown embarked on a series of foreign visits to win support for the British approach to the crisis. He argued that governments should not only provide the resources necessary to keep the financial system viable but increase the rate of stimulus in order to generate growth. The summit was viewed as a success for the Prime Minister, who secured a commitment of one trillion dollars to restore liquidity and support growth in the world economy, together with agreements on financial regulation and continued support for developing countries. An expression of collective political leadership underpinned by substantive agreement was welcomed by the markets. However, the belief that the summit implied a strong consensus in support of Brown's Keynesian approach to the crisis was questionable. The German and French governments took some persuasion to agree to the final communiqué. Both viewed the crisis as a product of Anglo-Saxon deregulation of the financial markets and Merkel, in particular, was reluctant to commit to anything that implied fiscal profligacy. In the end, European commitments to fiscal stimulus were small, particularly when compared to the US.

By 2009 the focus of the markets on government debt ran counter to arguments for increased economic stimulus. In November 2009, the new Greek socialist government came under scrutiny by the markets and by December it was clear that it had debts of 300 billion Euros, 113 per cent of GDP and nearly twice the Eurozone limit. The consequence was a downgrading of Greek government debt by credit agencies in December, unsustainable debt funding costs and, by May 2010, the implementation of a 110 billion IMF/EU rescue package conditional on major cuts in government spending.

The problems of debt within the Eurozone had been masked by a relatively benign environment up until the crisis of 2007. In fact huge trade and capital imbalances had built up between countries on the periphery (Ireland, Greece, Portugal and Spain) relative to the core (above all Germany). Unable to compete with the core, economic growth of the periphery increasingly depended on consumption and asset bubbles. The deregulation and integration of finance provided easy credit, resulting in large rises in corporate and household indebtedness. What is more, it enabled the fiscal positions of debtor states to be disguised by complex forms of securitisation (Dyson, 2010, p. 604). In all this, the risks normally associated with high levels of debt were ameliorated by the Eurozone's low interest rate and, ultimately, the strength of the euro as a global currency.

The crisis in the Eurozone was significant in shifting the focus of the financial crisis away from the global banking system towards problem states. The relationships between states in the Eurozone were reconfigured in terms of their status as creditors and debtors, or 'saints' and 'sinners', with power firmly in the hands of the former (p. 598). From this perspective the overriding problem was considered to be those countries with high levels of debt, and the solution was tighter surveillance and tougher sanctions (p. 604). The aim was to re-establish the guiding principles of EMU of sound money and sound finance that had been enshrined in the Maastricht Treaty and underpinned the European Central Bank. The emerging European response to the Greek crisis signalled a change from stimulus towards austerity as the hegemonic policy response.

The Eurozone crisis became a powerful reference point in British politics that proved decisive for the Labour government. In March 2009, the IMF released figures showing that Britain was heading for the worst fiscal deficit of the G7 at £165 billion; by the time of the pre-budget report in April it was actually £175 billion

(Seldon and Lodge, 2011, p. 684). The media began to focus on British debt levels, while the government grew increasingly concerned about market confidence (p. 684). The deficit was used by the Conservatives to attack Labour's record, particularly Brown's claims to prudence and sound financial management. The Conservatives dropped a proposal to match Labour's spending plans by 2008. In a speech to the Birmingham Chamber of Commerce, Cameron made a clean break with the economic policies of the New Labour years, apologising for Conservative complacency about debt and attacking an unbalanced economy characterised by unsustainable levels of debt and a massive welfare burden (Winnett, 2009). At the same time there were growing tensions inside government, as the Chancellor became exasperated with Brown's refusal to acknowledge the extent of the debt problem, to publicly acknowledge the necessity of cuts, and over optimistic growth forecasts (Darling, 2011, pp. 327–8). Seldon argues that the Treasury increasingly viewed Brown as wedded to Keynesianism and the belief that 'salvation would come from still further stimulus' (2011, p. 686). By the time of the 2010 election campaign, Brown had accepted the necessity of significant constraints on spending, but a core element of Labour's attack was the risked posed to economic recovery by Tory cuts. Meanwhile, on Channel 4 News, David Cameron compared Britain to Greece in his attacks on the government:

> This year, actually, we are borrowing more as a percentage of GDP than the Greeks are. Of course there are differences between Britain and Greece and you can see that in all sorts of ways. But Greece stands as a warning to what happens if you don't pay back your debts.[9]

Cameron's remarks were not just politicking but reflected the growing fear in the markets and amongst financial elites that Greece would spread contagion across Europe. Hence, when the British election result failed to produce a clear victory for any party, there was concern within the civil service that a prolonged negotiation would lead to market volatility. Sir Gus O'Donnell, the Cabinet Secretary, encouraged the Conservative and Liberal Democrat leaders to swiftly produce the most comprehensive agreement possible with the awareness that if they didn't the markets would make them pay the price. The 'instability in the markets' and the fear that what was unfolding in Greece and southern Europe could 'spread' to Britain was the context within which the Coalition agreement was negotiated (House of Commons Political and Constitutional Reform Committee, 2011, Ev. 4).

Conclusion

At the outset, the New Labour government was committed to the Europeanisation of British politics, which was consistent with the Third Way and its understanding

---

9 28 April 2010.

of globalisation. It was prepared to transfer policy competences to the European level and negotiated a reduced role for national governments in decision-making. However, this was devised to be consistent with traditional expressions of national interest and assertions of British power and influence. Indeed, Labour in power was more influential than any British government since the single market had been negotiated under Thatcher. In this respect, traditional diplomacy was very important and Labour oversaw the intensification of bilateral relations and negotiations. However, an approach that emphasised pragmaticism and 'realpolitik' was at the same time intensely ideological in terms of what came to be excluded. While interests could be Europeanised, values and identity for the most part could not. Instead, British/global values were constituted as essentially different from what Europe was at the time, although they were considered to be fundamental to what Europe could and should be. The latter meant Europe letting go of out of date welfarism, supranationalism and lack of openness to the rest of world. In this sense, Labour's *janus-faced* approach to the EU was not evidence of political inconsistency or confusion because the relationship between its Europeanism and its Euroscepticism was a necessary one. Its Europeanism was dependent on the capacity to influence European agendas and pursue British interests that could be presented as a reforming Anglo-Europe. This proved to be a very difficult circle to square, particularly when it came to the complexity and messiness of the Constitution and Lisbon processes. In a context in which integration continued apace and the Blair and Brown governments struggled to contain developments, the opportunity for Eurosceptic mobilisation once again arose. Developments were overshadowed by the 2008 financial crisis, which saw the Brown government exploit a new opportunity for British influence but, in the end, founder in the face of the ascendancy of austerity agendas. By the end of Labour's time in office, a Europeanisation of British politics had occurred, but one that was very different from that envisaged by Blair in 1997. On this view, Labour had put Britain at risk of becoming akin to a Eurozone 'sinner' state, only to be redeemed from the punishment of the markets by a Coalition government committed to cuts and deficit reduction. Europe emerged, once again, as the economic 'other' from which Britain had to be firmly kept apart. The remaking of Eurosceptic Britain was evident throughout Labour's period in office, but the economic crisis provided a new dynamic to its course that, as we will see, fully manifested in the populist Eurosceptic opposition to the Coalition government.

Chapter 8
The Eurosceptic Challenge to the Coalition Government

Introduction

The formation of a Coalition government in May 2010 brought together two parties, Conservatives and Liberal Democrats, with seemingly very different positions on Europe. In opposition, Euroscepticism was consolidated as the mainstream position within the Conservative party as the influence of Europhiles (Heseltine, Clarke, Patten) waned. Despite Cameron's modernisation agenda, he signalled his support for this trajectory by withdrawing Conservative MEPs from the main centre-right grouping (the European People's Party-European Democrats) and having them join the more marginal European Conservatives and Reformists. The damaging splits in the party of the Major era appeared to have been resolved in favour of the Eurosceptics. The party entered the 2010 election committed to a repatriation of powers and having ruled out membership of the Euro indefinitely. In contrast, the Liberal Democrats, under the former MEP Nick Clegg, were considered the most pro-European of the three main parties, with a manifesto stating that membership of the Euro continued to be in Britain's long term interests.

Nevertheless, Europe was not an insurmountable issue for party leaders when it came to negotiating the Coalition agreement. In fact, both parties appeared to have accepted the Brown government's pragmatic and realist approach to the EU; moreover, they were increasingly aligned on the referendum issue. Following Hague's failure to turn Europe into a popular cause in the 2001 election, the Conservative party had gradually moved to a position that was 'harder but quieter', which for the most part played down the issue (Bale, 2006, p. 388). The party leadership clearly viewed a virulent, ideological Euroscepticism as a barrier to electoral success and to reclaiming the centre ground of British politics from Labour. The decision not to pursue a referendum on the Lisbon Treaty was crucial in this respect, as it denied an opportunity for Eurosceptics to mobilise and once again put Europe centre stage.[1] As for the Liberal Democrats, they had not supported the initial Conservative calls for a referendum on Lisbon; however, they were committed to an IN/OUT referendum on any further transfer of power that meant the Conservative policy of a 'referendum lock' was unproblematic. Neither was the Euro a sticking point, the crisis in the Eurozone having left little space for

---

1 Albeit reinforcing a sense of betrayal by Cameron of the Eurosceptic cause following his 'cast iron guarantee' of a referendum. See Chapter 7.

Liberal Democrats to make the progressive case for membership. It was ruled out in the Coalition agreement for the duration of the parliament, as was any repatriation of powers. Most importantly, underlying the formal policy agreements was the consensus between the party leaders that the Eurozone crisis was an immediate threat to British political and economic survival and that austerity policies were a necessity. The change in position by the leaders of the Liberal Democrats on cuts was decisive in sealing the Coalition agreement which, while a response to events, also reflected the dominance of its centre-right leadership. Overall, notwithstanding the novelty of a British Coalition government, the structural and contingent factors at work in its formation enabled a governing elite to emerge that was remarkably consistent with the British political tradition.

The Coalition may have necessitated pragmatism; however, this was never likely to satisfy many Conservatives, which now included many of the 2010 intake of MPs for whom Euroscepticism was a matter of political faith. A parliamentary Eurosceptic opposition to the Coalition's European policy was quick to mobilise. However, echoing previous mobilisations, it was part of a broader based movement on the right of British politics that included the press, think tanks, interest and pressure groups and organisations. Of particular note was the continued rise of UKIP, providing a purer and harder Eurosceptic alternative to the Conservatives. The defining feature of this mobilisation was, once again, the populist re-working of British identity and interests, embodied in notions of sovereignty and 'the people', as antithetical to European integration, together with the targeting of governing elite policy towards the EU. A Conservative leadership compromised by being in Coalition, together with the Eurozone crisis and the emerging integrationist response, provided a unique opportunity for right wing Euroscepticism.

This chapter examines the Eurosceptic challenge to the Coalition government from 2010 to the end of 2013. It is viewed as a profound reassertion of Eurosceptic Britain, shaping agendas in a way that successfully establishes exit from the EU as part of the mainstream political debate.

Eurosceptic Mobilisation

A central plank of the Conservative party's Eurosceptic policy agenda, the 2010 European Union Bill, became the basis for a Eurosceptic rebellion, even though its objective was to demonstrate that the Tory leadership shared 'the rank and file's concern over the salami-slicing of Britain's sovereignty' (*The Daily Telegraph*, 2011). The Bill proposed to legislate for three coalition commitments: first, the 'referendum lock' required any future treaties transferring national powers to the European level to be subject to a referendum; second, significant transfers of power without treaty change, so called 'ratchet clauses', may also be subject to a referendum, an Act of Parliament or a parliamentary vote; third, the Bill introduced a sovereignty clause that attempted to counter claims that the EU represents a higher, autonomous legal order by stating the supremacy of parliament with regard to EU law.

During the Bill's passage, the veteran Eurosceptic, Bill Cash, was Chair of the European Scrutiny Committee, despite David Cameron's attempt to block the appointment. Cash oversaw a forensic examination of the Bill, which thoroughly critiqued its claims to 'lock' governments into a referendum on further integration; the argument was that the Bill contained significant exemptions that allowed governments to agree major changes without calling a referendum. Moreover, the House of Commons European Scrutiny Committee (2010) warned that reaffirmation of parliamentary sovereignty was an insufficient protection against the dominance of European law and its enforcement through the Courts by judicial activism. It concluded that the sovereignty clause simply re-stated the existing position regarding the legal relationship between parliament and the EU, which is that a treaty agreed by a government only comes into force once it is ratified by parliament. A particular concern for Cash was that the clause claimed that sovereignty was a common law principle and therefore subject to judicial authority. He proposed an amendment reaffirming parliamentary sovereignty as a legal and historic fact, which was backed by 27 Conservative MPs in January 2011.

In the autumn of 2011 the European budget issue came to the fore. Cash was supported in the October by the whips with his amendment rejecting the European Parliament's call for an increase. Another, proposed by Douglas Carswell and calling for the government to reduce British contributions, was not so fortunate but was, nevertheless, supported by 37 Conservative MPs. On this vote there was intensive activity by the whips reflecting the growing concern over Eurosceptic dissent during 2011 (Lynch, 2012, p. 85). The extent to which party discipline was breaking down over Europe was evident when the backbencher David Nuttall secured a Commons vote on a referendum on EU membership on 25 October. This followed the People's Pledge campaign that achieved 100,000 signatories on the government's e-petition site, therefore giving the issue parliamentary time under the new online initiative in public engagement. While the vote would not have affected government policy directly, a three line whip was imposed on Conservative MPs in a failed attempt to reassert party discipline. In the end, 81 Conservative MPs defied the whip, thus making it the largest rebellion ever by Conservatives on Europe. In defying the party leadership, Eurosceptics claimed popular legitimacy. Nuttall spoke of the 'the *vast* majority of the British people' wanting a vote in a referendum as evidenced by petitions and opinion polls (*Hansard*, Vol. 534, Col. 46).

The populist campaign for a referendum was successful in uniting MPs with different positions on Europe. Lynch and Whitaker noted that Conservative Eurosceptics were to be 'found along a spectrum ranging from outright rejectionists (favouring withdrawal), to maximalist revisionists (favouring a "Norway plus" relationship based on free trade and the single market), minimalist revisionists (favouring a limited repatriation of competences), and minimalists taking a "this far but no further" position' (2012a, p. 3). Notwithstanding these differences, the overall trajectory was a hardening of Euroscepticism in comparison to the Maastricht rebellions discussed in Chapter 6. Notably, Europhiles such as Ken

Clarke occupied a marginal position in the debate, having moderated their enthusiasm for the EU and accommodated to their party's Eurosceptic trajectory (Lynch, 2012, p. 86). This meant the right and centre-right of British politics was increasingly dominated by discourses that challenged the legitimacy of integration, whether or not this meant supporting complete British withdrawal. This ran counter to the governing position that Labour had defended while in office, which, for the most part, accepted the reality of integration as an ongoing process within which Britain could achieve a progressive accommodation. The challenge to the governing position on Europe was already signalled by the European Union Act, but it was reinforced by Eurosceptic mobilisation against the Coalition's depoliticised approach to the EU. Many Eurosceptics simply did not trust the Coalition government on the issue, believing that it would continue to allow Britain to be drawn deeper into a unified Europe, without being subject to domestic political accountability. Indeed, Douglas Carswell at one point complained that the government was the most pro-European since Heath (p. 86). The likelihood of elite betrayal remained a fundamental tenet of populist Euroscepticism.

By the time the Coalition was in power, Britain had witnessed a proliferation of Eurosceptic campaign groups and think tanks. Some were long standing, while others had been formed with the expectation of a referendum on the Euro or the Constitution. Some were directly linked to leading Eurosceptics in Westminster, such as the 'Better off Out' campaign for withdrawal and the influential Bruges Group, while others were closer to business such as the research based organisation OpenEurope and Business for Britain. Although predominantly a Conservative initiative, the Fresh Start Project was established in 2011 to work across party lines and with civil society organisations to push forward the case for the repatriation of powers, stating that 'our citizens want more control over their own lives'.[2] While many of these groupings were dominated by Eurosceptic Conservative MPs and politicians, their 'political party-ness' was often obscured by them being defined as cross-party and including the involvement of non party political figures, as well as figures from marginal parties (Usherwood, 2002, p. 223). Moreover, their partial externalisation to party politics was strategically important as they must at times be prepared to openly criticise and mobilise against the leadership because of the fundamental nature of the European issue. While they were neither continuously nor necessarily openly hostile, often looking to influence rather than undermine their leaders, their support was conditional and the European issue defined their relationship with government, even when they themselves were members of that government. Such groupings were central to building the capacity of Eurosceptics to mount sophisticated challenges to government policy. As Forster points out, the 'watershed' moment in this respect was Maastricht, since when Eurosceptic groupings developed a significantly improved 'capacity to provide autonomous analysis of policy-making, decisions and Treaty outcomes' (2002, p. 28).

---

2   See www.eufreshtstart.org.

The referendum campaign was indicative of the extent to which Euroscepticism was firmly established as a broad-based movement that could not be contained within the parliamentary arena. In this regard, Fitzgibbon (2013) demonstrated how civil society organisations became experts in mobilising publics on European issues, exploiting political opportunities and claiming to directly represent 'the people' on Europe. These actors positioned themselves outside of the political system, distrustful of its ability to represent their case, and have been at their most effective in making the referendum case (p. 115). By the time of the Coalition government they included 'I Want a Referendum', 'Vote UK out of the EU' and 'The People's Pledge'. While their focus was on establishing national campaigns for a referendum, they were for the most part motivated by the desire to see British withdrawal.

A hard Eurosceptic campaign for a referendum found support in the British press. Most notably *The Daily Express* launched a high profile populist campaign to 'get the UK out of the EU'. Meanwhile, the right wing press more generally stepped up the pressure for a redrawing of Britain's relationship with the EU, supporting calls for a referendum (*The Telegraph*, *The Daily Mail*, *The Daily Express*). Hawkins (2012) summarised the way in which the Eurosceptic discourse of the British right wing press had become organised around two principle themes: first, the view of the EU as a foreign power from which Britain is both separate and excluded, and secondly, the perspective of European politics as a zero-sum game in which Britain is presented as failing to protect its interests in face of a Franco-German dominated core Europe. Underlying this was a meta-narrative of the national political community as an essential and organic unity 'and thus the nation-state is the optimal form of political organization, buttressed by the shared identity which binds co-nationals together' (p. 569). Conversely, European integration represented an artificial ideal imposed on people against their wishes by utopian elites (p. 570). While the left wing press (*The Guardian*, *The Observer*, *The Mirror*) provided a counter-discourse, it was reactive to the dominant Eurosceptic agenda.

From inside the party system, UKIP was defined by its populist opposition to the mainstream parties and their elites. These were presented as undifferentiated ('LibLabCon') because of their continued support, no matter how qualified, for EU membership. Hence UKIP exploited its outsider status, appealing directly to voters disillusioned with the mainstream parties (Lynch and Whitaker, 2012b). It claimed to offer a purer Eurosceptic alternative to a Conservative party tainted by the compromises of government. Its rise, already evident in the winning of 12 seats in the 2004 European election, was confirmed by by-elections in 2012 and the extraordinary local elections results of 2013 when it captured 139 seats and a quarter of the vote. A crucial factor in broadening its appeal was its ability to position itself to the right of the Conservative leadership on issues such as same sex marriage. On immigration, it connected a salient public issue with EU membership, as free movement was opened up to those from the new member states of Bulgaria and Romania. Inferring from opinion poll results and anecdotally evidencing the deeply felt concerns and anxieties of 'the British people', the rise of UKIP consolidated a populist right-wing agenda fundamentally defined by its opposition to the European project. The difficulty posed by UKIP for the Conservative leadership was that, as Bale and Webb (2013) argued, many Conservative members and supporters were ideologically closer to UKIP than to their own party leaders.

By 2012 a hard Eurosceptic movement that cut across party lines was increasingly shaping the agenda on Europe. *Political Quarterly* noted that 'these radical Eurosceptics are the closest thing Britain has to the Tea Party. They cluster particularly thickly in the United Kingdom Independence party, but their tentacles also reach deep into the Conservative party' (Anon, 2012, pp. 1–3). It was this hard ideological Euroscepticism that had entered the British political mainstream. Ford summarised the situation as follows:

> In short, over the past decade it has become much easier for radical right politicians to argue that Europe is 'the problem'; the source of immigration threatening British jobs and cultural identity, the source of judicial rulings protecting terrorists and criminals who threaten British safety, the source of a corrupt and self-serving elite political culture, and the source of endless rules and legislation limiting British sovereignty and threatening British identity. (2012)

The mobilisation by Eurosceptics in opposition to the Coalition government demonstrated the extent to which Euroscepticism had become an *underpinning populist ideology* for a significant section of the British right. In so doing, core political constructs, such as the nation, sovereignty and 'the people', were rendered exclusive and essential. Moreover, despite employing an exclusory discourse, Eurosceptics could not be dismissed as out of touch, narrow nationalists, or 'little Englanders', as placing opposition to the EU at the forefront, their arguments and rhetoric had a particular contemporary resonance that broadened their appeal. As such, they remained open to transnational alliances, identifying with other nationally-based Eurosceptic movements. Of particular importance was the transatlantic dimension of British Euroscepticism, evident in its development in parallel with, if not close proximity to, the populist right in the US. In this regard we can point to Former Defence Secretary Liam Fox, who helped to establish close links between British politicians and American neo-conservatives through his Atlantic Bridge organisation. Fox (2012) had been particularly vocal in his attacks on the EU, which he described as 'a voraciously centralising entity – bureaucratic, expensive and wasteful – that is increasingly indifferent to if not contemptuous of ordinary Europeans'. He thus echoed the 'new sovereigntism' of influential academics and politicians in the US, who argued that emergent forms of global governance were illegitimate, undemocratic and contravene the principle of popular sovereignty (Ruggie, 2005; Goodhart and Taninchev, 2011). Global governance resulted in the ceding of power to unelected bodies, the erosion of the capacity of the state to represent the interests of 'the people' and normative commitments enshrined in international law, particularly human rights, that lacked any national constitutional basis (Goodhart and Taninchev, 2011, p. 1047). Such arguments had clear parallels with the constitutionalism of British Eurosceptics such as Bill Cash:

> Sovereignty is about giving ultimate power to the people's democratic representatives in Parliament, not to the courts and not to international bodies such as the European Union. (*Hansard*, Vol. 521, Col. 179)

This discourse of sovereigntism and its challenge to global governance became a defining feature of contemporary right wing Euroscepticism in Britain by 2013. Eurosceptic sovereigntists shared the view that European law lacked domestic legitimacy, was an affront to British parliamentary democracy and should be challenged by expressions of the popular will in referenda. In line with a broader opposition to global governance, their hostility was not confined to the EU but extended to human rights regimes such as the European Convention on Human Rights. The EU came to represent a dangerous expression of global governance, which had to be countered by a defence of national sovereignty, rooted in the democratic will of 'the people'. These themes resonated across national boundaries, enabling Eurosceptics to counter accusations of racism and xenophobia and qualifying their nationalism, evident in Fox's reference to 'ordinary Europeans'. Allegations of isolationism were further contradicted by a commitment to new economic opportunities outside of Europe; an over-regulated and crisis-ridden EU was now presented as a barrier to realising Britain's global economic potential. On this view, a more qualified defence of sovereignty, primarily concerned with securing the national interest within the existing European institutional arrangement, looked weak. Such arguments established a fundamental ideological dividing line concerning the politics of globalisation. The central proposition of this Chapter is that the Coalition government, and particularly the Conservative leadership, increasingly accommodated to this hard ideological Euroscepticism.

Vetoing the Fiscal Compact

A key focus for Eurosceptic opposition, and an opportunity around which to mobilise, continued to be the crisis within the Eurozone. While the Coalition agreement was being negotiated, Alistair Darling had attended an emergency meeting of European finance ministers in Brussels against the backdrop of the Greek crisis. While Darling refused to support any contribution to a new Eurozone support fund, earlier treaty obligations allowed member states to support each other when faced with exceptional circumstances. On this basis the European Financial Stabilisation Mechanism (EFSM) was established, together with the much larger European Financial Stabilisation Facility (EFSF) funded by the Eurozone member-states. The vote was based on a majority and therefore could not be blocked (Darling, 2011, p. 428). It left the British government liable for contributions of up to £6.6 billion towards any bailouts. Before the agreement was reached, Darling consulted Vince Cable and George Osborne and secured their agreement for his negotiating position, although this was later disputed by the new Chancellor (p. 428; Thompson, 2011, p. 3). The issue of British contributions to Eurozone bailouts was quickly picked up on by Eurosceptics when in November 2010 the Irish government was granted a £72 billion loan. Bill Cash claimed that the 'Darling guarantee mechanism with qualified majority voting involves, unnecessarily, both UK liability and sovereignty' (*Hansard*, Vol. 518, Col. 891). From the end of 2010 there was mounting opposition from Conservative Eurosceptics to government support for bailouts to the Eurozone, either via the EFSM or the IMF. In May 2011, with Portugal set to apply for support, Mark Reckless' motion called upon the government to negotiate the end of Britain's liability under the EFSM and was supported by 28 Conservative MPs. In July, 32 Conservatives joined the Labour party in opposing additional British contributions to IMF bailout funds by £9.3 billion. Commenting on the vote, the former Conservative Cabinet Minister, John Redwood, stated:

> Those in charge of the Euro scheme need to get a grip. It is doing a great deal of financial and economic damage, and they no longer seem to be in control of their project. The IMF should decline to bail out rich countries that have shackled themselves to a currency scheme that was badly put together and needs a thorough re-think. (2011)

Redwood reflected the view of many British Eurosceptics, who considered that they had been proved right in their opposition to EMU, which was now a failed project from which Britain must disentangle itself.

The Conservative leadership was therefore faced with mounting pressure from Eurosceptics to distance Britain from the Eurozone crisis. In the run up to the negotiations for a new European agreement on fiscal policy and financial regulation, Cameron declared that any new treaty would not involve any major transfer of power to the EU and therefore would not be subject to a referendum, despite claims to the contrary from Eurosceptics. The government entered negotiations having to win sufficient concessions, so that it could demonstrate the limited impact of any developments on Britain. Cameron declared that he would not sign a new treaty unless a protocol was included that re-asserted national control over further European fiscal competency and financial regulation, and provided protections to the interests of the City of London. Although presented as safeguarding the single market, Britain was viewed as seeking special arrangements. When these were rejected and Cameron vetoed a new EU treaty, Britain emerged from the negotiations isolated despite having earlier pressed its European partners to pursue further integration in the face of the crisis in the Eurozone.

The prominent role played by the Treasury in the preparation for the negotiations confirmed that the interests of finance were at the forefront of the British approach to the summit (Stephens, 2011). However, it was the combination of the defence of finance with that of sovereignty that defined the British position. The government did not demand 'opt-outs' but the right to maintain its veto in relation to those areas affecting financial services, because of its claim to vital national interests in this area. This was considered unreasonable, and at odds with negotiations that centred on a surrender of sovereignty on economic policy in the pursuit of regional macroeconomic stability (Van Rompuy, 2012). Sovereignty had become a problem, as it allowed individual member states to pursue policies that potentially undermined regional macroeconomic stability, and placed limitations on the intervention by European institutions to address member-states' structures and policies. Instead, an integrated fiscal and financial framework was initiated by the fiscal compact, which began the move towards more extensive macroeconomic governance under the increased control and surveillance of the European institutions, although there remained significant differences between the member-states on how this was to be achieved and what the end point would look like. Alongside this was the partial reversal of the liberalisation of financial markets, which had occurred as a direct result of a large body of European legislation associated with the completion of the single market (Grahl, 1997; Story and Walter, 1997). The lack of European oversight in this area meant that the stabilising objectives of EMU were from the outset compromised by the uncertainties of demand and investment that were characteristic of globally integrating financial markets. In re-regulating financial services and markets three European developments stood out: first, proposals for a single supervisory mechanism (SSM) under which all national banks would be subject to supervision of the European Central Bank by 2014; second, revisions to European financial service regulations would enforce transparency in the 'dark pools' of liquidity within the derivatives trading system that involve multiple third party interests; finally, controversial proposals for a European Financial levy that would tax trade in bonds and derivatives, which was given the go ahead by 11 Eurozone members in January 2013. The latter was designed to curb the excessive cross-border activities that were seen to have contributed most to the financial crisis. From the British perspective, the transaction tax was indicative of the potential threat to City interests posed by European reforms.

The British government vetoed the final agreement for a fiscal compact when its demands for retaining national control in the areas of financial regulation were not met. However this did not prevent treaty negotiations from going ahead, albeit nominally outside of the European Union, thereby excluding Britain from further negotiations. It was therefore a decision that marginalised British influence, in which an overt expression of sovereignty was viewed as consistent with the defence of economic interests. This was questionable, not least for many in the City who saw in the government's position an explicit loss of influence, as a Senior Credit Executive at Norddeutsche Landesbank pointed out: 'the City can only maintain its ascendancy in financial services if the UK is a committed member of the European Union' (Brown, 2011, p.12). The limitations of the veto became fully apparent when a new intergovernmental treaty went ahead using

EU institutions without Britain's involvement. In vetoing, the British government therefore appeared to pursue a narrow conception of the national interest over an issue that seemed to merit a more flexible approach.

The veto challenged the Coalition compromise on Europe. While initially backing Cameron's position, Nick Clegg later criticised him for leaving Britain isolated as a consequence of diplomatic incompetence. Nevertheless, the veto was met with jubilation on the part of Eurosceptics at home and opinion polls indicated support for Cameron's position. This short respite from European troubles signalled to the Conservative leadership that it was possible to regain the political initiative on Europe. By early summer 2012, Cameron (2012) announced that there would be a 'national audit' reviewing the balance of EU competences 'to spell out in more detail the parts of our European engagement we want and those that we want to end'. The review was presented by William Hague (2012) as a 'serious British contribution to the public debate across Europe about how the EU can be reformed, modernised and improved'. Yet it clearly raised the issue of the legitimacy of the EU in the national context and the possibility of a repatriation of powers. Hague referred directly to the disillusionment of 'the people' with Europe and their experience of integration as 'a one way process, a great machine that sucks up decision-making from national parliaments to the European level until everything is decided by the EU'. The leadership therefore responded to the Eurosceptic challenge by shifting in a more Eurosceptic direction and intensifying its own populist rhetoric. Yet without a commitment to a referendum, it was clear by the end of 2012 that divisions on Europe would continue to have the potential to derail the Cameron leadership.

Cameron's Bloomberg Speech

In a long awaited speech at Bloomberg in London in January 2013, Cameron (2013) finally set out his position on the future of Britain's role in Europe. He argued that a renegotiated relationship could be agreed as part of a new European settlement that was necessary as the EU was being transformed by the crisis in the Eurozone. This would be a flexible and open Europe that would keep Britain in the EU but out of the fiscal compact, and would include a repatriation of powers to Westminster. The 2015 Conservative Manifesto would therefore ask for a mandate to pursue a new European settlement that would be presented to the British public in a referendum by 2017.

Cameron's speech was an attempt to regain the political initiative by asserting a revised governing position on Europe. In his essentialist assertions of national identity, Cameron presented a classic defence of British exceptionalism:

> We have the character of an island nation – independent, forthright and passionate in defence of our sovereignty. We can no more change this British sensibility than we can drain the English Channel. And because of this sensibility, we

come to the European Union with a frame of mind that is more practical than emotional. (2013)

This British 'national character', defined by its openness, independence and pragmatism, was the starting point for outlining a distinctly British vision of a 'flexible, adaptable and open European Union'. This 'flexible union' was to have the single market as its central focus, overseen by 'free member-states who share treaties and institutions and pursue together the ideal cooperation'. Hence it was this British vision he claimed could underpin a new European settlement and, notably, challenge the fundamental principle of integration: 'ever close union among the peoples of Europe'. In the end it was only national parliaments that could command democratic authority. European institutions were over-extended, beyond what was legitimate and consequently powers had to be returned.

In challenging both the constitutional and popular bases of the EU, Cameron aligned himself with a harder Euroscepticism. Nevertheless, at the same, he attempted to present a constructive vision for the EU's future that included full British membership. The dilemmas of the Prime Minister's approach were discussed in-depth in a House of Commons Foreign Affairs Committee Report that came out in May 2013. The report commended aspects of the Prime Minister's agenda including the deepening of the single market, free trade agreements with third countries, and improving the EU's regulatory practice (2013, p. 8). It agreed 'that, in principle, a more flexible and differentiated model of integration might accord better with the demands of diversity and democratic consent in the EU than the traditional homogenising model' (p. 9). It argued that the veto of the fiscal compact had not necessarily left Britain isolated and marginalised. There were considerable differences of opinion amongst the member-states providing opportunities for Britain to build alliances, exert influence and play a constructive role in European reform. In this respect, the December 2012 agreement on a Single Supervisory Mechanism (SSM), which would make the ECB the supervisor of all Eurozone banks, was cited as evidence of the Britain's ability to protect its position within the single market. The British government not only opted out of this further step towards a European banking union but was influential in establishing the 'double majority' principle, which meant that certain decisions could only be passed if there was a majority of both SSM and non-SSM states in favour. However, this issue also highlighted a central dilemma for the British government, which was how Britain could continue to have influence in a EU that was dominated by the Eurozone members. The possibility of renegotiating and repatriating powers as part of new broad-based EU settlement looked questionable considering the dynamic of further integration that was embedded within EMU and had been re-affirmed by the Eurozone crisis. As the report pointed out:

> Assuming that it remains in the EU, the UK is likely to be part of a sizeable group of Member States outside the Eurozone for at least another decade. However, most other non-Eurozone states are under a Treaty obligation to adopt

the Euro at some point, and appear to wish and expect to do so. The assumption that they will one day be in the Eurozone does not at all rule such states out as allies for the UK in particular EU policy areas. However, it is likely to push their longer-term orientation in the EU away from the UK and towards the Eurozone 'core'. (p. 40)

In many respects, the report endorsed the established governing position on European integration. It recommended constructive engagement and attempting to shape the course of events from the inside. In this regard, it supported the incorporation of the Treaty on Stability, Coordination and Governance in the Economic and Monetary Union (TSCG) into the EU legal order, albeit with appropriate British safeguards. Nevertheless, the report clearly identified the significant challenges in pursuing an agenda of differentiated integration and repatriation, and the risks of isolation that this posed.

The whole idea of a reformed relationship was more forcefully challenged by the former Chancellor, Nigel Lawson, when he argued that any changes secured by a British government would be inconsequential because 'to make exceptions for one member state would inevitably lead to similar demands from others and threaten a general un-ravelling' (2013). Lawson stated that he would vote 'out' in a referendum. EMU inevitably meant full economic and political union and was antithetical to British identity and interests: 'we are now becoming increasingly marginalised as we are doomed to being consistently outvoted by the eurozone bloc'. Lawson's criticisms highlighted the extent to which Cameron's reform and repatriation agenda depended on the support from other member-states. There was little sign of this by the end of 2013, apart from a Dutch government review of subsidiarity. Meanwhile Angela Merkel's re-election saw the formation of a grand coalition with the social democrats that included pressing forward on a tax to cover all financial transactions in the Eurozone.

Conservative party problems with Eurosceptic rebels were not quelled by the referendum commitment. In May 2013, 114 Conservative MPs voted against the government in support of an amendment regretting the lack of inclusion of a Referendum Bill in the Queen's Speech. The Conservative leadership chose to support a Private Members' Bill, introduced by James Wharton, that would guarantee a referendum would be held before December 2017. In introducing the Bill, Wharton was consistent with a populist Eurosceptic position: 'It is an honour to introduce a Bill that has at its heart the heart of our democracy. Power should reside with the people. In introducing the Bill, I speak for many in the House, but I speak for millions more outside the House' (*Hansard*, 5 July 2013 Vol. 565, Col. 1169).

The underpinning premise of the referendum proposal was therefore that it was something 'the people' were demanding. However, the problems with this became evident in October 2013, when the Electoral Commission was required to test the intelligibility of the question proposed in the bill: 'do you think the United Kingdom should be a member of the European Union?' (The Electoral Commission 2013, p. 5). It was apparent from their research that participants had little understanding of the EU. Indeed, some demonstrated no knowledge whatsoever, including not knowing that Britain was a member. While they were confident with their initial response to a question, as the interviews progressed it was clear that their knowledge of the subject matter was limited (p. 4). What is more, polling evidence consistently demonstrated the low salience of the issue with voters, with between 3 to 7 per cent identifying it as important. Eurosceptics pointed to polls consistently showing majorities in favour of a referendum and for leaving the EU, yet failed to mention that for a large majority it was an issue on which they were ill-informed and cared little about. Nevertheless, while the popular credentials of populist Euroscepticism were questionable, they had effectively established the idea that British membership of the EU was now illegitimate until it was supported in a referendum.

Challenging Euroscepticism

In July 2013, the first reports were published from the review of the 'balance of competences' undertaken by the FCO.[3] They provided little support for Eurosceptic arguments of unnecessary interference and regulation from Brussels. Stephens (2013) identified three broad conclusions. Firstly, that the single market was the basis for high levels of economic integration that depended on common standards and regulations. These were rules that it would be impossible to opt out of and to do so would be of considerable risk to business and investment in Britain. Secondly, European and global economic activities were complementary, with Europe providing the basis on which to develop and realise global strategies. Thirdly, British governments often chose to work through Brussels, even in areas such as foreign and defence policy where there was no obligation to do so. While the reports provided a number of instances where reforms were necessary, the overriding conclusion was that British governance in its broadest sense was intimately connected with the EU in ways that were profoundly important for a number of key stakeholders in British economy and society.

In October 2013, the position of business and finance on British EU membership and the referendum proposal was outlined in two reports. The first, *The City Speaks* (The City UK, 2013), was based on a survey carried out by IPSOS Mori. It found that leaders within financial and related services were overwhelmingly supportive of British membership of the European Union and argued that the economic benefits were 'compelling'. However, 41 per cent agreed that the prospect of a referendum created a climate of uncertainty that affected business decisions. While endorsing the government's reform agenda, it implicitly reflected concerns of isolation arguing for 'the UK to use its place at the EU table'. These sentiments were echoed in a more comprehensive CBI report (The Confederation

---

3   See Foreign and Commonwealth Office 'Review of the Balance of Competences', https://www.gov.uk/review-of-the-balance-of-competences.

of British Industry, 2013), which was unequivocal in support for the benefits of EU membership and the direct benefits to British citizens, which it estimated at £3,000 per household (p. 11). It argued that Britain could continue to be influential in the context of a changing EU, claiming that 'if the UK continues to build alliances across Europe to protect the Single Market, as it has done in the past, further integration is compatible with, and indeed can support, the UK's global future' (p. 13). It consequently rejected alternatives to EU membership, none of which provided the advantages or influence that full membership could and which were simply 'unrealistic' (p. 16). While in some respects supporting the Prime Minister's reform agenda, it argued that this was only possible by from within the EU. It called for a comprehensive engagement strategy: 'the UK should increase interaction with EU issues, policy and politics at home to allow for better engagement in Europe and a better relationship with the EU overall' (p. 20).

Eurosceptic Labour?

The CBI report represented a more pro-European vision for Britain's role in the EU than was being articulated by political elites in 2013. In addressing the CBI Conference, Ed Balls (2013), Shadow Chancellor, stated that he shared the vision of a prosperous Britain inside a 'reformed global Europe', but also recognised that the CBI had challenged 'politicians to maintain British influence'. However, compared to the Blair years, Labour's Europeanism had become far more muted. The crisis in the Eurozone had certainly put an end to any lingering support for British membership of the single currency and the dominance of allies of Gordon Brown at the top of the party meant a firm commitment to his brand of Eurorealism. Douglas Alexander (2011), Shadow Foreign Secretary, echoed this view in a major speech on Britain and Europe when he called for 'pragmatism and not dogmatism' in European negotiations and 'a hard-headed view of Britain's national interest'. Meanwhile, the Labour Leader, Ed Miliband (2012), argued for 'One Nation in Europe', repeating the economic case for membership while criticising pro-Europeans for having 'turned a blind eye' to the EU's failings. While the 'One Nation' Miliband spoke of was imbued with images of a shared national community, Europe was primarily discussed in terms of strategic interests and in need of reform. Labour therefore defended a traditional governing position whilst accommodating to Euroscepticism. First, while opposed to the IN/OUT referendum it refused to rule out the possibility and, second, it acknowledged that in the context of further integration in the Eurozone Britain's relationship with the EU would have to change. The strength of Euroscepticism across British politics seemed to offer little space for the Labour leadership to do much more than defend British membership, albeit with an implicit acceptance of declining influence in a multi-speed Europe. Yet without a referendum commitment, its claims to represent British citizens on the issue remained open to challenge from Eurosceptic opponents.

By the end of 2013, the European issue was publicly reignited by the prospect of Romanian and Bulgarian immigration to Britain, as the seven-year restrictions on their free movement expired on 1 January 2014. The government rushed through three-month restrictions on their access to benefits, which were supported by Labour who matched their rhetoric on 'welfare tourism'. In addition, Cameron announced that Britain would pursue reform of the EU's free movement principle, arguing that this should not be an unqualified right. Equally, Labour began to suggest that EU immigration could be restricted to those with a firm offer of a job.

Conclusion

From the beginnings of the Coalition government, Euroscepticism shaped the British political agenda on Europe. The 2011 European Union Act was the most significant piece of Eurosceptic legislation in British history and placed considerable obstacles to further engagement in the process of integration. The December 2011 veto and the Conservative leadership's support for an IN/OUT referendum signalled significant moves in a Eurosceptic direction. There emerged a consensus that no further integration of Britain into the EU could take place without a referendum of some kind, and that the relationship would have to be renegotiated in response to the changes initiated by the Eurozone crisis. Nevertheless, traditional British objectives remained: the belief that the EU could be reformed in line with a British vision of an intergovernmentally controlled globalised Europe. However such a view underestimated the extent to which 'more Europe' firmly under German leadership was the dominant EU position. Moreover, there remained a residing belief that the Anglo-Saxon model of deregulated finance, whose interests Cameron seemed so keen to protect, had been a significant causal factor of the Eurozone's problems. In this context, the possibility that British elites had the political capital to lead a European reform agenda looked unlikely. The British economy had come perilously close to unravelling in 2008 and by 2013 it was only finally beginning to come out recession, albeit dangerously dependent on the housing market. The economy continued to be characterised by low levels of productivity and high levels of external exposure far in excess of national income. Conversely, Eurosceptics continued to re-imagine Britain as a bastion of openness, enterprise and stability against a crisis-ridden, over-regulated European Union. In this sense, Euroscepticism perpetuated the hyper-reality of British exceptionalism in a context in which, as a number of reports indicated, the interdependence of Britain with the dynamics of integration was increasingly fixed. What marked the period in question was the accommodation of governing and mainstream party elites to the hardening of Euroscepticism. This was particularly evident with the growing criticisms of the principle of free movement and the attacks on immigration from Bulgaria and Romania.

A consistent solution to the dilemmas of Eurosceptic Britain for governing elites has been the possibility of British leadership in Europe. However, the Coalition government's period in office seemed to signal the end of any progressive accommodation to integration compatible with maintaining and extending British influence. The political mainstream shifted to a position that saw Britain's relationship with the EU as increasingly conditional and potentially marginal to the integrationist dynamic. In short, the British governing code on Europe unravelled in the face of populist Eurosceptic opposition.

Conclusion

This book has placed Euroscepticism at the centre of Britain's relationship to European integration. It has attempted to understand Euroscepticism as integral to the trajectory of the British political order; an embedded and institutionalised facet of its contemporary history. This not only means a persistent opposition to the idea of an integrated European political and economic order but a deeper and more fundamental reproduction of Britain and Britishness in opposition to the integrationist project. In a context of global change and domestic political crisis, Eurosceptic Britain emerges as an essentialist articulation of distinct and exceptional interests and identities.

To begin with this argument, as set out in Chapters 2–4, depended on the explication of Britain's post-imperial crisis and its resolutions in a form that favoured continuity within change. For much of the 1950s, British elites encountered European integration as antithetical to Britain as a global power, operating in partnership with the US in pursuit of a liberal economic order. For all of the changes brought about by the post-war settlement, the state retained an outlook that was cosmopolitan and imperial rather than national and corporatist. The post-imperial crisis was a consequence of the closing stages of this regime, characterised by absolute political and relative economic decline in the face of global Fordism under *pax Americana*. It was in this sense a crisis of modernisation and the 'turn to Europe' represented a highly contested and problematic response to this situation. It contrasted with post-war European reconstruction that successfully linked national projects of modernisation with the political and economic organisation of Western Europe (Milward 1992). Post-Suez the Europe option was therefore an elite strategy associated with decline and failure. For the Macmillan government it emerged as the only option for retaining some degree of British influence in the world and economic survival, as the Commonwealth option receded. When the Wilson government decided to renew the British application, it was a response to its own governing crisis in the wake of the failure of its plan for national modernisation. Following the failure of the second application, the fragile consensus on membership that had been established across the political class fractured. By the end of the 1960s and early 1970s, Europe was firmly established as a threat to the nation by politicians of the left and right who began to appeal to the popular sovereignty of 'the people' in opposition to their party leaders. Thus, despite the Heath government achieving British membership in 1973, the issue was divisive in both main political parties and public opinion was unconvinced. The success of the first wave of Eurosceptic populist mobilisation was demonstrated by Wilson's decision to concede to calls for a referendum on membership. By the time Britain had become a new member-state, Europe was a strategy associated with crisis management; in particular, the need to reassure large scale capital and expand the opportunities for the City. Moreover managing Europe meant depoliticising the issue as much as possible by firmly linking it to narrow conceptions of the national interest, particularly economic, and eschewing the more fundamental issues of sovereignty and identity.

The early Thatcher governments successfully depoliticised the European issue. They exploited the budgetary issue and the drive for the single market. The leadership faced little opposition from within the Conservative party and was able to occupy the political mainstream in the face of Labour's leftwing Euroscepticism. However, with the second wave of European integration initiated by Delors, the British government's global neo-liberalism looked increasingly at odds with a programme of European politico-economic organisation. The Thatcher governments were not just representing distinctive national interests in the process of European integration, but had become a vehicle for a kind of globalisation that many European governments viewed as a threat. Britain was distinctive, in the extent to which globalisation manifested not as an external force but as the interplay between an institutional heritage, active policy decisions, and the changing structure of opportunities within the global financial economy. It was also continuous with a post-imperial period, in which British European policy was directly affected by the pursuit of an integrated transatlantic political economy and the structural position of financial interests in the state.

In the face of the drive for economic and monetary unification, Thatcherism was reconfigured as a right wing populist Euroscepticism that asserted a globalised free market nationalism in opposition to a regulated social Europe. The issue became fundamental and divisive within the Conservative party. The Major government struggled to maintain governing autonomy in the face of party rebellions and Eurosceptic mobilisations. Moreover, Britain's ejection from the ERM reasserted a national approach to monetary policy that put paid to joining EMU in the first wave. The consolidation of Thatcherism in Britain effectively marginalised the European cause in Britain. It was consistent with the identification of British patriotic and national interest with an unstable US global hegemony. The Tory Europeanism of Macmillan and Heath, also associated with a new wave of modernisers such as Heseltine and Clarke, was the main casualty of the European wars of the Conservative party during the 1990s.

This dominance of an institutionalised Euroscepticism was evident in the failure of Labour under Blair and Brown to establish its European credentials, and the Eurosceptic nationalism that came to typify its dealings with the EU. While Labour was prepared to Europeanise policy and accept a reduced role for national governments in decision-making, this was legitimated on the belief in British leadership and influence. This was an attempt to renew the governing strategy on Europe in the guise of Third Way modernisation. While it affirmed Britain's continued membership of the European Union, it was also complicit in the reproduction of Eurosceptic Britain. This was illustrative of how British governments have not just expressed distinctive national interests in the process of European integration, but have been a vehicle for international and global projects that represent an alternative model of politico-economic development. Labour's attempt to remodel British-Europeanism depended upon constructing an Anglo-Europe rooted in its project of a financially-driven but progressive globalisation. This proved increasingly difficult to sustain outside of the Euro and in the face of new integrationist developments, particularly the Constitutional and Lisbon Treaties. Such developments provided new opportunities for Eurosceptic mobilisations, backed by the virulent anti-Europeanism of large sections of the press, particularly those owned by Rupert Murdoch, which fuelled the scepticism of British public opinion. In the end the financial crisis swept away Labour's European vision, discrediting its Third Way political economy (Ryner, 2010). Meanwhile, the Eurozone crisis was successfully constituted as a threat to British economic recovery, and a dangerous experiment from which Britain must be kept apart. The 'sinner' states of the Eurozone provided a justification for the austerity measures of the new Coalition government.

The only viable option for the Coalition government was to attempt to depoliticise the European issue and turn it into a pragmatic issue of government. For the Conservative leadership, the hope was that the European Union Bill would placate Eurosceptics by putting a halt on any further integration without a referendum. The Eurosceptic surge that followed was consistent with the pattern that was seen in earlier mobilisations. It was an extra-parliamentary populist movement, constituted in opposition to the governing position. It was, however, particularly successful in mainstreaming the possibility of British withdrawal as a legitimate position. Notably, the low salience of EU issues for domestic public opinion was challenged by high profile concerns about immigration, as controls on the free movement Bulgarians and Romanians came to an end. The rise of UKIP in polls and elections signalled the coming of age of an anti-establishment, Eurosceptic populism to which the Conservative leadership struggled to find a response to. The concession by Cameron of a future referendum on membership left the Conservative leadership in the unenviable position of having to achieve significant EU reform in line with British ideas of an open and flexible EU. This looked increasingly unlikely in the face of other member-states resistance to treaty change. Moreover, a competences review designed to provide the basis for a possible reform agenda largely supported the status quo. It demonstrated the extent to which British governance and policy had become transnational and Europeanised largely in line with the ideas of functional integration that the European founding fathers had envisaged. Nevertheless, Eurosceptic arguments for a post-exit Britain along the lines of Switzerland and Norway began to enter the public debate as serious alternatives to the governing position. British political and economic power could not be ignored by the EU, so the argument went, and would enable a successful renegotiation on favourable terms. On this view, freed from the constraints of the EU, Britain would be able to revive its global mission by building on its connections with the Anglosphere and fully exploiting global economic opportunities. Most importantly sovereignty and British democracy would be reclaimed. The arguments were reminiscent of the reasons for keeping out of the EC in the 1950s, and implied a return to Britain's true vocation before the fateful wrong 'turn to Europe'.

In one sense, Eurosceptic populists made explicit what depoliticised governing elites had for the most part denied, that European integration was not simply a matter of national interest but a choice over political values and identities. It meant a commitment to shaping a European political economy, which was always more than a single market, and a European cosmopolitan civil society that challenged national communities of fate.

This book has argued that the problems of Britain's relationship with European integration are a structural effect of post-imperial change. We have seen the establishment of a political culture within which Europe becomes antithetical to what Britain is and can become. This has aligned with a belief in the post-imperial renaissance of Britain's globalised political economy as an alternative to EMU. While elites have continued to affirm membership, they have asserted British exceptionalism from Europe, and have been complicit in the reproduction of Eurosceptic Britain. The Eurosceptic populist challenge has been countered by the possibility that Britain would lead the way to a reformed and de-federalised Anglo-Europe. Yet elite attempts to accommodate Britain to Europe look increasingly exhausted. Even if British exit from the European Union is unfeasible, the opportunities to challenge Eurosceptic Britain have become unremittingly narrow.

Bibliography

Addison, P., 1994. *The Road to 1945, British Politics and The Second World War*. London: Pimlico.
Aglietta, M., 1979. *A Theory of Capitalist Regulation: the US Experience*. London: New Left Books.
Alber, J., 1988. Continuities and Change in the Idea of the Welfare State. *Politics and Society*, 16 (4), pp. 451–68.
Alexander, D., 2011. Speech to Baltic and Nordic Ambassadors. *The Guardian*, 14 November. Available at: http://www.guardian.co.uk/politics/interactive/2011/nov/14/douglas-alexander-speech-policy-eu [Accessed 12 June 2013].
Alexandre-Collier, A., 2009. John Major vs. the 'Bastards' ou la Puissance de la Mobilisation Eurosceptique Contre le Traité de Maastricht. *Observatoire de la Société Britannique. La Revue*, 7, pp. 63–83.
Anderson, B., 1991. *Imagined Communities*. London, New York: Verso.
Anderson, P., 1992. *English Questions*. London: New York: Verso.
Anderson, P., 1997. Under the Sign of the Interim. In: P. Anderson and P. Gowan (eds), *The Question of Europe*. London: New York: Verso.
Anon, 2012. Comment: Britain's Tea Party. *Political Quarterly*, 83 (1), pp. 1–3.
Anthias, F. and Yuval Davis, N., 1992. *Racialised Boundaries, Race, Nation, Gender, Colour and Class and the Anti-racist Struggle*. London: Routledge.
Arrighi, G., 1994. *The Long Twentieth Century, Money, Power and the Origins of our Times*. London: Verso.
Arrighi, G., 1999. The Global Market. *Journal of World-Systems Research*, 5 (2), pp. 217–51.
Arrighi, G., 2003. Tracking Global Turbulence. *New Left Review*, 20 (second series), pp. 5–71.
Aspinwall, M., 2000. Structuring Europe: Power-sharing Institutions and British Preferences on European Integration. *Political Studies*, 48 (3), pp. 415–42.
Aspinwall, M., 2003. Britain and Europe: Some Alternative Economic Tests. *The Political Quarterly*, 74 (2), pp. 146–57.
Aspinwall, M., 2004. *Rethinking Britain and Europe: plurality elections, party management and British policy on European integration*. Manchester: Manchester University Press.
Bacon, R.W. and Eltis, W., 1978. *Britain's Economic Problem: Too Few Producers*. London: Macmillan.
Baker, D., 2003. Britain and Europe: Treading Water or Slowly Drowning. *Parliamentary Affairs*, 56 (2), pp. 237–54.

Baker, D. and Seawright, D. (eds), 1998. *Britain for and against Europe: British politics and the question of European integration*. Oxford: Oxford University Press.

Baker, D. and Sherrington, P., 2004. Britain and Europe: Europe and/or America? *Parliamentary Affairs*, 57 (2), pp. 347–65.

Baker, D., Gamble, A. and Ludlam, S., 1993a. 1846 ... 1906 ... 1996? Conservative Splits and European Integration. *The Political Quarterly*, 64 (4), pp. 420–34.

Baker, D., Gamble, A. and Ludlam, S. 1993b Whips and Scorpions? Conservative MPs and the Maastricht Paving Motion Vote, *Parliamentary Affairs*, 46 (2), 151–66.

Baker, D., Gamble, A. and Ludlam, S., 1994. The Parliamentary Siege of Maastricht 1993, Conservative Divisions and British Ratification. *Parliamentary Affairs*, 47 (1), pp. 37–60.

Baker, D., Gamble, A. and Seawright, D., 2002. Sovereign Nations and Global Markets: Modern Conservatism and Hyperglobalism. *British Journal of Politics and International Relations*, 4 (3), pp. 399–428.

Bale, T., 2006. Between a Soft and a Hard Place? The Conservative Party, Valence Politics and the Need for a New 'Euro-realism'. *Parliamentary Affairs*, 59 (3), pp. 385–400.

Bale, T. and Webb, P. 2013 Lots of Conservative Party Members Prefer UKIP's Policies. *The Daily Telegraph*, 8 July. Available at: http://www.telegraph.co.uk/news/politics/ukip/10166693/Lots-of-Conservative-Party-members-prefer-Ukips-policies.html [Accessed 8 September 2013].

Balls, E., 2006. *Speech by Economic Secretary to the Treasury, Ed Balls MP, to the Hong Kong General Chamber of Commerce and the British Chamber of Commerce: Financial Services, a UK Perspective*. 13 September. Available at: http://webarchive.nationalarchives.gov.uk/+/http:/www.hm-treasury.gov.uk/2277.htm. [Accessed 15 July 2013].

Balls, E., 2007. *Britain and Europe: A City Ministers Perspective*. London: Centre for Economic Reform.

Balls, E., 2013. Speech to the Confederation of British Industry Conference. *The New Statesman online*, 4 November. Available at: http://www.newstatesman.com/politics/2013/11/ed-ballss-speech-cbi-full-text [Accessed 2 December 2013].

Barnett, C., 1986. *The Audit of War*. London: Macmillan.

Barrow, C., 2005. The Return of the State: Globalization, State Theory and the New Imperialism. *New Political Science*, 27 (2), pp. 123–45.

Bates, S. 1993. Grassroot Complaints Hearten Eurosceptics. *The Guardian*, 19 April, p. 3.

Batory, A. and Sitter, N., 2004. Cleavages, Competition and Coalition-building: Agrarian Parties and the European Question in Western and East Central Europe. *European Journal of Political Research*, 43 (4), pp. 523–46.

Beer, S., 1982. *Modern British Politics: Parties and Pressure Groups in the Collectivist Age*. London: Faber & Faber.

Beloff, N., 1963. *The General Says No*. Harmondsworth: Penguin.
Benn, T., 1974. The Common Market: Loss of Self-Government. In: M. Holmes (ed.), 1996. *The Eurosceptical Reader*. Basingstoke: Macmillan, pp. 38–41.
Benn, T., 1996. *The Benn Diaries, New Single Volume Edition*. London: Arrow.
Berrington, H. and Hague, R., 1998. Europe, Thatcherism and Traditionalism: Opinion, Rebellion and the Maastricht Treaty in the Backbench Conservative Party 1992–1994. *West European Politics*, 21 (1), pp. 44–71.
Bilski, R., 1977. The Common Market and the Growing Strength of Labour's Left Wing. *Government and Opposition*, 12 (3), pp. 306–31.
Black, I., 2000. Blair Sees 20m net Jobs. *The Guardian*, 25 March Available at: http://www.theguardian.com/business/2000/mar/25/europeanunion.efinance [Accessed 18 July 2013].
Blair, A., 1999. *Dealing with Europe: Britain and the Negotiation of the Maastricht Treaty*. Aldershot: Ashgate.
Blair, A., 2012. The UK and Lisbon. In: F. Laursen (ed.), *The Making of the EUs Lisbon Treaty*. Bern: Peter Lang, pp. 97–121.
Blair, T., 1997. Speech at the Lord Mayor's Banquet. 10 November. Available at: http://www.number10.gov.uk/output/Page1070.asp [Accessed 1 June 2008].
Blair, T., 2003. Tony Blair's speech in Warsaw. *The Guardian*, 30 May. Available at: http://www.theguardian.com/world/2003/may/30/eu.speeches [Accessed 19 July 2013].
Blair, T., 2005. Blair's European Speech. *The BBC*, 23 June. Available at: http://news.bbc.co.uk/1/hi/uk_politics/4122288.stm [Accessed 19 July 2013].
Blair, T., 2011. *A Journey*. London: Arrow Books.
Bonefield, W., 2002. European Integration, the Market, the Political and Class. *Capital and Class*, 77, pp. 117–42.
Bonefield, W. and Burnham, P., 1996. Britain and the Politics of the Exchange Rate Mechanism. *Capital and Class*, 60, pp. 5–38.
Brivati, B. and Jones, H (eds), 1993. *From Reconstruction to Integration: Britain and Europe since 1945*. Leicester: University of Leicester.
Broomhead, P. and Shell, D., 1977. The British Constitution in 1976. *Parliamentary Affairs*, 30 (2), pp. 143–60.
Broomhead, P. and Shell, D., 1979. The British Constitution in 1978. *Parliamentary Affairs*, 32 (2), pp. 125–42.
Brown, G., 2003a. British values can help shape a Europe for the 21st century. *The Daily Telegraph*, 3 June. Available at: http://www.telegraph.co.uk/comment/personal-view/3592144/British-values-can-help-shape-a-Europe-for-the-21st-century.html [Accessed 12 July 2013].
Brown, G., 2003b. Speech given by the Chancellor, Gordon Brown, to the Labour Party Conference in Bournemouth. *The Guardian*, 29 September. Available at: http://www.theguardian.com/politics/2003/sep/29/labourconference.labour1 [Accessed 12 July 2013].
Brown, G., 2003c. Flexibility, Not Federalism, is Key to this Competitive New World. *The Daily Telegraph*, 5 November. Available at: http://www.telegraph.

co.uk/comment/personal-view/3598501/Flexibility-not-federalism-is-key-to-this-competitive-new-world.html [Accessed 12 July 2013].

Brown, G., 2004. Speech given by the Chancellor, Gordon Brown, at the Mansion House London. *The Guardian*, 17 June. Available at: http://www.theguardian.com/politics/2004/jun/17/economy.uk [Accessed 13 July 2013].

Brown, T., 2011. City of London Owes its Dominance to the EU. *The Financial Times*, 11 December. p. 12.

Brubaker, W.R., 1989. *Immigration and the Politics of Citizenship in Europe and North America*. London: University Press of America.

Brubaker, W.R., 1992. *Citizenship and Nationhood in France and Germany*. Cambridge: Cambridge University Press.

Bruter, M. and Harrison, S., 2012. *How European do we Feel? The Psychology of European Identity*. London: Lansons Communications in association with London School of Economics and Opinium.

Buiter, W., 2008. There is no excuse for Britain not to join the Euro. *The Financial Times*, 2 June. Available at: http://www.ft.com/cms/s/0/fa2a465a-30bc-11dd-bc93-000077b07658.html#axzz2tDjujGXh [Accessed 5 August 2013].

Buller, J., 2000a. *National Statecraft and European Integration: The Conservative Government and the European Union, 1979–1997*. London: Continuum.

Buller, J., 2000b. Understanding Contemporary Conservative Euroscepticism, Statecraft and the Problem of Governing Autonomy. *The Political Quarterly*, 71 (3), pp. 319–27.

Buller, J., 2006. Contesting Europeanisation: Agents, Institutions and Narratives in British Monetary Policy. *West European Politics*, 29 (3), pp. 389–409

Buller, J. and Flinders, M., 2005. The Domestic Origins of Depoliticisation in the Area of British Economic Policy. *The British Journal of Politics & International Relations*, 7 (4), pp. 526–43.

Buller, J. and Gamble, A., 2008. Britain: The Political Economy of Retrenchment. In: K. Dyson (ed.), *The Euro at Ten: Europeanization, Power, and Convergence*. Oxford: Oxford University Press, pp. 258–73.

Bulmer, S., 1992. Domestic Politics and European Integration: of Sovereignty, Slow Adaptation and Semi-Detachment. In: S. George (ed.), *Britain and the European Community, the Politics of Semi-detachment*. Oxford: Clarendon Press, pp. 1–29.

Bulpitt, J., 1992. Conservative Leaders and the 'Euro-Ratchet': Five Doses of Scepticism. *The Political Quarterly*, 63 (1), pp. 258–75.

Burk, K. and Cairncross, A., 1992. *Goodbye Great Britain: The 1976 IMF Crisis*. New Haven and London: Yale University Press.

Burn, G., 1999. The State, the City and Euromarkets. *Review of International Political Economy*, 6 (2), pp. 225–61.

Butler, D., 1979. Public Opinion and Community Membership. *The Political Quarterly*, 50 (1), pp. 151–6.

Butler, D. and Kitzinger, U.W., 1976. *The 1975 Referendum*. Basingstoke: Macmillan.

Butler, M., 1986. *Europe, More Than A Continent*. London: Heinemann.
Cain, P.J. and Hopkins, A.G., 1993a. *British Imperialism: Innovation and Expansion 1688–1914*. London: Longman.
Cain, P.J. and Hopkins, A.G., 1993b. *British Imperialism: Decline and Deconstruction 1914–1990*. London: Longman.
Cain, P.J., 1997. British Capitalism and the State: An Historical Perspective. *The Political Quarterly*, 63 (1), pp. 95–9.
Callaghan, J., 2000. Rise and Fall of the Alternative Economic Strategy, From Internationalisation of Capital to Globalisation. *Contemporary British History*, 14 (3), pp. 105–30.
Cameron, D., 2012. We need to be clear about the best way of getting what is best for Britain. *The Daily Telegraph*, 30 June Available at: http://www.telegraph.co.uk/news/politics/david-cameron/9367479/David-Cameron-We-need-to-be-clear-about-the-best-way-of-getting-what-is-best-for-Britain.html [Accessed 10 September 2013].
Cameron, D., 2013. Speech on Plans for a Referendum on British Membership of the EU. *The Guardian*, 23 January. Available at: http://www.guardian.co.uk/politics/2013/jan/23/david-cameron-eu-speech-referendum [Accessed 8 July 2013].
Campbell, J., 1993. *Edward Heath*. London: Johnathan Cape.
Camps, M., 1964. *Britain and the European Community 1955–63*. London: Oxford University Press.
Canovan, M., 1981. *Populism*. London: Junction Books.
Canovan, M., 1999. Trust the People! Populism and the Two Faces of Democracy. *Political Studies*, 47 (1), pp. 2–16.
Carter, N., Evans, M., Alderman, K. and Gorham, S., 1998. Europe, Goldsmith and the Referendum Party. *Parliamentary Affairs*, 51 (3), pp. 470–85.
Castle, B., 1980. *The Castle Diaries, 1974–1976*. London: Weidenfeld and Nicolson.
Cecchini, P., 1988. *The European Challenge 1992: The Benefits of the Single Market*. Aldershot: Wildwood House.
The City UK, 2013. *The City Speaks: A Milestone Study of the Views of Financial and Related Professional Services Leaders on the EU*. London: The City UK.
Clark, D., 2005. Labour's New Divide. *The Guardian*, 15 August. Available at: http://www.theguardian.com/politics/2005/aug/15/labour.uk [Accessed 27 March 2013].
Coates, D., 1980. *Labour in Power 1974–1979*. London: Longman.
Coates, D., 1989. *The Crisis of Labour, Industrial Relations and the State in Contemporary Britain*. Deddington: Philip Allan.
Coates, D. and Hillard, J., 1986. *The Economic Decline of Modern Britain: The Debate between Left and Right*. Brighton: Wheatsheaf.
Cochrane, A. and Anderson, J.(eds), 1989. *Restructuring Britain: Politics in Transition*. London: Sage.
The Confederation of British Industry, 2013. *Our Global Future: the Business Vision for a Reformed EU*. London: CBI.

The Conservative Party, 1970. *Conservative Party General Election Manifesto A Better Tomorrow*. Available at: http://www.conservative-party.net/manifestos/1970/1970-conservative-manifesto.shtml [Accessed 20 March 2013].

Cook, R., 2005. Blair can get Europe Behind him. *The Guardian*, 24 June. Available at: http://www.theguardian.com/world/2005/jun/24/eu.politics3 [Accessed 20 July 2013].

Cox, H., 1997. The Evolution of International Business Enterprise. In: R. John and G.L. Gillies (eds), *Global Business Strategy*. London: International Thomson Press, pp. 9–46.

Craig, F.W.S., 1990. *British General Election Manifestos, 1959–1987*. Aldershot: Dartmouth.

Cronin, J.E., 1991. *The Politics of State Expansion: War, State, and Society in Twentieth-century Britain*. New York: Routledge.

Crook, S. Pakulski, J. and Waters, M., 1992. *Postmodernization: Change in Advanced Society*. London: Sage.

Crossman, R., 1979. *The Crossman Diaries: Selections from the Diaries of a Cabinet Minister 1964–1970*. London: Magnum.

Crouch, C., 1993. *Industrial Relations and European State Traditions*. Oxford: Clarendon.

Crouch, C., 2009. Privatised Keynesianism: An Unacknowledged Policy Regime. *The British Journal of Politics & International Relations*, 11 (3), pp. 382–99.

Crouch, C. and Streeck, W. (eds), 1997. *Political Economy of Modern Capitalism*. London: Sage.

Crowson, N.J., 2007. *The Conservative Party and European Integration since 1945*. London and New York: Routledge.

Daddow, O., 2011. *New Labour and the European Union: Blair and Brown's logic of history*. Manchester: Manchester University Press.

Daddow, O., 2012. Margaret Thatcher, Tony Blair and the Eurosceptic Tradition in Britain. *The British Journal of Politics & International Relations*, 15(2), pp. 210–27, doi: 10.1111/j.1467-856X.2012.00534.x. (published online first: 19 September 2012).

The Daily Mail, 2005. Blair's Surrender. *The Daily Mail*, 17 December. Available at: http://www.dailymail.co.uk/news/article-371925/Blairs-surrender.html [Accessed 15 July 2013].

The Daily Telegraph, 2011. European Union Bill: Brussels Will Not be Blocked by One Bill Alone. *The Daily Telegraph*, 2 January. Available at: http://www.telegraph.co.uk/comment/telegraph-view/8235326/European-Union-Bill-Brussels-will-not-be-blocked-by-one-Bill-alone.html [Accessed 8 September 2013].

Darling, A., 2011. *Back from the Brink*. London: Atlantic Books.

de Wilde, P., and Trenz, H.J., 2012. Denouncing European integration Euroscepticism as polity contestation. *European Journal of Social Theory*, 15 (4), pp. 537–54.

Deighton, A., 1993. Britain and The Cold War 1945–55: An Overview. In: B. Brivati and H. Jones (eds), *From Reconstruction to Integration: Britain and Europe since 1945*. Leicester: University of Leicester, pp. 7–17.

Dell, E., 1995. *The Schuman Plan and the British Abdication of Leadership in Europe*. Oxford: Oxford University Press.

Delors, J., 1992. *Le Nouveau Concert Européen*. Paris: Odile Jacob.

Dyson, K., 2010. Norman'ss Lament: The Greek and Euro Area Crisis in Historical Perspective. *New Political Economy*, 15 (4), pp. 597–608.

The Economist, 1977. Labour Closes Ranks – At Least Until the Election, *The Economist*, 8 October, p. 18.

Edwards, G. and Wallace, H., 1977. EEC, The British Presidency in Retrospect. *The World Today*, 33 (8), pp. 283–6.

The Electoral Commission, 2013. *Referendum on the United Kingdom's Membership of the European Union*. London: Electoral Commission Publications.

Elliott, L., 2003. An Impressive Way to Say No. *The Guardian*, 10 June. Available at http://www.theguardian.com/business/2003/jun/10/theeuro.politics3 [Accessed 10 July 2013].

Ellison, J.R.V., 2000. Accepting the Inevitable: Britain and European Integration. In: W. Kaiser and G. Staerck (eds), *British Foreign Policy, 1955–64*. Basingstoke and London: Macmillan, pp. 171–89.

European Communities – Commission, 1987. *Treaties Establishing the European Communities (ECSC, EEC, EAEC) – Single European Act – Other Basic Instruments*. Luxembourg: Office for Official Publications of the European Communities.

Evans, D., 1975. *While Britain Slept: The Selling of the Common Market*. London: Gollancz.

Falkner, G., 1998. *EU Social Policy in the 1990s, Towards a Corporatist Policy Community*. London and New York: Routledge.

Fella, S., 2006a. New Labour, Same Old Britain? The Blair Government and European Treaty Reform. *Parliamentary Affairs*, 59 (4), pp. 621–37.

Fella, S., 2006b. Robin Cook, Tony Blair and New Labours Competing Visions of Europe. *The Political Quarterly*, 77 (3), pp. 388–401.

Fieldhouse, D.K., 1984. The Labour Governments and the Empire-Commonwealth, 1945–1951. In: R. Overdale (ed.), *The Foreign Policy of the British Labour Government 1945–51*. Leicester, pp. 83–120.

Fine, B. and Harris, L., 1985. *The Peculiarities of the British Economy*. London: Lawrence Wishart.

Fitzgibbon, J., 2013. Citizens Against Europe? Civil Society and Eurosceptic Protest in Ireland, the United Kingdom and Denmark. *JCMS: Journal of Common Market Studies*, 51 (1), pp. 105–21.

Ford, R., 2012. Euroscepticism is now a Powerful Force for the Radical Right – and UKIP is Well Placed to Harness it. *British Policy and Politics at LSE*, 21 June. Available at: http://blogs.lse.ac.uk/politicsandpolicy/archives/24622 [Accessed 9 September 2013].

Forster, A., 1999. *Britain and the Maastricht Negotiations*. New York and Oxford: St. Martin's Press in association with St. Anthony's College, Oxford.

Forster, A., 2002. *Euroscepticism in British Politics*. New York: Routledge.

Fox, L., 2012. *Speech for Open Europe at the Royal United Services Institute: Britain and the European Union – An Emerging Consensus*. 10 December. Available at: http://www.liamfox.co.uk/news/liam-fox-speech-eu [Accessed 9 September 2013].

Frey, C.W., 1968. Meaning Business: The British Application to Join the Common Market, November 1966–October 1967. *JCMS: Journal of Common Market Studies*. 6 (3), pp. 197–230.

Gaitskell, H., 1962. The Common Market. In: M. Holmes (ed.), 1996. *The Eurosceptical Reader*. Basingstoke: Macmillan, pp. 13–37

Gallagher, J., 1982. *The Decline, Revival and Fall of The British Empire, The Ford Lectures and Other Essays*. Cambridge: Cambridge University Press.

Gamble, A., 1974. *The Conservative Nation*. London: Routledge and Paul Kegan.

Gamble, A., 1988. *The Free Economy and the Strong State, the Politics of Thatcherism*. Basingstoke: Macmillan Press.

Gamble, A., 1993. The Entrails of Thatcherism. *New Left Review*, 198, pp. 117–28.

Gamble, A., 1994. *Britain in Decline, Economic Policy, Political Strategy and the British State*. Basingstoke: Macmillan.

Gamble, A., 1995. The Crisis of Conservatism. *New Left Review*, 214, pp. 3–25.

Gamble, A., 2003. *Between Europe and America: The Future of British Politics*. Basingstoke: Palgrave.

Gamble, A. and Kelly, G., 2000. The British Labour Party and Monetary Union. *West European Politics*, 23 (1), pp. 1–25.

George, S., 1990. *An Awkward Partner, Britain in the European Community*. Oxford: Oxford University Press.

George, S., 1991. *Britain and European Integration since 1945*. Oxford: Blackwell.

George, S., 1994. *An Awkward Partner, Britain in the European Community*. Second Edition. Oxford: Oxford University Press.

George, S., 2000. Britain: Anatomy of a Eurosceptic State. *Journal of European Integration*, 22 (1), pp. 15–33.

George, S. and Haythorne, D., 1996. The British Labour Party. In: J. Gaffney (ed.), *Political Parties in The European Union*. London and New York: Routledge, pp. 110–21.

Geyer, R.R., 2000. *Exploring European Social Policy*. Cambridge: Polity Press.

Giddens, A., 1998. *The Third Way*. Cambridge: Polity.

Gifford, C., 2006. The Rise of Post-Imperial Populism: The Case of Right Wing Euroscepticism. *European Journal of Political Research*, 45 (5), pp. 851–69.

Gifford, C., 2007. Political Economy and the Study of Britain and European Integration: A Global-National Perspective. *British Journal of Politics and International Relations*, 9 (3), pp. 461–76.

Gifford, C., 2010. The United Kingdom and the European Union: Dimensions of Sovereignty and the Problem of Eurosceptic Britishness. *Parliamentary Affairs*, 63 (2), pp. 321–38.

Gifford, C. 2014. The People against Europe: The Eurosceptic Challenge to the United Kingdom's Coalition Government. *JCMS: Journal of Common Market Studies*, 52 (3), pp. 512–28.

Gilroy, P., 1987. *'There Ain't No Black in the Union Jack': The Cultural Politics of Race and Nation*. London: Hutchinson.

Glyn, A. and Harrison, J., 1980. *The British Economic Disaster*. London: Pluto Press.

Goodhart, M., and Taninchev, S.B., 2011. The New Sovereigntist Challenge for Global Governance: Democracy Without Sovereignty. *International Studies Quarterly*, 55 (4), pp. 1047–68.

Gowan, P., 1987. The Origins of the Administrative Elite. *New Left Review*, 162, pp. 4–34.

Gowan, P., 1997. British Euro-solipsism. In: P. Gowan, and P. Anderson (eds), *The Question of Europe*. London: Verso, pp. 91–103.

Gowan, P., 1999. *The Global Gamble: Washinghton's Faustian Bid for World Dominance*. London: Verso.

Gowland, D. and Turner, A. 2000a. *Reluctant Europeans: Britain and European Integration 1945–1998*. Harlow: Pearson Education.

Gowland, D. and Turner, A. 2000b. *Britain and European Integration 1945–1998, A Documentary History*. London: Routledge.

Grahl, J., 1997. *After Maastricht: A Guide to Monetary Union*. London: Lawrence and Wishart.

Grant, C., 1994. *Delors: Inside the House that Jacques Built*. London: Brealey Publishing.

Gray, J., 1986. *Liberalism*. Milton Keynes: Oxford University Press.

Gray, J., 1998. *False Dawn: The Delusions of Global Capitalism*. London: Granta Books.

Greenwood, S., 1992. *Britain and European Cooperation Since 1945*. Oxford: Blackwell.

Greider, W., 1997. *One World, Ready or Not: The Manic Logic of Global Capitalism*. New York: Touchstone.

Grimmond, J. and Neve, B., 1975. *The Referendum*. London: Rex Collings.

Grosser, A., 1980. *The Western Alliance: European-American Relations since 1945*. Basingstoke: Macmillan.

Grote, J.R. and Schmitter, P., 1999. The Renaissance of National Corporatism, unintended side-effect of European Economic and Monetary Union or Calculated Response to the Absence of European Social Policy? *Transfer*, 5 (1–2), pp. 34–63.

The Guardian, 1993a. When the Writ of Parliament doesn't Run. *The Guardian*, 15 February, p. 20.

The Guardian, 1993b. Social Chapter Ploy Trips up Sceptics. *The Guardian*, April 16, p. 24.
The Guardian, 1993c. Mr Major as the Heir of Ted Heath. *The Guardian*, 23 April, p. 19.
Haack, W.G.C.M., 1972. The Economic Effects of Britain's Entry Into The Common Market. *JCMS: Journal of Common Market Studies*, 11 (2), pp. 136–51.
Habermas, J., 1976. *Legitimation Crisis*. London: Heinemann.
Habermas, J., 1999. The European Nation-State and the Pressures of Globalization. *New Left Review*, 235, pp. 46–60.
Habermas, J. and Derrida, J., 2005. February 15, or, What Binds Europeans Together: Plea for a Common European Policy, Beginning in Core Europe. In: D. Levy, M. Pensky and J. Torpey (eds), *Old Europe, New Europe, Core Europe: Transatlantic Relations After the Iraq War*, London and New York: Verso, pp. 3–13.
Hague, W., 2012. *Speech to the Körber Foundation Conference Europe at a Crossroads: What Kind of Europe do we Want?* 23 October. Available at: https://www.gov.uk/government/speeches/europe-at-a-crossroads-what-kind-of-europe-do-we-want [Accessed 10 September 2013].
Hall, C., 1994. Rethinking Imperial Histories, The Reform Act of 1867. *New Left Review*, 208, pp.3–29.
Hall, S., 1979. The Great Moving Right Show. *Marxism Today*, January, pp. 14–20.
Hall, S. and Jacques, M. (eds), 1983. *The Politics of Thatcherism*. London: Lawrence and Wishart.
Hall, S. and Jacques, M. (eds), 1989. *New Times*. London: Lawrence Wishart.
Halsey, A.H., 1986. *Changes in British Society*. Oxford: Oxford University Press.
Hansen, R., 2000. *Citizenship and Immigration in Post-War Europe*. Oxford: Oxford University Press.
Harvey, D., 1989. *The Condition of Postmodernity*. Oxford: Blackwell.
Harvey, D., 2010. *The Enigma of Capital: And the Crises of Capitalism*. London: Profile Books.
Hasse, R. and Leiulfsrud, H., 2002. From Disorganized Capitalism to Transnational Fine Tuning?, Recent Trends in Wage Development, Industrial Relations, and 'Work' as a Sociological Category. *British Journal of Sociology*, 53 (1), pp. 107–26.
Hawkins, B., 2012. Nation, Separation and Threat: An Analysis of British Media Discourses on the European Union Treaty Reform Process. *JCMS: Journal of Common Market Studies*, 50 (4), pp. 561–77.
Hay, C., 1994. The Structural and Ideological Contradictions of Britain's Post-War Reconstruction. *Capital and Class*, 54, pp. 25–59.
Hay, C., 1996. *Re-stating Social and Political Change*. Buckingham: Open University Press.
Hay, C., 1999. *The Political Economy of New Labour: Labouring under False Pretences?* Manchester: Manchester University Press.

Hay, C., 2011. Pathology without Crisis? The Strange Demise of the Anglo-Liberal Growth Model. *Government and Opposition*, 46 (1), pp. 1–31.

Hay, C. and Rosamond, B., 2001. Globalisation, European Integration and the Discursive Construction of European Imperatives: A Question of Convergence. *Queen's Papers on Europeanisation*, No. 1/2001.

Hay, C., Watson, M. and Wincott, D., 1999. Globalisation, European Integration and the Persistence of the Social Model. *One Europe or Several?*, working paper 3/99.

Hay, C. and Wincott, D., 1998. Structure, Agency and Historical Institutionalism. *Political Studies*, 46 (5), pp. 951–7.

Heath, E., 1970. *Old World, New Horizons: Britain, the Common Market, and the Atlantic Alliance*. London: Oxford University Press.

Heath, E., 1998. *The Autobiography of Edward Heath: The Course of My Life*. London: Hodder and Stoughton.

Heffernan, R., 1999. *New Labour and Thatcherism: Political Change in Britain*. New York: St. Martin's Press.

Held, D., 1995. *Democracy and the Global Order: From the Modern State to Cosmopolitan Democracy*. Cambridge: Polity Press.

Hennessy, P., 2000. *The Prime Minister: The Office and Its Holders since 1945*. London: Penguin.

Heseltine, M., 2000. *Life in the Jungle: My Autobiography*. London: Hodder and Stoughton.

Hill, M., 2007. The Parliamentary Conservative Party: The Leadership Elections of William Hague and Iain Duncan Smith. Unpublished PhD thesis, University of Huddersfield.

Hirst, P., 1989. *After Thatcher*. London: Collins.

Hirst, P. and Thompson, G., 1999. *Globalization in Question: The International Economy and the Possibilities of Governance*. Cambridge: Polity Press.

Hirst, P. and Thompson, G., 2000. Globalization in One Country? The Peculiarities of the British. *Economy and Society*, 29 (3), pp. 335–56.

Hix, S., 2002. Britain, the EU and the Euro. In: P. Dunleavy, A. Gamble, R. Heffernan, I. Holliday and G. Peele (eds), 2002. *Developments in British Politics 6*. Revised edition. Basingstoke: Palgrave, pp. 47–68.

Hobsbawm, E.J., 1995. *Age of Extremes: The Short Twentieth Century, 1914–1991*. London: Abacus.

Hogg, S. and Hill, J., 1995. *Power and Politics, John Major in No. 10*. London: Little Brown.

Holland, R.F., 1984. The Imperial Factor in British Strategies from Attlee to Macmillan, 1945–1963. *Journal of Imperial and Commonwealth History*, 12 (2), pp. 165–86.

Hollingsworth, J.R. and Streeck, W., 1994. Countries and Sectors, Concluding Remarks on Performance, Convergence and Competitiveness. In: J.R. Hollingsworth, P.C. Schmitter and W. Streeck (eds), *Governing Capitalist*

Economies. Performance and Control of Economic Sectors. New York/Oxford: Oxford University Press, pp. 270–300.

Holmes, M. (ed.), 1996. *The Eurosceptical Reader*. Basingstoke: Macmillan.

Hooghe, L. and Marks, G., 1997. The Making of a Polity, The Struggle over European Integration, *European Integration Online Papers EioP*, 1 (004). Available at: http://eiop.or.at/eiop/ps/1997-004.ps [Accessed 26 March 2004].

Hooghe, L. and Marks, G., 2005. Calculation, Community and Cues: Public Opinion on European Integration. *European Union Politics*, 6 (4), pp. 419–43.

Hooghe, L. and Marks, G., 2007. Sources of Euroscepticism. *Acta Politica*, 42 (2), pp. 119–27.

Hooghe, L. and Marks, G., 2009. A Postfunctionalist Theory of European Integration: From Permissive Consensus to Constraining Dissensus. *British Journal of Political Science*, 39 (1), pp. 1–23.

House of Commons European Scrutiny Committee, 2007. *European Union Intergovernmental Conference: Follow-up Report. Third Report of Session 2007–2008*. London: HMSO.

House of Commons European Scrutiny Committee, 2010. *The EU Bill and Parliamentary Sovereignty*. London: HMSO.

House of Commons Foreign Affairs Committee, 2013. *The Future of the European Union: UK Government Policy, Volume 1*. London: HMSO.

House of Commons Political and Constitutional Reform Committee, 2011. *Lessons from the process of Government formation after the 2010 General Election: Fourth report of session 2010–11*. London: HMSO.

Howe, G., 1990. Sovereignty and Interdependence, Britain's Place in the world. *International Affairs*, 66 (4), pp. 675–95.

Howe, G., 1995. *Conflict of Loyalty*. London: Macmillan.

Hutton, W., 1995. *The State We're In*. London: Johnathan Cape.

Hutton, W., 2002. *The World We're In*. London: Little Brown.

Hutton, W., 2008. It Might be Politically Toxic – But we Must Join the Euro Now. *The Observer*, 16 November. Available at: http://www.theguardian.com/commentisfree/2008/nov/16/comment-will-hutton-euro [Accessed 5 August 2013].

The Independent on Sunday (1992). Leading Article: The End of Another British Delusion. 20 September. Available at http://www.independent.co.uk/voices/leading-article-the-end-of-another-british-delusion-1552441.html [Accessed 16 February 2014].

Ingham, G., 1984. *Capitalism Divided? The City and Industry in British Social Development*. London: Macmillan.

Ingham, G., 2002. Shock therapy in the City. *New Left Review*, 2 (14), pp. 152–8.

Ionescu, G. and Gellner, E. (eds), 1969. *Populism: Its Meaning and National Characteristics*. London: Weidenfeld and Nicolson.

Jenkins, R., 1989. *European Diary, 1977–1981*. London: Collins.

Jenkins, R., 1991. *A Life at the Center*. London: Macmillan.

Jessop, B., 1980. The Transformation of the State in Post-war Britain. In: R. Scase (ed.), *The State in Western Europe*. London: Croom, Helm, pp. 23–93.

Jessop, B., 1991. Thatcherism and Flexibility: The White Heat of a Post-Fordist Revolution. In: B. Jessop, H. Kastendiek, K. Nielson and O.K. Pedersen (eds), *The Politics of Flexibility, Restructuring State and Industry in Britain, Germany and Scandinavia*. Aldershot: Edward Elgar, pp. 135–61.

Jessop B., Bonnett, K., Bromley, S. and Ling, T., 1988. *Thatcherism: A Tale of Two Nations*. Cambridge: Polity Press.

Kaiser, W., 1996. *Using Europe, Abusing the Europeans, Britain and European Integration, 1945–1963*. Basingstoke: Macmillan.

Kaiser, W., 2002. A Never-ending Story: Britain in Europe. *The British Journal of Politics & International Relations*, 4 (1), pp. 152–65.

Kennedy, P., 1989. *The Rise and Fall of the Great Powers: Economic Change and Military Conflict from 1500–2000*. London: Fontana.

Kumar, K., 2008. The Question of European Identity: Europe in the American Mirror. *European Journal of Social Theory*, 11 (1), pp. 87–105.

Kynaston, D., 2002. *City of London, Vol. 4: A Club No More 1945–2000*. London: Pimlico.

Laclau, E., 2005. Populism: What's in a Name? In: F. Panizza (ed.), *Populism and the Mirror of Democracy*. London and New York: Verso, pp. 32–49.

Lawson, N., 1992. *The View From No. 11. Memoirs of a Tory Radical*. London: Corgi.

Lawson, N., 2013. I'll be Voting to Leave the EU. *The Times*, 7 May. Available at: http://www.thetimes.co.uk/tto/opinion/columnists/article3757 562.ece [Accessed 10 September 2013].

Lazer, H., 1976. British Populism: The Labour Party and the Common Market Parliamentary Debate. *Political Science Quarterly*, 91 (2), pp. 259–77.

Lee, J.M., 1977. Forward Thinking and the War, the Colonial Office during the 1940s, *Journal of Imperial and Commonwealth History*, 6 (1), pp. 64–79.

Lee, S., 2006. Gordon Brown and the British way. *The Political Quarterly*, 77 (3), pp. 369–78.

Lee, S., 2009. The Rock of Stability? The Political Economy of the Brown Government. *Policy Studies*, 30 (1), pp. 17–32.

Leys, C., 1983. *Politics in Britain, An Introduction*. London: Heinemann Educational.

Leys, C., 1990. Still a Question of Hegemony. *New Left Review*, 181, pp. 119–28.

Lipgens, W., 1982. *A History of European Integration / Vol.1: The Formation of the European Unity Movement*. Oxford: Clarendon.

Lipietz, A., 1985. *Mirages and Miracles: The Crisis of Global Fordism*. London: Verso.

Lord, C., 1993. *British Entry to the European Community under the Heath Government of 1970–1974*. Aldershot: Dartmouth.

Lord, C., 1996. *Absent at the Creation, Britain and the Formation of the EC 1950–1952*. Aldershot: Dartmouth.

Louis, W.R. and Owen, R. (eds), 1989. *Suez 1956: The Crisis and its Consequences*. Oxford: Clarendon.

Lowe, R., 1990. The Second World War: Consensus and the Foundation of the Welfare State. *Twentieth Century British History*, 1, pp. 152–82.

Luo, C., 2003. A Choice between Two Paradigms, What the Euro Implies for the City of London as a World Financial Centre. *University Association for Contemporary European Studies UACES Studies On-line Essays*, July. Available at: www.uaces.org [Accessed 22 June 2006].

Lynch, P., 2012. European Policy. In: T. Heppell and D. Seawright (eds), *Cameron and the Conservatives: The Transition to Coalition Government*. London: Palgrave, pp. 74–88.

Lynch, P. and Whitaker, R., 2012a. Where There is Discord, Can They Bring Harmony? Managing Intra-party Dissent on European Integration in the Conservative Party. *The British Journal of Politics & International Relations*, 15(3), pp. 317-339 doi: 10.1111/j.1467-856X.2012.00526.x [published online first: 20 August 2012].

Lynch, P., and Whitaker, R., 2012b. Rivalry on the Right: The Conservatives, the UK Independence Party UKIP and the EU issue. *British Politics*, 8 (3), pp. 285–312 doi: 10.1057/bp.2012.29 [published online first 17 December 2012].

Macartney, H. and Moran, M., 2008. Banking and financial market regulation and supervision. In: K. Dyson (ed.), *The Euro at Ten: Europeanization, Power, and Convergence*. Oxford: Oxford University Press, pp. 325–40.

McCrone, D. and Kiely, R., 2000. Nationalism and Citizenship. *Sociology*, 34 (1), pp. 19–34.

McGrew, A., 2002. Between Two Worlds: Europe in a Globalizing Era. *Government and Opposition*, 37 (3), pp. 343–58.

Magnette, P. and Nicolaidis, K., 2004. The European Convention: Bargaining in the Shadow of Rhetoric. *West European Politics*, 27 (3), pp. 381–404.

Mair, P., 2000. Partyless Democracy: Solving the Paradox of New Labour? *New Left Review*, 2 (2), pp. 21–35.

Mair, P., 2002. Populist Democracy versus Party Democracy. In: Y. Meny and Y. Surel (eds), *Democracies and the Populist Challenge*. Basingstoke: Palgrave, pp. 81–92.

Majone, G., 1996. *Regulating Europe*. London: Routledge.

Major, J., 1993. Raise Your Eyes, There is a Land Beyond. *The Economist*, 25 September, p.29.

Major, J., 1999. *The Autobiography*. London: Harper Collins.

Marks, G. and Wilson, C.J., 2000. The Past in the Present: A Cleavage Theory of Party Based Response to European integration. *British Journal of Political Science*, 30 (3), pp. 433–59.

Marquand, D., 1981. Club Government – the Crisis of the Labour Party in the National Perspective. *Government and Opposition*, 16 (1), pp. 19–36.

Marquand, D., 1988. *The Unprincipled Society*. London: Cape.

Marquand, D., 1991. Crab-Like Into The Future. *Marxism Today*, October, pp. 38–42.

Marquand, D., 1999. *The Progressive Dilemma: From Lloyd George to Blair*. Second Edition. London: Phoenix.
Marsh, D. and Rhodes, R.A.W., 1992. *Implementing Thatcherite Policies: An Audit of an Era*. Buckingham: Open University Press.
Marsh, D., 2008. Understanding British government: Analysing Competing Models. *The British Journal of Politics & International Relations*, 10 (2), pp. 251–68.
Martell, L., 2008. Britain and Globalization. *Globalizations*, 5 (3), pp. 449–66.
Meehan, E., 1993. *Citizenship and the European Community*. London: Sage.
Meny, Y. and Surel, Y., 2002. The Constitutive Ambiguity of Populism. In: Y. Meny and Y. Surel (eds), *Democracies and the Populist Challenge*. Basingstoke: Palgrave, pp. 1–21.
Middlemas, K., 1979. *Politics in Industrial Society, The Experience of the British System Since 1911*. London: André Deutsch.
Miliband, E., 2012. *Speech to the Confederation of British Industry: One Nation in Europe*. 19 November. Available at: http://www.labour.org.uk/one-nation-in-europe [Accessed 13 June 2013].
Miliband, R., 1973. *The State in Capitalist Society, The Analysis of the Western System of Power*. London: Quartet.
Milward, A.S., 1992. *The European Rescue of the Nation-State*. London: Routledge.
Milward, A.S., 1996. Approach Reality, Euro-Money and the Left. *New Left Review*, 216, pp. 55–65.
Milward, A.S., 1997. The Springs of Integration. In: P. Anderson, P. and P. Gowan (eds), *The Question of Europe*. London: New York: Verso, pp. 5–20.
Milward, A.S., 2002. *The UK and The European Community, Vol. 1: The Rise and Fall of a National Strategy, 1945–1963*. London and Portland: Whitehall History Publishing in association with Frank Cass.
Milward, A.S. and Sorenson, V., 1993. Interdependence or Integration? A National Choice. In: A. S. Milward, F. Romero, F.M.B. Lynch and R. Ranieri (eds), *The Frontier of National Sovereignty*. London: Routledge, pp. 1–32.
Moon, J., 1985. *European Integration in British Politics 1950–63: A Study of Issues of Change*. Aldershot: Gower.
Morris. P., 1996. The British Conservative Party. In: Gaffney, J. (ed.), *Political Parties in The European Union*. London and New York: Routledge, pp. 122–38.
Mouffe, C., 2005. The 'End of Politics' and the Challenge of Right-wing Populism. In: F. Panizza (ed.), *Populism and the Mirror of Democracy*. London and New York: Verso, pp. 50–71.
Mudde, C., 2010. The Populist Radical Right: A Pathological Normalcy. *West European Politics*, 33 (6), pp. 1167–86.
Mudde, C., 2012. The Comparative Study of Party-based Euroscepticism: the Sussex Versus the North Carolina School. *East European Politics*, 28 (2), pp. 193–202.
Nairn, T., 1973. *The Left Against Europe*. Harmondsworth: Penguin.

Nairn, T., 1977. The Twilight of the British State. *New Left Review*, 101/102, pp. 3–61.
Nairn, T., 1979. The Future of Britain's Crisis. *New Left Review*, 113/114, pp. 43–69.
Nairn, T., 1994. The Sole Survivor. *New Left Review*, 200, pp. 41–7.
Nairn, T., 2000. *After Britain, New Labour and the Return of Scotland*. London: Granta.
Nairn, T., 2001. Mario and the Magician. *New Left Review*, 9, pp. 5–30.
Northcott, J., 1995. *The Future of Britain and Europe*. London: Policy Studies Institute.
Northedge, F.S., 1974. *Descent from Power, British Foreign Policy 1943–1973*. London: Allen and Unwin.
Norton, P. (ed.), 1996. *The Conservative Party*. London: Prentice Hall.
Nugent, N., 1994. *The Government and Politics of the European Union*. Third Edition. London: Macmillan.
Offe, C., 1984. *Contradictions of the Welfare State*. London: Hutchinson.
Offe, C., 1996. *Modernity and the State: East, West*. Cambridge: Polity Press.
Ohmae, K., 1990. *The Borderless World: Power and Strategy in the International Economy*. London: Fontana.
Osborne, P., 1996. Times (Modern) Modernity (Conservative): Notes on the Persistence of a Temporal Motif. *New Formations*, 28, pp. 132–41.
Overbeek, H., 1986. The Westland Affair, Collision over the Future of British Capitalism. *Capital and Class*, 29, pp. 12–26.
Overbeek, H., 1990. *Global Capitalism and British Decline: The Thatcher Decade in Perspective*. London: Unwin, Hyman.
Owen, D., 1991. *Time To Declare*. London: Michael Joseph.
Panitch, L., 1976. *Social Democracy and Industrial Militancy: The Labour Party, The Trade Unions and Incomes Policy, 1945–1974*. Cambridge: Cambridge University Press.
Panitch, L., 2000. The New Imperial State. *New Left Review*, 2 (2), pp. 5–22.
Panizza, F., 2005. Introduction: Populism and the Mirror of Democracy. In: F. Panizza (ed.), *Populism and the Mirror of Democracy*. London and New York: Verso, pp. 1–31.
Peterson, J., 1995. Decision Making in the European Union: Towards a Framework for Analysis. *Journal of European Public Policy*, 2 (1), pp. 69–93.
Pierson, C., 1991. *Beyond the Welfare State*. Cambridge: Polity Press.
Pimlott, B., 1988. The Myth of Consensus. In: L.M. Smith (ed.), *The Making of Britain, Echoes of Greatness*. London: Macmillan, pp. 129–41.
Pimlott, B., 1993. *Harold Wilson*. London: Harper Collins.
Pinder, J., 1991. *European Community, The Building of a Union*. Oxford and New York: Oxford University Press.
Pollard, S., 1980. *The Wasting of the British Economy*. London: Croom Helm.
Poulantzas, N., 1975. *Classes in Contemporary Capitalism*. London: New Left Books.

Powell, E., 1971. *The Common Market – The Case Against*. Kingswood: Elliot Right.
Preston, P., 2007. Freedom from 'Britain': A Comment on Recent Elite-Sponsored Political-Cultural Identities. *British Journal of Politics and International Relations*, 9 (1), pp. 158–64.
Quaglia, L., 2009. The British Plan as a Pace-Setter: The Europeanization of Banking Rescue Plans in the EU? *JCMS: Journal of Common Market Studies*, 47 (5), pp. 1063–83.
Ray, L., 1999. Measuring Party Orientations Towards European Integration: Results From an Expert Survey. *European Journal of Political Research*, 36 (2), pp. 283–306.
Redwood, J., 2011. Parliament Backs Bail Outs. *John Redwood's Diary*, 12 July. Available at: http://johnredwoodsdiary.com/2011/07/12/parliament-backs-bail-outs/ [Accessed 9 September 2013].
Reyes, O., 2005. Skinhead Conservatism: A Failed Populist Project. In: F. Panizza (ed.), *Populism and the Mirror of Democracy*. London and New York: Verso, pp. 99–117.
Rhodes, M., 2000. Desperately Seeking a Solution: Social Democracy, Thatcherism and the Third Way in British Welfare. *West European Politics*, 23 (2), pp. 161–86.
Riddell, P., 1992. The Conservatives after 1992. *The Political Quarterly*, 63 (4), pp. 422–31.
Ritchie, R. (ed.), 1978. *Enoch Powell*. London: Batsford.
Ross, G., 1992. Confronting the New Europe. *New Left Review*, 191, pp. 49–68.
Ruggie, J., 2005. American Exceptionalism, Exemptionalism and Global Governance. In: M. Ignatieff (ed.), *American Exceptionalism and Human Rights*. Princeton: Princeton University Press, pp. 304–38.
Rustin, M., 1989. The Politics of Post-Fordism, or the Trouble with New Times. *New Left Review*, 174, pp. 4–78.
Ryner, M., 2010. An Obituary for the Third Way: The Financial Crisis and Social Democracy in Europe. *The Political Quarterly*, 81 (4), pp. 554–63.
Sanders, D., 1990. *Losing an Empire, Finding a Role, British Foreign Policy Since 1945*. London: Macmillan.
Schenk, C., 2002. Sterling, International Monetary Reform and Britain's Application to Join the European Economic Community in the 1960s. *Contemporary European History*, 11 (3), pp. 349–69.
Schmidt, V.A., 2006. Adapting to Europe: Is it Harder for Britain? *The British Journal of Politics and International Relations*, 8 (1), pp. 15–33.
Seldon, A., 1998. *Major: A Political Life*. London: Phoenix.
Seldon, A., 2005. *Blair*. London: Free Press.
Seldon, A. and Lodge, G., 2011. *Brown at 10*. London: Biteback
Sherrington, P., 2006. Confronting Europe: UK Political Parties and the EU 2000–2005. *The British Journal of Politics and International Relations*, 8 (1), pp. 69–78.

Sitter, N., 2001. The Politics of Opposition and European Integration in Scandinavia: Is Euro-Scepticism a Government-Opposition Dynamic? *West European Politics*, 24 (4), pp. 22–39.

Skidelsky, R., 1993. *Interests and Obsessions: Historical Essays*. London: Macmillan.

Smith, J., 2005. A Missed Opportunity? New Labour's European policy 1997–2005. *International Affairs*, 81 (4), pp. 703–21.

Spiering, M., 2004. British Euroscepticism. *European Studies: A Journal of European Culture, History and Politics*, 20 (1), pp. 127–49.

Stephens, P., 1996. *Politics and the Pound: The Conservatives Struggle with Sterling*. London and Basingstoke: Macmillan.

Stephens, P., 2011. Was this the Moment UK Stumbled out of Europe? *The Financial Times*, 13 December. Available at: http://www.ft.com/cms/s/0/ef3c98b4-24b6-11e1-ac4b-00144feabdc0.html#axzz2tICXqmxn [Accessed 9 September 2013].

Stephens, P., 2013. Facts Finally Collide with Ideology. *The Financial Times*, July 22. Available at: http://www.ft.com/cms/s/0/96074de6-f2d9-11e2-a203-00144feabdc0.html#axzz2tICXqmxn [Accessed 10 September 2013].

Story, J. and Walter, I., 1997. *Political Economy of Financial Integration in Europe: The Battle of the System*. Manchester: Manchester University Press.

Strange, G., 2006. The Left Against Europe? A Critical Engagement with New Constitutionalism and Structural Dependence Theory. *Government and Opposition*, 41 (2), pp. 197–229.

Strange, G., 2012. The Euro, EU Social Democracy, and International Monetary Power: A Critique of New Constitutionalism. *Globalizations*, 9 (2), pp. 257–72.

Strange, G., 2013. Depoliticisation, the Management of Money and the Renewal of Social Democracy: New Labour's Keynesianism and the Political Economy of 'Discretionary Constraint'. *New Political Economy*, 19 (1), pp. 138–54. doi: 10.1080/13563467.2013.779648. [published online first: 29 April 2013].

Strange, S., 1967. *Sterling and the Problem of the Six*. London: Chatham House.

Strange, S., 1971. *Sterling and British Policy: A Political Study of an International Currency in Decline*. London: Oxford University Press.

Streeck, W., 1995. From Market Making to State Building, Reflections on the Political Economy of European Social Policy. In: S. Liebfried and P. Pierson (eds), *European Social Policy, Between Fragmentation and Integration*. Washington D.C.: Brookings Institution, pp. 389–431.

Streeck, W. and Schmitter, P., 1991. From National Corporatism to Transnational Pluralism, Organaized Interests in the Single European Market. *Politics and Society*, 19 (2), pp. 134–64.

Szczerbiak, A. and Taggart, P., 2000. Opposing Europe, Party Systems and Opposition to the Union, the Euro and Europeanisation. *Sussex European Institute, Working Paper No. 36*. Brighton: University of Sussex.

Szczerbiak, A. and Taggart, P., 2003. Theorising Party-Based Euroscepticism, Problems of Definition, Measurement and Causality. *Sussex European Institute, Working Paper No. 69*. Brighton: University of Sussex.

Szczerbiak A and Taggart P. (eds), 2008a. *Opposing Europe? The Comparative Party Politics of Euroscepticism Volume 1: Case Studies and Country Surveys*, Oxford: Oxford University Press.

Szczerbiak, A. and Taggart, P. (eds), 2008b. *Opposing Europe? The Comparative Party Politics of Euroscepticism Volume 2: Comparative and Theoretical Perspectives*. Oxford: Oxford University Press.

Taggart, P., 1998. A Touchstone of Dissent: Euroscepticism in Contemporary Western European Party Systems. *European Journal of Political Research*, 33, pp. 363–88.

Taggart, P., 2002. Populism and the Pathology of Representative Politics. In: Y. Meny and Y. Surel (eds), *Democracies and the Populist Challenge*. Basingstoke: Palgrave, pp. 62–80.

Taggart, P., 2004. *European Parliament Election Briefing No. 14: The European Parliament Election in the United Kingdom June 10 2004*. University of Sussex: European Parties Elections and Referendums Network.

Taggart, P. and Szczerbiak, A., 2004. Contemporary Euroscepticism in the Party Systems of the European Union Candidate States of Central and Eastern Europe. *European Journal of Political Research*, 43, pp. 1–27.

Talani, L.S., 2012. *Globalization, Hegemony and the Future of the City of London*. Basingstoke: Palgrave Macmillan.

Tempest, M., 2007. Blair Sets Out Red Lines of EU Constitution. *The Guardian*, 18 June. Available at: http://www.theguardian.com/world/2007/jun/18/eu.politics [Accessed 23 July 2013].

Thatcher, M., 1993. *The Downing Street Years*. London: Harper Collins.

Thatcher, M., 1995. *The Path to Power*. London: Harper Collins.

Thatcher, M., 2002. *Statecraft, Strategies for a Changing World*. London: Harper Collins.

Thompson, G., 2011. *The European Financial Stabilisation Mechanism*. House of Commons Library Standard Note, 29 May 2011.

Tomlinson, B.R., 1982. The Contraction of England: National Decline and the Loss of Empire. *Journal of Imperial and Commonwealth History*, 11 (1), pp. 58–72.

Turner, J., 2000. *The Tories and Europe*. Manchester: Manchester University Press.

Usherwood, S., 2002. Opposition to the European Union in the UK, The Dilemma of Public Opinion and Party Management. *Government and Opposition*, 37 (2), pp. 211–30.

Usherwood, S. and Startin, N., 2013. Euroscepticism as a Persistent Problem. *JCMS: Journal of Common Market Studies*, 51 (1), pp. 1–16.

Van Rompuy, H., 2012. *Towards a Genuine Economic and Monetary Union*. Available at: http://www.consilium.europa.eu/uedocs/cms_Data/docs/press data/en/ec/134069.pdf [Accessed 9 September 2013].

Walby, S., 1999. The New Regulatory State: The Social Powers of the European Union. *British Journal of Sociology*, 50 (1), pp. 118–40.

Wall, S., 2008. *A Stranger in Europe: Britain and the EU from Thatcher to Blair.* Oxford: Oxford University Press.

Wall, S., 2013. *The Official History of Britain and the European Community, Volume II: From Rejection to Referendum, 1963–1975.* Abingdon and New York: Routledge.

Wallace, H., 1981. The Contradictions of Democracy. *Government and Opposition,* 16 (1), pp. 120–23.

Wallace, H., 1995. Britain out on a Limb? *Political Quarterly,* 166 (1), pp. 46–58.

Wallace, H., 2000. Europeanisation or Globalisation, Complementary or Contradictory Trends. *New Political Economy,* 5 (3), pp. 369–82.

Wallace, W., 1990. *The Transformation of Western Europe.* London: Pinter.

Wallace, W., 1991. Pride and Prejudice. *Marxism Today,* October, pp. 28–31.

Wallace, W., 1994. Foreign Policy. In: D. Kavanagh and A. Seldon (eds), *The Major Effect.* London: Macmillan.

Wallace, W., 1997. The Nation-State, Rescue or Retreat. In: P. Anderson and P. Gowan (eds), *The Question of Europe.* London, New York: Verso, pp. 21–50.

Wallace, W. and Wallace, H., 1990. Strong State or Weak State in Foreign Policy? The Contradiction of Conservative Liberalism 1979–1987. *Public Administration,* 68 (1), pp. 83–101.

Warde, A., 1982. *Consensus and Beyond: The Development of Labour Party Strategy Since the Second World War.* Manchester: Manchester University Press.

Watson, M. and Hay, C., 2002. The Discourse of Globalisation and the Logic of no Alternative, Rendering the Contingent Necessary in the Political Economy of New Labour. *Policy and Politics,* 31 (3), pp. 289–305.

Watt, N., 2008. Economy at 60-year Low, Says Darling. And it Will Get Worse. *The Guardian,* 30 August. Available at: http://www.theguardian.com/politics/2008/aug/30/economy.alistairdarling [Accessed 2 August 2013].

Watt, N. and Wintour, M., 2009. David Cameron to Shed 'Cast Iron' Pledge on Lisbon Treaty. *The Guardian,* 3 November. Available at: http://www.theguardian.com/world/2009/nov/03/david-cameron-lisbon-treaty-referendum. [Accessed 13 February 2014].

Wearden, G. and Seager, A., 2008. Pound Falls to Five-Year Low as Bank Head Admits Recession is Here. *The Guardian,* 22 October. Available at: http://www.theguardian.com/business/2008/oct/22/pound-recession-interest-rates [Accessed 4 August 2013].

Wellings, B., 2010. Losing the Peace: Euroscepticism and the Foundations of Contemporary English Nationalism. *Nations and Nationalism,* 16 (3), pp. 488–505.

Wellings, B., 2012. *English Nationalism and Euroscepticism: Losing the Peace.* Bern: Peter Lang.

White, M., 1993. Major the European Comes out of the Closet. *The Guardian,* 23 April 1993, p. 1.

Wilkes, G., 1997. *Britain's Failure to Enter the European Community, 1961–63: The Enlargement Negotiations and crises in European, Atlantic, and Commonwealth Relations.* London and Portland: Frank Cass.

Wilkes, G. and Wring, D., 1998. The British Press and European Integration, 1948–1996. In: D. Baker and D. Seawright (eds), *Britain For and Against Europe, British Politics and the Question of Europe.* Oxford: Clarendon Press, pp. 185–205

Willetts, D., 1992. Modern Conservatism. *The Political Quarterly*, 63 (4), pp. 413–21.

Winnett R., 2009. David Cameron Apologises For Not Holding Labour to Account. *The Daily Telegraph*, 13 March. Available at: http://www.telegraph.co.uk/news/politics/david-cameron/4986760/David-Cameron-apologises-for-not-holding-Labour-to-account.html [Accessed 6 August 2013].

Young, H., 1998. *This Blessed Plot: Britain and Europe from Churchill to Blair.* London: Macmillan.

Young, J., 1973. *Britain, France and the Unity of Europe.* Leicester: Leicester University Press.

Young, J., 1993. *Britain and European Unity, 1945–1992.* London: Macmillan.

Young, J., 1995. British officials and European integration 1944–1960. In: A. Deighton (ed.), *Building Postwar Europe, National Decision-makers and European Institutions, 1948–63.* Basingstoke: Macmillan, pp. 87–106.

Ziltener, P., 1997. The Relaunch of European Integration, Explaining the Single European Act as a Package Deal. Paper presented for the *Third European Sociological Association Conference*, University of Essex, 27 to 30 August 1997.

Index

1975 referendum 1, 11, 53, 70, 71, 72–3, 77, 171–2

Anglo-American Europe 38, 51, 59, 141, 146
Anglo-American nationalism 39, 82, 84, 87, 90, 97, 110
Anglo-Americanism 11, 47, 77, 138, 148
Anglo-Europe 129, 131, 139–40, 142, 146, 153, 173
Attlee government 21–2, 33, 34–5, 36

Baker, D., Gamble, A. and Ludlam, S. 83, 116, 121
Bank of England 18, 21, 24, 25, 105, 113, 135
Benn, T. 55n2, 57, 58, 70, 71, 120
Bevin, E. 33, 34, 37
BIE (Britain in Europe) campaign 11, 71, 72
Blair, T. 131, 132, 134, 140, 145–6, 147, 148, 172
   Constitutional Treaty 143, 144, 145
Blair government 4–5, 11–12, 132–3, 134, 139, 143, 145, 146–7, 153
   Constitutional Treaty 144, 145, 146
   Iraq War 12, 131, 140–41, 142, 143, 144n7
   Social Chapter 131, 138
British contributions, European budget 64, 65, 66, 70, 85–6, 89, 145–6, 157
British exceptionalism 11, 29, 97, 101, 127, 128, 139–40, 164–5, 169, 174
British rebate 86, 145–6
Brown, G. 132–3, 135, 138n5, 139, 140, 168, 172
   EMU 134, 135, 136, 137
   financial crisis 150–51, 152
   Treaty of Lisbon 147, 148–9
Brown government 4–5, 12, 147–8, 153, 155
   financial crisis 12, 149–50, 152, 153
Bruges Group 97, 108, 148, 158

Burn, G. 24
Bush administration 141

Callaghan, J. 73, 76
Callaghan government 25, 68, 73–4, 75–6, 77, 85
Cameron, D. 148, 152, 155, 157, 164–5, 169
   fiscal compact 162, 164
   IN/OUT referendum 1, 12, 164, 169, 173
CAP (Common Agricultural Policy) 65, 70, 75, 145
Cash, B. 116, 117, 123, 157, 162
   Maastricht Treaty 124–5, 126
Churchill, W.S. 33, 37
Churchill government 20, 37–8, 39–40
City of London 18, 21, 23–4, 25, 47, 48, 63–4, 75, 91, 93, 137–8
   EMU 105, 109, 134
   fiscal compact 162, 163
civil society organisations 158, 159
Clarke, K. 83, 105, 111, 157–8, 172
Coalition government 1, 7, 12, 152, 153, 155–6, 158, 162–3, 169–70, 173
   European Union Bill 156–7, 173
   Euroscepticism 155, 156, 159, 160, 161, 169, 173–4
   fiscal compact 163–4, 165
   IN/OUT referendum 1, 7, 12, 157, 158–9, 166–7, 169, 173
Common Agricultural Policy, *see* CAP
Commonwealth 25, 26, 34, 35, 40, 42, 57
   EC membership 45, 46, 48–9, 50, 51, 54, 64, 70
Community budget, *see* European budget
consensus 19–20, 21, 28, 31, 33, 35
Conservative party 1, 12, 67–8, 77, 79, 103–4, 123–5, 133, 144, 155, 172
   EU membership *83*, 83–5, 129, 157
   Euroscepticism 4, 106, 116, 156, 166

IN/OUT referendum 157, 164, 166–7
Constitutional Treaty 143–5, 146, 147, 148, 149, 153, 173
Crossman, R. 54, 55, 58, 59, 61n10

Darling, A. 149–50, 161–2
de Gaulle, C. 43, 44, 46, 50–51, 54, 60, 62
Delors, J. 2, 11, 79, 89, 90, 95, 97, 107–8, 139, 172
  Maastricht Treaty 111, 117
Delors Report 93, 94

EC (European Community) 16–19, 31, 93
EC (European Community) membership 5, 7, 8–9, 27–9, 44–51, 53–5, 58–62, 63–7, 68–73, 75–7
  1975 referendum 1, 11, 53, 70, 71, 72–3, 77, 171–2
ECSC (European Coal and Steel Community) 31–3, 34–5, 36, 37, 38, 39
EDC (European Defence Community) 37–8, 39
Eden, A. 37, 38, 41
EFTA (European Free Trade Area) 41, 43–4, 45
EMS (European Monetary System) 74–5
EMU (European Monetary Union) 93, 105, 112, 126, 135–6, 151, 162, 163, 165, 166, 174
  Major government 106, 109, 110, 111, 114, 115, 128, 129, 172
  New Labour government 134–5, 136, 137, 140
  Thatcher 90, 93–4, 98
ERM (Exchange Rate Mechanism) 90–91, 93–4, 112
  Major government 103, 105, 106, 107, 111, 112, 113–15, 118, 172
  Thatcher government 91, 92, 93, 94, 98
EU (European Union) membership 1, *83*, 83–5, 124–7, 129–30, 156–61, 165–8, 169–70, 171–4
  IN/OUT referendum 1, 7, 12, 155, 157, 158–9, 164, 166–7, 168, 169, 173
euro 12, 136, 137–8, 150, 151, 155
Eurodollar market 24–5, 48, 63, 64
European budget 11, 86, 157

British contributions 64, 65, 66, 70, 85–6, 89, 145–6, 157
British rebate 86, 145–6
European Coal and Steel Community, *see* ECSC
European Commission 54, 62, 70, 85, 96, 97, 107–8, 126, 138
European Communities Bill 65, 67, 70, 72
European Community, *see* EC
European Constitution, *see* Constitutional Treaty
European Defence Community, *see* EDC
European Foundation 123
European Free Trade Area, *see* EFTA
European integration 1, 2–4, 6, 10–12, 15, 16–19, 28–9, 31–6, 37–41, 171–4
European Monetary System, *see* EMS
European Monetary Union, *see* EMU
European Parliament 76, 109, 147
European Union Act 158, 169
European Union Bill 156–7, 173
Eurosceptic mobilisation 121–2, 171–2
  Maastricht Treaty 116, 118, 119–22, 123–5, 126, 127
Eurosceptic Thatcherism 79, 95, 97, 126, 129, 133, 172
Euroscepticism 1–6, 7, 9, 28, 129, 155, 159, 160, 161, 168, 169–70
  hard 2, 5, 6, 77, 134, 156, 159, 160
  populist 7–8, 11, 12–13, 53, 68, 69, 71–2, 126–7, 133, 167, 171–2, 173–4
  soft 2, 5
Eurosceptics 3–4, 6, 12–13, 116, 123, 157–8, 160, 162, 169, 173; *see also* Eurosceptic mobilisation
  EC membership 61–2, 97
  IN/OUT referendum 166, 167
Eurozone 134, 135, 136, 150, 165–6
Eurozone crisis 12, 131, 151, 155–6, 161–2, 164, 168, 169, 173
Exchange Rate Mechanism, *see* ERM
extended government 83, *83*, 84

federal Europe 17, 32, 34n1, 39, 50, 66, 99, 107, 143–4
financial crisis 12, 131, 149–52, 153, 163, 173

fiscal compact 162, 163–4, 165
Forster, A. 3, 72, 107, 108, 116, 158
Fox, L. 160, 161
France 17, 37, 40, 43–4, 54, 118, 141
    Constitutional Treaty 143, 145
    ECSC 31–2, 33–4
    EDC 37, 38
Franco-German Europe 67, 97, 140, 141, 142, 159
Fresh Start Group 122–3, 158

Gaitskell, H. 49–50, 53
Germany 16, 17, 37, 38, 66, 74–5, 96, 97, 107, 141, 143
    ECSC 31–2, 33
    ERM 112, 113–14
global governance 21, 36, 132, 160–61
globalisation 9–10, 81–2, 93, 131, 132, 136, 137–8, 150, 172
Goldsmith, J. 123, 126
governing code 7–8, 9, 10

Habermas, J. and Derrida, J. 141, 142
Hague, W. 132n1, 133, 155, 164
hard Euroscepticism 2, 5, 6, 77, 134, 156, 159, 160
Heath, E. 43, 45, 62–3, 73, *83*, 86, 97
    EC membership 46, 62, 63, 64, 65–6, 67, 76–7
    Treaty of Rome 1, 53
Heath government 66–8, 77, 97
    EC membership 11, 62, 63, 65, 66–7, 171
Heseltine, M. *83*, 84, 87, 99, 100, 111, 172
Hoon, G. 146, 147
Howe, G. *83*, 84, 88, 91–2, 94, 98–9
Hurd, D. *83*, 98, 106, 109, 111, 128
    Maastricht Treaty 119, 121

IMF (International Monetary Fund) 25, 68, 73–4, 75, 137, 151–2, 162
IN/OUT referendum 1, 7, 12, 155, 157, 158–9, 164, 166–7, 168, 169, 173
interdependence 9, 64, 83, *83*, 84, 169
Iraq War 12, 131, 140–42, 143, 144n7
Italy 17, 38, 88, 140

Keynesian welfare state 15–16, 21, 23, 74, 77, 80, 137

Labour party 20, 21, 27, 34, 134, 169; *see also* New Labour government
    EC membership 11, 49–50, 53, 59, 68–71, 76, 77
Lamfulussy Process 139
Lamont, N. *83*, 112, 113
Lawson, N. *83*, 91, 92, 93, 94, 97, 98, 166
    ERM 91, 92, 94
Liberal Democrats 12, 152, 155–6
Lisbon Agenda 138–9, 140
Lisbon Treaty 146–9, 155, 173
Lisbon Treaty referendum 147, 148, 155

Maastricht Treaty 7, 111, 112, 117, 118, 126, 151, 158
    Eurosceptic mobilisation 116, 118, 119–22, 123–5, 126, 127
    Major government 7, 11, 103, 106, 108–9, 110–11, 115, 118, 119–22, 123–5, 126, 127
Macmillan, H. 38, 41–2, 43, 45–6, 48, 59, 73
Macmillan government 22, 31, 41–4, 47–8, 71
    EC membership 1, 11, 28, 45, 48–9, 50, 51, 171
Major, J. *83*, 98, 100, 101, 103, 104, 107, 111, 122, 127–8
    Maastricht Treaty 109, 110–11, 117, 118, 120
Major government 11, 84, 103–6, 110, 111–14, 127, 128–9, 130
    EMU 106, 109, 110, 111, 114, 115, 128, 129, 172
    ERM 103, 105, 106, 107, 111, 112, 113–15, 118, 172
    Eurosceptic mobilisation 116, 118, 119–22, 123–5, 126, 127, 172
    Maastricht Treaty 7, 11, 103, 106, 108–9, 110–11, 115, 118, 119–22, 123–5, 126, 127
    Social Chapter 109–10, 121
Merkel, A. 151, 166
Messina Resolution 39–40
Miliband, D. 147–8
Miliband, E. 168
Milward, A.S. 10, 15, 16, 17, 18, 19, 29, 32, 38

minimal government 83, *83*, 84
monetarism 91–2, 93
Monnet, J. 31–2, 39

Nairn, T. 21, 69, 71–2
National Referendum Campaign, *see* NRC
New Labour government 4–5, 11–12, 131–4, 138–40, 143, 145–6, 152–3, 158, 168, 172–3
    Constitutional Treaty 144, 145, 146
    EMU 134–5, 136, 137, 140
    financial crisis 12, 149–50, 152, 153
    Iraq War 12, 131, 140–41, 142, 143, 144n7
    Lisbon Treaty 146–9, 155, 173
    Social Chapter 131, 138
    Third Way 12, 132, 139, 140, 152–3, 172, 173
North Carolina School 2
NRC (National Referendum Campaign) 71, 72

OEEC (Organisation for European Economic Cooperation) 33, 36, 39n3, 40, 43, 44

Patten, C. 84, 103, 106–7, 109, 110
Pompidou, G. 61, 62, 64
populism 6–7, 12, 69
populist Euroscepticism 7–8, 11, 12–13, 53, 68, 69, 71–2, 126–7, 133, 167, 171–2, 173–4
post-imperial crisis 15
Powell, E. 77, *83*, 97, 116
    EC membership 61, 67, 70, 71, 72, 73, 77

Schuman Declaration 31, 32, 33–4, 35, 36
SEA (Single European Act) 87–8, 89, 116
Shore, P. 61, 70, 71
single currency, *see* EMU; euro
Single European Act, *see* SEA
single market 8, 11, 87–9, 128, 163, 165, 167, 172
Single Supervisory Mechanism, *see* SSM

Social Chapter 109–10, 121, 131, 138
soft Euroscepticism 2, 5
sovereignty 5, 9, 63, 65, 71, 83, *83*, 84, 124, 156–7
Spaak Committee 39–40
SSM (Single Supervisory Mechanism) 163, 165
Suez crisis 41, 42, 43
supranationalism 31, 32, 33–4, 38–9, 50–51, 54, 126
Sussex School 2

Thatcher, M. 77, *83*, 84, 85, 89, 90, 95–7, 98, 99, 101, 116–17
    EMU 90, 93–4, 98
    ERM 92, 93–4, 98
    Maastricht Treaty 119, 121, 125
Thatcher governments 11, 79, 82, 85–7, 91–2, 93, 97–8, 99–101, 172
    ERM 91, 92, 93, 94, 98
    SEA 87–8, 89, 116
    Westland Affair 85, 87, 89
Thatcherism 11, 79–81, 82, 84, 85, 87, 93, 98, 100–101, 103, 104, 126, 172
    Eurosceptic 79, 95, 97, 126, 129, 133, 172
Third Way 12, 132, 139, 140, 152–3, 172, 173
Treasury 18, 21, 24, 25, 40, 45, 47, 56, 112, 134, 135, 152, 162–3
Treaty of Amsterdam 131
Treaty of Lisbon 147, 148–9, 153, 155, 173
Treaty of Rome 1, 17, 43, 50, 53, 70

UKIP (United Kingdom Independence Party) 12, 144, 156, 159–60, 173
US (United States) 21, 22, 46–7, 63, 64, 81–2, 87, 140–41, 149

Westland Affair 85, 87, 89
WEU (Western European Union) 38, 39
Wilson, H. 53, 54, 58–9, 70, 72–3, 171–2
Wilson governments 56–8, 61, 68, 73, 85
    EC membership 11, 53, 54–5, 58, 59, 60, 70, 171